McCALL'S Big Book OF CROSS-STITCH

McCALL'S Big Book OF CROSS-STITCH

The Editors of McCall's Needlework & Crafts Magazine

Chilton Book Company

Radnor, Pennsylvania

Copyright © 1983 ABC Needlework and Crafts Magazines, Inc.

Published in Radnor, Pennsylvania 19089,
by Chilton Book Company

Library of Congress Cataloging in Publication Data

Main entry under title:
　　McCall's big book of cross-stitch.

　　Includes index.
　　　1. Cross-stitch—Patterns.　　I. McCall's needlework &
crafts magazine.
TT778.C76M34 1983　　　746.44　　　82-73539
ISBN 0-8019-7363-5 (pbk.)

Manufactured in the United States of America

1 2 3 4 5 6 7 8 9 0 　 2 1 0 9 8 7 6 5 4 3

CONTENTS

****

A "pewter" tankard holds an Autumn Bouquet for any wall in
your home. Simple cross-stitches are worked on even-weave fabric
with six-strand embroidery floss. Also see Spring Bouquet, page 33.
Directions for Seasons' Bouquets on page 17.

Stitch an old-fashioned memory from the pages of the past. Jewel-bright colors in easy cross-stitch work up quickly. Skaters directions on page 19.

*It's a great day for walking—even
the family pet agrees! Quick and
easy cross-stitch picture is
worked with DMC embroidery floss
on 11-count even-weave cloth. "Frame" in double rows
of cross-stitch, mount on stretchers. Design area
is 7 $\frac{3}{4}$" × 16 $\frac{1}{2}$". Springtime Stroll, page 24.*

*Welcome springtime with this beautiful verse from
the Song of Solomon. A bluebird in flight and delicate
spring blossoms echo the hope and happiness of the season.
Cross-stitch is worked on 18 threads-to-the-inch
even-weave fabric with embroidery floss.
For directions, see page 23.*

Assisi work creates a picture in reverse—
cross-stitch fills in the background,
and the design is left plain. Our three
pictures are worked with floss on
even-weave fabric. Each is 10″ × 8″.
Two petaled pillows are worked on
Aida cloth, one in Assisi, and the other
in traditional cross-stitch.
Directions for all begin on page 28.

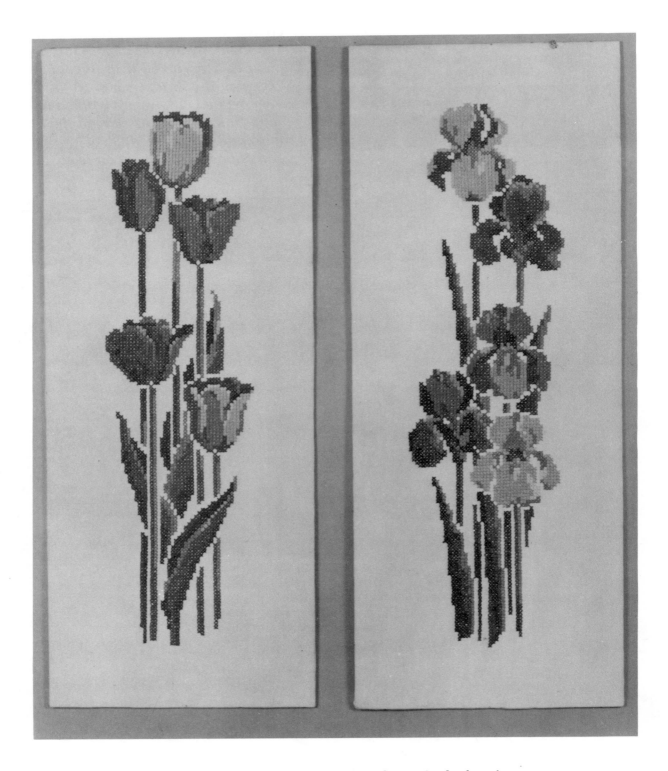

Tall tulips and irises announce the arrival of spring.
Seven crosses-to-the-inch; each panel is 7" × 23".
Tulips and Irises, directions on page 25.

SEASONS' BOUQUETS

Shown on pages 9 and 33

SIZE: Design area, approximately 10″ × 13″.
EQUIPMENT: Masking tape. Scissors. Embroidery needle. Pencil. Ruler. Straight pins. Embroidery hoop (optional).
MATERIALS: White or cream-colored linen 18

threads-to-the-inch, at least 16″ × 18″ (allows for background area around design and margins for mounting only). DMC six-strand embroidery floss: one skein of each color listed in Color Key.

DIRECTIONS: (See Contents for all General Directions.) Tape fabric edges to prevent raveling. Place fabric on smooth, hard surface. Using a pencil, lightly mark design area 10″ × 13″ in cen-

- DEEP GRAY 645
- DARK GRAY 646
- MEDIUM GRAY 647
- LIGHT GRAY 648
- PALE GRAY 3072
- WHITE
- DEEP BROWN 3371
- RED-LILAC 315
- DEEP ORANGE 918
- DARK ORANGE 919
- RED-ORANGE 920
- ORANGE 900
- LIGHT ORANGE 608
- STARK YELLOW 444
- PALE YELLOW 445
- MEDIUM YELLOW 307
- LIGHT WARM YELLOW 743
- MEDIUM WARM YELLOW 725
- DARK WARM YELLOW 783
- ORANGE-YELLOW 740
- RED 350
- YELLOW 402
- DARK PALE GREEN 3011
- MEDIUM PALE GREEN 732
- LIGHT PALE GREEN 734
- DARK BROWN 898
- DARK RED-BROWN 801
- LIGHT RED-BROWN 632
- DARK ORANGE-BROWN 976
- PALE BROWN 841
- GREEN-BROWN 610
- CREAM 746
- STARK GREEN 988
- DUSTY GREEN 3053
- DARK BRIGHT GREEN 367
- MEDIUM BRIGHT GREEN 368
- LIGHT BLUE-GREEN 503
- DARK BLUE-GREEN 501
- DEEP YELLOW-GREEN 937
- MEDIUM YELLOW-GREEN 470
- LIGHT YELLOW-GREEN 471
- PALE YELLOW-GREEN 472
- LIGHT GREEN-BROWN 832
- LIGHT RED-BROWN 975
- ROSE 819
- RED-BROWN 300
- DARK GREEN 890
- LIGHT LILAC 3042

ter of fabric. Then find center of design area by folding fabric in half horizontally and vertically. Mark center with pin.

Refer to "Four Methods of Cross-Stitching," specifically reading "On Even-Weave Fabric." Each square on chart represents two threads horizontally and two threads vertically. To begin embroidery, find center square on chart (center rows marked by arrows). Following chart and color key, embroider outward. Do not make knots; see "Embroidery Basics."

Spring Bouquet: Refer to "Stitch Details." Using three strands of floss in embroidery needle, work backstitch (colors in parentheses) as follows: Outline corn marigold (976), red lily (918), pansies (327), peony (817), iris (801), milfoil (9367), marguerite (648), lily stamen (976); outline between the flower leaves (645), peony leaves (319); outline handle (739) and bottom (434) of earthenware pot.

Autumn Bouquet: Refer to "Stitch Details." Using three strands of floss in embroidery needle,

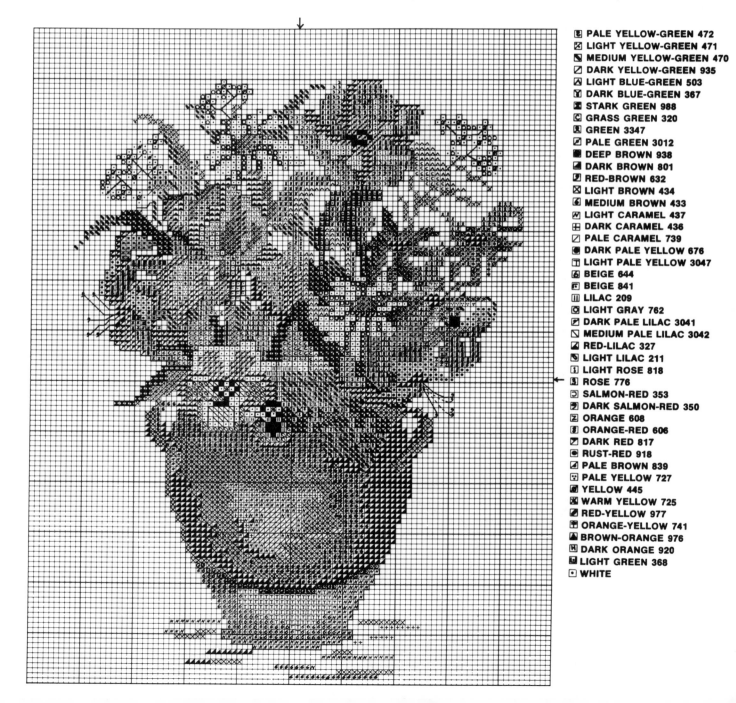

PALE YELLOW-GREEN 472
LIGHT YELLOW-GREEN 471
MEDIUM YELLOW-GREEN 470
DARK YELLOW-GREEN 935
LIGHT BLUE-GREEN 503
DARK BLUE-GREEN 367
STARK GREEN 988
GRASS GREEN 320
GREEN 3347
PALE GREEN 3012
DEEP BROWN 938
DARK BROWN 801
RED-BROWN 632
LIGHT BROWN 434
MEDIUM BROWN 433
LIGHT CARAMEL 437
DARK CARAMEL 436
PALE CARAMEL 739
DARK PALE YELLOW 676
LIGHT PALE YELLOW 3047
BEIGE 644
BEIGE 841
LILAC 209
LIGHT GRAY 762
DARK PALE LILAC 3041
MEDIUM PALE LILAC 3042
RED-LILAC 327
LIGHT LILAC 211
LIGHT ROSE 818
ROSE 776
SALMON-RED 353
DARK SALMON-RED 350
ORANGE 608
ORANGE-RED 606
DARK RED 817
RUST-RED 918
PALE BROWN 839
PALE YELLOW 727
YELLOW 445
WARM YELLOW 725
RED-YELLOW 977
ORANGE-YELLOW 741
BROWN-ORANGE 976
DARK ORANGE 920
LIGHT GREEN 368
WHITE

work backstitch (colors in parentheses) as follows: Outline Japanese quince and chestnuts (3011), ivy (890), blackberry (315), snowberry (3042) rowan berry (918), climbing-thread of Virginia Creeper (610) and the pewter tankard (844).

To Finish: See directions for blocking and mounting under "Embroidery Basics."

SKATERS
Shown on pages 10–11

EQUIPMENT: Scissors. Embroidery needle. Embroidery hoop. Masking tape. Pencil. Ruler. T-square. Soft wooden board. Brown wrapping paper. Thumbtacks. Tack hammer. Towel.

⊡ PALE PINK #963	☑ LIGHT ROSE #957
Ⓢ SHOCKING PINK #603	⊞ DEEP ROSE #956
⊙ GOLD #977	⊠ MEDIUM BLUE #793
▼ STEEL GRAY #414	⬛ DEEP BLUE #792
⊟ LIGHT BEIGE #842	⊛ CLARET #600
⊞ LIGHT BLUE #794	■ BLACK #310
◺ TAUPE #840	◪ DARK BLUE GREEN #924

MATERIALS: White or off-white even-weave fabric: 14″ × 11″ for each picture (allows for background area around design, plus margins for mounting). DMC six-strand embroidery floss: one 8.7-yard skein of each color listed in color key (enough for both pictures). Stiff white mounting cardboard, ⅛″ thick, in size desired for finished picture (determine size by blocking off amount of white space you desire around embroidery). Short straight pins. Masking tape. Wooden frame (optional).

DIRECTIONS: (See Contents for all General Directions.) Tape edges of fabric to prevent raveling. Place area to be worked in an embroidery

⊡ PALE PINK #963	◩ DARK BLUE GREEN #924	
⊟ LIGHT BEIGE #842	⊟ EMERALD GREEN #910	
⑤ SHOCKING PINK #603	ⓥ STEEL GRAY #414	
◳ TAUPE #840	ⓗ WHITE	
◪ GRAY BLUE #926	◉ GOLD #977	
⊞ LIGHT PINK #605	■ BLACK #310	
ⓥ MEDIUM GREEN #912	◉ CLARET #600	

RUNNING STITCH

STRAIGHT STITCH

BACKSTITCH

CROSS-STITCH

hoop, so fabric is held smoothly without distortion. Work cross-stitch first, following charts, then trace actual-size patterns for background and transfer patterns to fabric using dry ball-point pen and dressmaker's tracing (carbon) paper; place patterns on fabric so that X's for skaters' heads correspond to cross-stitches already worked.

Begin by leaving an end of floss on back and working over it to secure; end by running strand through stitches on back. Do not make any knots.

Work embroidery as follows, referring to "Stitch Details." Work skaters and foreground in cross-stitch, using three strands of floss in needle. Work background with two strands of black floss; use running stitch for sky and similar details; use backstitch for outlines of houses, hills, tree trunks, bridge, and people. Work bridge design with a combination of cross-stitch and running stitch; make crosses first, then connect ends of crosses at top and bottom with running stitches. Work remaining areas in straight stitch.

When embroidery is complete, block and mount as indicated below.

BLOCKING: Cover wooden board with brown wrapping paper; secure in place with thumbtacks.

Draw the exact original size of the fabric on brown paper for guidelines. Use T-square at corners. Mark center of each side on guidelines. Place embroidery right side up on paper.

Stretch and tack cloth to wooden surface on guidelines. Tack corners first, then place tacks at center of each side, matching center marks of fabric and guide; work toward corners, dividing and subdividing the spaces between the tacks already placed. Repeat until there is a solid border of thumbtacks around the entire edge. Hammer in tacks or they will pop out as linen dries.

Cover embroidery with damp towel; allow towel and embroidery to dry thoroughly.

MOUNTING: Stretch blocked fabric right side up over mounting cardboard. Be sure lines of stitches are straight horizontally and vertically, and embroidery is centered. Push pins through fabric partway into sides of board. Use same procedure as for blocking, but space pins about $\frac{1}{4}''$ apart all around picture. When design is even, drive pins into board edge with tack hammer. If a pin does not go in straight, it should be removed and reinserted. Tape excess fabric to back. Insert mounted embroidered picture in frame.

SONG OF SOLOMON
Shown on page 14

SIZE: Design area, $13\frac{1}{2}'' \times 5\frac{1}{2}''$; framed plaque, $17\frac{1}{2}'' \times 10\frac{1}{2}''$.

EQUIPMENT: Pencil. Ruler. Scissors. Embroidery hoop and needle. Sewing needle.

MATERIALS: Zweigart Ainring cloth, cream, 18 threads-to-the-inch, $17\frac{1}{2}'' \times 9\frac{1}{2}''$. DMC six-strand embroidery floss: two skeins of brown; one skein each light green, medium green, light blue, medium blue, white, yellow; scraps of gold, peach, orange, gray. Foamcore board, $13\frac{1}{2}'' \times 5\frac{1}{2}''$ and $17'' \times 10''$. Blue twisted cord, 3 yards. Sewing thread to match cord. Yellow cotton fabric, $21'' \times 14''$. Straight pins. Masking tape. Glue.

DIRECTIONS: Read "Four Methods of Cross-Stitching" and see "Stitch Details." (See Contents for all General Directions.) With short edges of cream fabric at sides, measure $2\frac{3}{4}''$ in and $3\frac{1}{2}''$ down from upper right corner for placement of first cross-stich, indicated on chart by arrows; mark mesh with pin. Insert fabric in hoop. Follow How-To's, stitch detail, color key, and chart to work all cross-stiches, using two strands of floss in needle; each stitch is worked over one vertical and one horizontal fabric thread. Solid lines on chart represent backstitches, each worked over a single fabric thread with one strand of floss in needle: Outline flower petals in gray, centers in orange, bird details in medium blue; work brown straight stitches over flower centers (see illustration).

Place finished embroidery face down on well-padded surface and steam-press lightly from center outward. When dry, center small foamcore board on wrong side of embroidered fabric; fold raw edges over board and tape in place. Cut 40" length of cord; glue or stitch ends to prevent raveling; slip-stitch to fabric around edge of board; overlap and trim ends.

Center large foamcore board on wrong side of yellow fabric; fold raw edges over board and tape in place. Cut 56" length of cord; attach as for small board. Glue small board to center of large board.

Brown | Light Blue | Medium Blue | Light Green | Medium Green | Yellow | White | Gold | Peach

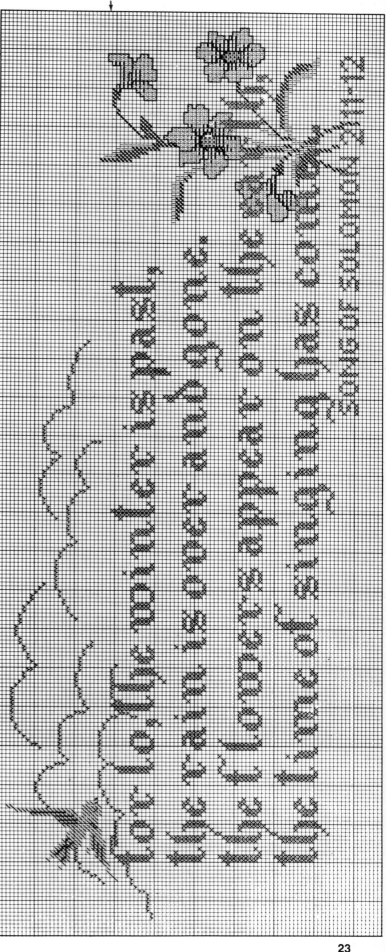

SPRINGTIME STROLL
Shown on pages 12–13

SIZE: Design area: $7\frac{3}{4}'' \times 16\frac{1}{2}''$.

EQUIPMENT: Masking tape. Embroidery scissors. Tailor's chalk. Ruler. Embroidery hoop (optional). Embroidery needle. Steam iron. Hammer.

MATERIALS: Aida cloth 11 threads-to-the-inch, $12'' \times 20\frac{1}{2}''$. DMC six-strand embroidery floss in colors listed in color key, one skein each. **For Mounting:** Heavy white cardboard, $9\frac{3}{4}'' \times 18\frac{1}{2}''$. Straight pins. Frame to fit.

DIRECTIONS: (See Contents for all General Directions.) Tape raw edges of cloth to prevent raveling. With tailor's chalk, mark design area in center of cloth. This marks the outside of the blue border. Be careful to keep cloth clean.

NOTE: Aida cloth consists of groups of thread woven in a square pattern which creates definite holes in which to make the cross-stitches.

To work cross-stitch, refer to "Stitch Details." Use three strands of floss in needle and work each cross-stitch over one group of threads of Aida cloth; each square on chart represents one stitch over one group of threads horizontally and vertically. Work all underneath stitches in one direction, and all top stitches in opposite direction. Keep stitches as even as possible; be sure the ends of all crosses meet in same hole of cloth.

To begin, find the center along one side of fabric at edge of marked border; mark with pin. Place fabric in hoop, if desired. Work border following chart, beginning at center and working from right to left. Finish one quarter of border; repeat to complete.

Work center motif following chart and color key. Steam-press when finished.

To mount, center and stretch finished embroidery over cardboard. Push pins partially into edge of cardboard, at the four corners, then at centers of sides and all along edges until there is a border of pins about $\frac{1}{4}''$ apart. When satisfied that the design is even, drive pins into cardboard edge with hammer. Frame as desired.

◹ Ivory #739	⊡ Turquoise #806
☑ Dusty Rose #3688	▭ Navy #823
⬈ Red #349	◩ Dark Brown #433
◸ Lt. Salmon #754	☒ Olive Green #470
⊙ Bright Yellow #725	◺ Gray #318
⊞ Yellow Ochre #783	◼ Black #310
◿ Burnt Orange #922	
⬕ Eggplant Purple #3685	
⊡ Orchid #209	
⊟ Light Blue #519	
⊠ Medium Blue #826	

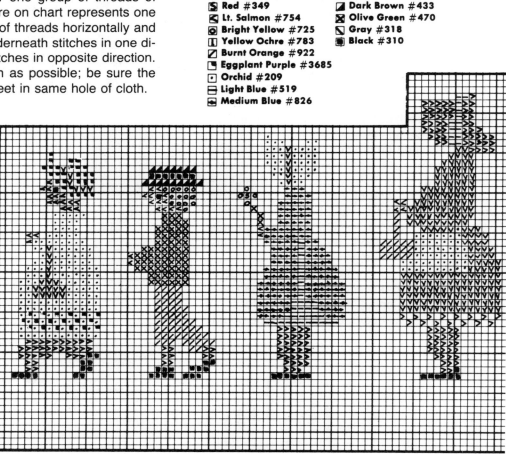

TULIPS AND IRISES

Shown on page 16

SIZE: Design area for each picture, approximately 7″ × 23″.

EQUIPMENT: Pencil. Ruler. Embroidery scissors. Embroidery and sewing needles. Tweezers. Penelope (or cross-stitch) canvas, 7 mesh-to-the-inch, approximately 9″ × 25″. Embroidery hoop and picture frame (optional).

For Blocking: Sewing thread. Soft wooden surface. Brown wrapping paper. T-square. Thumbtacks.

MATERIALS: White or cream linen, at least 15″ × 31″ for each picture. DMC six-strand embroidery floss:

For Irises Only: 1 skein each of bottle green #895, yellow #725, orange #740, light pink #818, wine #3685, deep purple #550, and lavender #210; 2 skeins each of yellow-green #703, medium green #701, dark emerald green #699, medium rose #603, dark rose #601, purple #552, and violet #208; 3 skeins of rose pink #605. **For Tulips Only,** 1 skein each of bottle green, yellow, orange, light pink, wine, deep purple, and lavender; 2 skeins each of yellow-green, dark emerald green, rose pink, medium rose, dark rose, purple and violet; 3 skeins of medium green. **For**

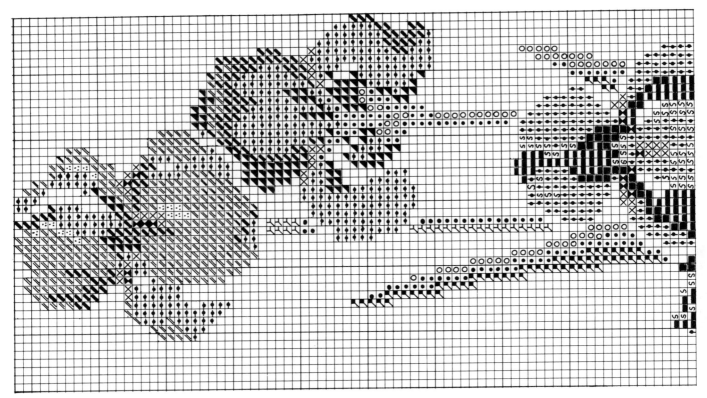

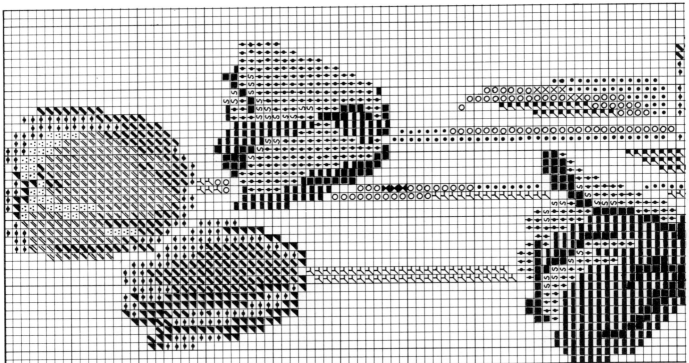

Mounting: Stiff cardboard for picture size desired. Small straight pins. Masking tape.

DIRECTIONS: See "Four Methods of Cross-stitching." (See Contents for all General Directions.) Center canvas on linen and baste in place.

Following charts and color key, work cross-stitch design over canvas mesh and through linen. Work all cross-stitches using six strands of floss in needle. Each filled-in square on chart is equal to one cross-stitch.

When embroidery is complete, remove canvas threads carefully. Block and mount picture, following directions for "Embroidery Basics." Frame as desired.

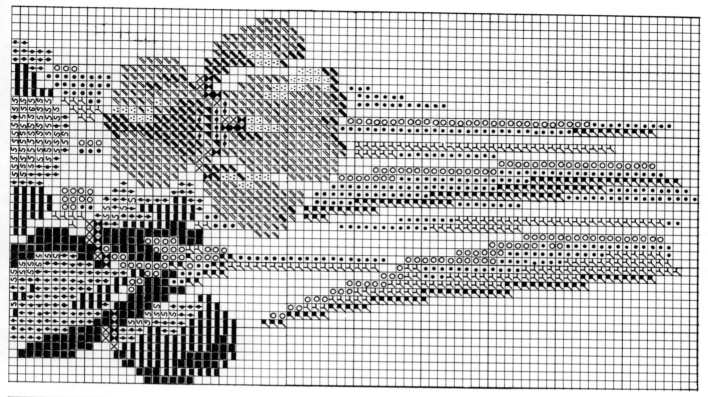

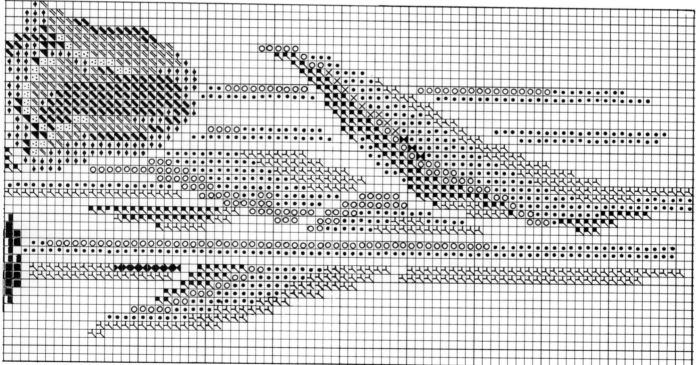

◨ YELLOW-GREEN ◉ MED. GREEN ▨ DK. EMERALD GREEN ◣ BOTTLE GREEN ⊠ YELLOW ◆ ORANGE ⊡ LT. PINK ▧ ROSE PINK ◨ MED. ROSE ✦ DK. ROSE ◺ WINE Ⓢ LAVENDER ◈ VIOLET ▮ PURPLE ■ DP. PURPLE

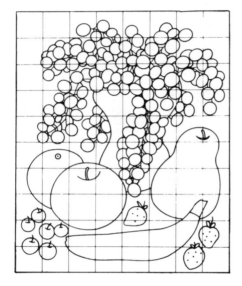

ASSISI PICTURES
Shown on page 15

EQUIPMENT: Pencil. Paper for patterns. Ruler. Scissors. Tracing paper. Dressmaker's tracing (carbon) paper. Embroidery hoop. Embroidery needle. Masking tape. Padded ironing board.

MATERIALS: For each: White Aida cloth or even-weave linen 22 threads-to-the-inch, 11″ × 9″. Six-strand embroidery floss in colors shown or desired (about four skeins for each background, one skein or less for outlining details). Cardboard, 10″ × 8″. Frame.

GENERAL DIRECTIONS: (See Contents for all General Directions for cross-stitch and embroidery.) Tape raw edges of cloth to prevent raveling. Enlarge designs by copying on paper ruled in 1″ squares. Center pattern on cloth, and with dressmaker's carbon between, go over lines with pencil to transfer to fabric. Place cloth in embroidery hoop, being sure not to distort threads.

See "Stitch Details" and "Four Methods of Cross-Stitching." Following pattern and individual directions, embroider all outlines in backstitch, all dots in French knots. Use two strands of floss in needle for all embroidery.

Working over two threads vertically and horizontally, fill in background with cross-stitches.

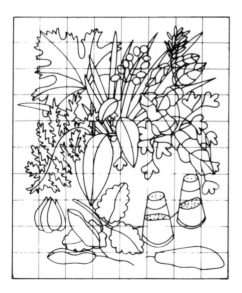

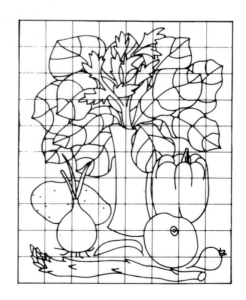

Fruit Picture: Use gold for pear and banana; red for apple, cherries, and strawberries; orange for orange; two purple shades for grapes; turquoise for vase; brown for stems; dark green for leaves on strawberries. Fill in background with mint green floss.

Vegetable Picture: Use various shades of green for pepper, spinach, celery, asparagus, string bean, and leaves on radish and onion. Use magenta for radish; red for tomato; gold for onion; tan for potato, French knots and onion roots; turquoise for vase; brown for stems on pepper and tomato. Fill in background with yellow floss.

Spice Picture: Use various shades of green for leaves; red for pepper and berries; tan for garlic; brown for stems; gold for allspice, salt and pepper shaker tops; light gold for mustard buds; light and dark grays for salt and pepper bottoms and French knots; light blue for vase. Fill in background with orange floss.

To Finish: See "Embroidery Basics."

PETALED PILLOWS
Shown on page 15

SIZE: 9" square.

EQUIPMENT: Pencil. Paper for patterns. Ruler. Scissors, Embroidery and sewing needles. Straight pins. Dressmaker's tracing (carbon) paper. Masking tape. Embroidery hoop (optional).

MATERIALS: For each: White Aida cloth 9 threads to the inch, 10" square. Linen or cotton fabric for backing, 10" square. Muslin, 10½" × 21" for inner pillow. Polyester fiberfill for stuffing. **For Assisi Pillow:** Embroidery cotton, one skein deep wine. Six-strand embroidery floss, six skeins lavender. **For Cross-Stitch Pillow:** No. 5 pearl cotton, one skein (27.3 yds.) or less: red, deep wine, orange, yellow, green, purple.

GENERAL DIRECTIONS: (See Contents for all General Directions for cross-stitch and details.) Enlarge pattern for flower design by copying on paper ruled in 1" squares. Using dressmaker's carbon and pencil, transfer outline of flower to center of cloth. Tape edges of cloth to prevent raveling. If desired, place fabric in hoop.

Following individual directions, embroider design. To work cross-stitch on Aida cloth, see "Four Methods of Cross-Stitching." Work each cross-stitch over one group of threads of cloth horizontally and vertically.

Assisi Pillow: Refer to "Stitch Details." Using one strand of deep wine embroidery cotton in needle, work complete outline of flower in backstitch. Using three strands of lavender floss in needle, fill in background, petal centers, and inner circle with cross-stitch.

Cross-Stitch Pillow: Follow color key and numbers given on pattern. Using one strand of pearl cotton in needle for all cross-stitches, begin stitching in flower center. Fill in entire center area, then embroider outward as numbered. Work all petals in the same manner as numbered petal. Use the purple last and outline all around each flower petal with one row of cross-stitches.

To Finish: With right sides facing, pin embroidered cloth and fabric backing together. Making ½" seams, sew together, leaving a 6" opening in center of one side. Turn to right side. Push out corners.

For inner pillow, cut two pieces of muslin 10½" square. Making ¼" seams, stitch together all around, leaving an opening along one side. Turn right side out; stuff firmly. Turn in open edges and slip-stitch closed. Insert inner pillow into embroidered pillow cover. Turn raw edges in and slip-stitch closed.

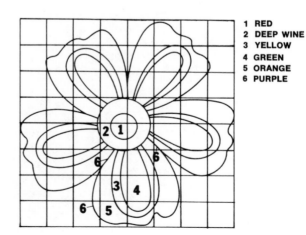

1	RED
2	DEEP WINE
3	YELLOW
4	GREEN
5	ORANGE
6	PURPLE

FRONT ROOM
Shown on page 40

SIZE: Design area, 10″ × 12½″ (108 × 135 stitches).

EQUIPMENT: Ruler. Embroidery scissors, needle and hoop. Masking tape. Steam iron.

MATERIALS: Zweigart's Hardanger #1008 even-weave fabric, 22 threads-to-the-inch, cream, 15″ × 17½″ piece. DMC six-strand embroidery floss, one skein of each color in color key, unless otherwise listed in parentheses. **Note:** For larger cross-stitches, use Zweigart's "Ainring" #3793, 18 threads-to-the-inch Aida cloth, cream, 17″ × 20″ piece; design area will be 12″ × 15″. For a closer match to the fabric used in the 1944 original shown in photograph, use Zweigart's "Belfast" #3609 cream linen, 31 threads-to-the-inch, 16″ × 18½″ piece; design area will be 11″ × 13½″. If using either of these fabrics, see modifications in directions below.

DIRECTIONS: (See Contents for all General Directions.) Tape all raw edges of fabric to prevent raveling. Measure and mark design area in center of fabric by running a line of basting all around; there should be a 2½″ margin on all sides. Cut floss into 18″ lengths; separate strands and work with three strands in needle. (For Ainring Aida cloth, use four strands in needle.) Read "Four Methods of Cross-Stitching."

Each square on chart represents two horizontal and two vertical fabric threads. Each symbol represents one cross-stitch; different symbols represent different colors (see color key). Work stitches over two threads in each direction. (For Belfast linen, each square represents three fabric threads in each direction; work cross-stitches over three threads.) Always bring needle up to front and down to back of work between two adjacent threads; do not split fabric threads. Long straight lines on chart indicate additional embroidery; work as directed after all cross-stitches are completed.

To Stitch: With short fabric edges at top and bottom, place upper left corner of design area in hoop, making fabric taut and keeping threads straight and even. Begin by working "window" and "wallpaper" flowers, counting two fabric threads (three, if using Belfast linen) in each direction for each blank square on chart between stitches. Continue working, following chart and color key, and moving hoop as needed, until all cross-stitches are completed. Using a single strand of black floss, work backstitch for lamp and sail outlines, and straight stitch for ship's rigging. Using four strands of black floss in needle, work straight stitch for knitting needles. Remove basting.

Place finished embroidery, face down, on well-padded surface and steam-press lightly from center outward. Mount and frame as desired.

PUMPKIN PICTURE
Shown on page 34

SIZE: Design area, 11″ × 12″.

EQUIPMENT: Masking tape. Scissors. Embroidery needle. Pencil. Ruler. Straight pins. Embroidery hoop.

MATERIALS: White or cream-colored linen 18 threads-to-the-inch, at least 15″ × 16″ (allows for background area around design and margins for mounting only. To determine amount you will need, measure desired frame rabbet size and add 2″ extra all around for turning under). DMC six-strand embroidery floss: one skein of each color listed in color key unless otherwise noted in parentheses. Stiff white mounting cardboard, ⅛″ thick, the same as frame rabbet size. Short straight pins. Frame to fit.

DIRECTIONS: Tape fabric edges to prevent raveling. Place fabric on smooth hard surface. Using a pencil, lightly mark design area 11″ × 12″ in center of fabric. Then find center of design area by folding fabric in half horizontally and vertically. Mark center with pin.

☑ Snow White (5)		⊞ Apple Green #703	
� Light Gray #762 (2)		⌷ Medium Green #3347	
⊠ Medium Gray #318 (2)		⋈ Dark Green #3345	
◉ Black #310 (2)		⋎ Pale Yellow #745	
⊠ Sky Blue #800		△ Deep Yellow #743	
⊡ Medium Blue #798		⊎ Goldenrod #742	
◩ Pink #963 (2)		⊡ Beige #738	
⊡ Medium Rose #962 (2)		⊡ Toast #950	
⊟ Bright Rose #335		⊞ Honey #437	
◪ Red #326		⋈ Light Brown #407	
◣ Garnet #815		⟆ Medium Brown #435	
⊡ Nile Green #966 (2)		◤ Dark Brown #801	

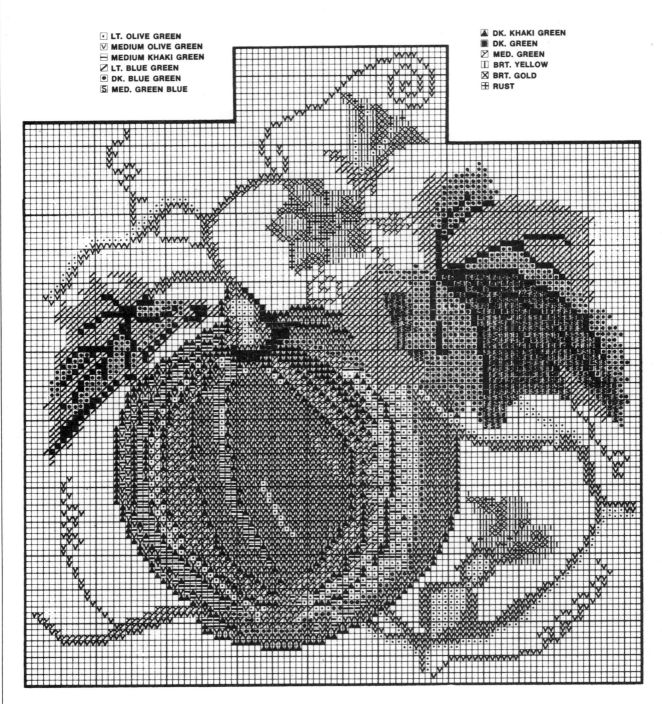

Color Key:

- ⊡ LT. OLIVE GREEN
- Ⅴ MEDIUM OLIVE GREEN
- ⊟ MEDIUM KHAKI GREEN
- ⊿ LT. BLUE GREEN
- ◉ DK. BLUE GREEN
- Ⓢ MED. GREEN BLUE
- ▲ DK. KHAKI GREEN
- ◼ DK. GREEN
- ⊠ MED. GREEN
- Ⅱ BRT. YELLOW
- ✕ BRT. GOLD
- ⊞ RUST

Entire picture is worked in cross-stitch. See "Four Methods of Cross-Stitching". Each square on chart represents two threads horizontally and two threads vertically. To begin embroidery, find center square on chart (center rows marked by arrows). Following chart and color key, embroider outward. Use three strands of six-strand floss in needle. Do not make knots. Begin by leaving 1″ of floss end on back and working over it to secure; to end, run strand through stitches on back. When embroidery is finished, block and mount following directions for "Embroidery Basics." Frame as desired.

*A "pottery" bean pot becomes the perfect vase for
a delightful assortment of spring flowers.
Stitches are worked with embroidery floss in more than
twenty colors. Also see page 9, Autumn Bouquet.
Directions for Seasons' Bouquets on page 17.*

A gardenful of cross-stitch can be yours at just the count of a thread! Leafy pumpkin with tiny yellow blossoms is stitched with floss on an 18 thread-to-the-inch fabric (design area: 11″ × 12″). Giant Rose is a dramatic wall panel stitched on a much heavier fabric with soft yarn. The finished panel measures 44″ × 30″. Directions for Pumpkin Picture, page 31, and Giant Rose, page 45.

*A Chinese Ring-Necked Pheasant perches above its mate, resplendent
in the hues of autumn foliage. The long-tailed game bird
came to this country in the 19th century. Design size, 16" × 20"; to work
over Penelope canvas. Directions for Pheasants, page 45.*

*Wild and free, the mallard duck is found from Nova Scotia to
California. Here, a pair break their migratory flight to rest in a marsh;
he rises to display a flash of vivid blue wing. Design area, on
7 crosses-to-the-inch fabric, is 16" × 20". Mallard directions on page 45.*

Buds and blossoms of pink and blue are arranged in a stylized bouquet, 13½″ × 18½″, worked with more than 20 colors of floss over Penelope canvas. Roses and Delphiniums, page 41.

A new sampler, bordered with the names of the original thirteen states repeated over and over in cross-stitch, is centered with a spray of official state flowers. Embroidery is worked on linen with DMC floss for a picture 19″ square. State Flowers Sampler, directions on page 42.

"Front Room" is a nostalgic scene to cross-stitch, perfect for any cozy corner.
Details are added with backstitch and straight stitch. Design
measures 10" × 12½"; for directions, see page 31.

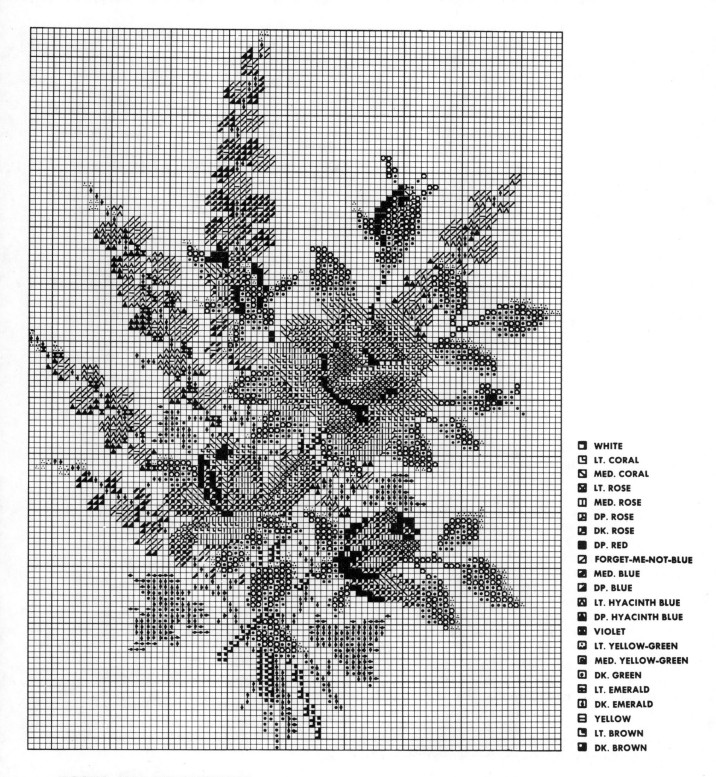

□	WHITE
◨	LT. CORAL
◩	MED. CORAL
◪	LT. ROSE
◫	MED. ROSE
▨	DP. ROSE
◰	DK. ROSE
■	DP. RED
▨	FORGET-ME-NOT-BLUE
◲	MED. BLUE
◳	DP. BLUE
◱	LT. HYACINTH BLUE
▩	DP. HYACINTH BLUE
◍	VIOLET
◌	LT. YELLOW-GREEN
◎	MED. YELLOW-GREEN
◐	DK. GREEN
◒	LT. EMERALD
◑	DK. EMERALD
◓	YELLOW
◔	LT. BROWN
◕	DK. BROWN

ROSES AND DELPHINIUMS
Shown on page 38

SIZE: Design size, approxiately 13½″ × 18½″.
EQUIPMENT: Pencil. Ruler. Embroidery scissors. Embroidery and sewing needles. Tweezers. Penelope (or cross-stitch) canvas, 7 mesh-to-the-inch, approximately 15″ × 20″. Embroidery hoop and picture frame (optional). **For Blocking:** Sewing thread. Soft wooden surface. Brown wrapping paper. T-square. Thumbtacks.

MATERIALS: White or cream linen, at least 21″ × 26″. DMC six-strand embroidery floss: 1 skein each of white, light coral #818, medium coral #3326, light rose #776, medium rose #899, deep rose #335, dark rose #309, deep red #815, medium blue #334, deep blue #825, light hyacinth blue #799, deep hyacinth blue #797, violet #552, light yellow-green #907, light emerald #913, dark emerald #911, yellow #743, light brown #435, and dark brown #801; 2 skeins each of forget-me-not blue #827, medium yellow-green #905, and dark green #319. **For Mounting:** Stiff mounting cardboard (size of picture). Small straight pins. Masking tape.

DIRECTIONS: See "Four Methods of Cross-Stitching." (See Contents for all General Directions.) Center canvas on linen and baste in place.

Following chart and color key above, work cross-stitch design over canvas mesh and through linen. Work all cross-stitches using six strands of floss in needle. Each filled-in square on chart is equal to one cross-stitch.

When embroidery is complete, remove canvas threads carefully. Block and mount picture, following directions under "Embroidery Basics." Frame as desired.

STATE FLOWERS SAMPLER
Shown on page 39

SIZE: 18½" square, mounted.
EQUIPMENT: Pencil. Ruler. Scissors. Paper for patterns. Dressmaker's tracing (carbon) paper. Tracing wheel or dry ball-point pen. Embroidery scissors, needle, and hoop. **For Blocking and Mounting:** T-square. Soft wooden surface. Brown wrapping paper. Rustproof thumbtacks. Tack hammer. Towel.
MATERIALS: Cream-colored linen, 22" square. DMC six-strand embroidery floss, one 8.7 yard skein each of: #550 dk. purple, #208 purple, #209 lavender, #310 black, #938 dk. brown, #801 brown, #436 camel, #444 yellow, #725 gold, #746 cream, #893 bright pink, #605 pink, #776 lt. pink, #761 pale rose, #754 pale peach, #351 coral, #906 bright green, #904 forest green, #469 olive green, #937 dk. olive; seven skeins of #907 chartreuse. **For Blocking and Mounting:** Heavy mounting cardboard, 18½" square. Small straight pins. Masking tape. Frame with 18½" rabbet size.
DIRECTIONS: Enlarge pattern by copying on paper ruled in 1" squares. With dressmaker's tracing carbon and dry ball-point pen, center and transfer design to linen.
To Embroider Floral Design: Place upper right area of floral design in embroidery hoop, holding the fabric firmly without distortions. Refer to flower embroidery chart. Following chart, thread needle with specified number of strands according to the area of the flower being worked. Cut strands about 18"–20" long for all embroidery. Work flower area in designated color and stitch, referring to "Stitch Details."

To begin a strand, take a tiny backstitch to anchor it; to end a strand, run underneath stitches on underside of linen. Do not use knots. To facilitate the many color changes, keep several needles threaded to be used as needed. Fasten off thread when ending each motif, rather than carrying it to another motif. As work proceeds, reposition linen in the embroidery hoop.

When floral design is complete, begin background. For all background cross-stitches, thread needle with three strands of chartreuse.

To Block and Mount: See directions under "Embroidery Basics."

FLOWER EMBROIDERY CHART

Flower Area	Stitch	Color	Strands
#1 CHEROKEE ROSE			
Petals	Split	746 Cream	3
Petal edges	Straight	907 Chartreuse	2
Petal lines	Outline	907 Chartreuse	2
Inner center	French knot	907 Chartreuse	3
Outer center	Straight	444 Yellow	2
Sepal	Satin	907 Chartreuse	2
Stems	Outline	907 Chartreuse	3
Leaves	Split	907 Chartreuse	3
Veins	Outline	904 Forest Green	2
#2 BLACK-EYED SUSAN			
Petals	Satin	725 Gold	3
Centers	French knot	938 Dk Brown	3
Outlines	Running	938 Dk. Brown	1
Stem	Outline	904 Forest Green	3
Sepal	Satin	904 Forest Green	3
#3 DOGWOOD			
Petals	Split	746 Cream	3
Petal trim	Satin	801 Brown	3
Outlines	Running	310 Black	1
Centers	French knot	907 Chartreuse	3
Leaves	Split	907 Chartreuse	3
Veins	Outline	937 Dk. Olive	2
#4 PEACH BLOSSOMS			
Petals	Satin	893 Bright Pink	2
Leaves, Sepal	Satin	906 Bright Green	2
Stems	Chain	801 Brown	3

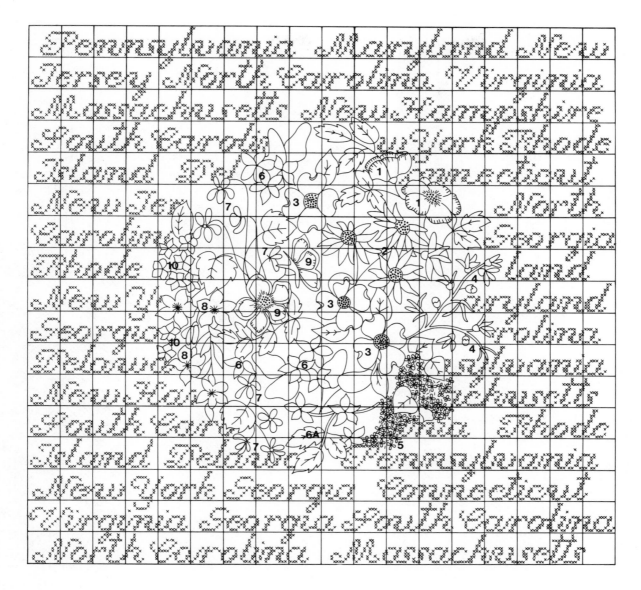

#5 LILACS

Petals	Lazy daisy	208 Purple and 209 Lavender (alternate)	2
Centers	French knot	444 Yellow	3
Leaves	Split	937 Dk. Olive	3
Veins	Outline	310 Black	2

#6 ARBUTUS

Petals	Split	605 Pink	3
Petal lines	Straight	310 Black	1
Centers	French knot	725 Gold	3
Leaves	Split	904 Forest Green	3
Stems	Outline	904 Forest Green	3

#6A LEAVES

Leaves	Split	907 Chartreuse	3
Veins	Outline	937 Dk. Olive	2
Stems	Chain	907 Chartreuse	3

#7 VIOLETS

Petals	Satin	550 Dk. Purple	2
Centers	Satin	725 Gold	2
Leaves	Split	937 Dk. Olive	3
Veins	Outline	310 Black	2
Stems	Outline	937 Dk. Olive	3

#8 JASMINE

Petals	Split	444 Yellow	3
Petal lines	Straight	436 Camel	3
Centers	French knot	436 Camel	3
Leaves	Satin	907 Chartreuse	2
Stems	Outline	907 Chartreuse	2

#9 WILD ROSE

Petals (main)	Split	754 Pale Peach	3
Petal edges	Split	761 Pale Rose	3
Center lines	Straight	893 Bright Pink and 351 Coral (alternate)	3
Centers (open flower only)	French knot	444 Yellow and 496 Camel (alternate)	3
Leaves	Split	906 Bright Green	3
Veins	Outline	937 Dk. Olive	2

#10 MOUNTAIN LAUREL

Petals	Satin	776 Lt. Pink	2
Petal lines	Straight	893 Bright Pink	2
Leaves	Split	469 Olive	3
Veins	Outline	310 Black	2

GIANT ROSE
Shown on page 35

SIZE: About 44″ × 30″.
EQUIPMENT: Large-eyed tapestry needle. Scissors. Ruler. Pencil. Straight pins. Iron.
MATERIALS: Zweigart Turkestan even-weave jute, 4 threads-to-the-inch, beige, 47″ × 33″. Heavy rug yarn, 2-ounce skeins (60 yards), one skein of each color listed in color key, unless otherwise noted in parentheses.

For Mounting: Fiberboard 44″ × 30″. Large straight pins. Masking tape.
DIRECTIONS: (See Contents for all General Directions.) Tape fabric edges to prevent raveling. Using a pencil, mark a design area 44″ × 30″ centered on fabric. Then find center of design area by folding fabric in half horizontally and vertically. Mark center with pin.
EMBROIDERY: Refer to "Stitch Details," and "Four Methods of Cross-Stitching." The picture is worked in cross-stitch with French knots around center of large flower. Use one strand of yarn in needle and work each cross-stitch over one group of threads; each square on chart represents one cross-stitch worked over one group of threads horizontally and vertically.

To begin embroidery, find center square on chart (center rows marked by arrows). Following chart and color key, embroider from center outward. Embroider roses and leaves first; then fill in the background to marked design area.

When cross-stitch is completed, make French knots randomly around flower center and small straight stitches radiating from the center with saffron color yarn (refer to illustration as a guide).

Do not make knots. Begin by leaving an end of yarn on back and working over it to secure; to begin and end successive strands, run yarn end through stitches on back.

Block and mount, following directions in "Embroidery Basics."

PHEASANTS
Shown on page 36

SIZE: Design area, approximately 16″ × 20″.
EQUIPMENT: Pencil. Ruler. Embroidery scissors. Embroidery and sewing needles. Tweezers. Penelope (or cross-stitch) canvas, 7 mesh-to-the-inch, approximately 18″ × 22″. Embroidery hoop and picture frame (optional). **For Blocking:** Sewing thread. Soft wooden surface. Brown wrapping paper. T-square. Thumbtacks.
MATERIALS: White or cream linen, at least 24″ × 28″. DMC Six-Strand Embroidery Floss: 1 skein each of white, light gray #318, taupe #644, light wheat #738, medium brown #435, light buttercup #743, dark buttercup #741, light rust #922, bright rose-rust #919, yellow-green #907, light emerald #913, dark emerald #911, turquoise #518, peacock #517, cornflower blue #826, royal blue #820, bright salmon #758, bright red #326, dark red #816, rose #335, and deep wine rose #815; 2 skeins each of medium gray #414, black #310, wheat #436, deep brown #801, and deep rust #918.

For Mounting: Stiff mounting cardboard (size of picture). Small straight pins. Masking tape.
DIRECTIONS: See "Four Methods of Cross-Stitching." (See Contents for all General Directions.) Center canvas on linen and baste in place.

Following chart and color key, work cross-stitch design over canvas mesh and through linen. Work all cross-stitches using six strands of floss in needle. Each filled-in square on chart is equal to one cross-stitch.

When embroidery is complete, remove canvas threads carefully. Block and mount picture, following directions under "Embroidery Basics." Frame as desired.

MALLARDS
Shown on page 37

SIZE: Design area, approximately 16″ × 20″.
EQUIPMENT: Pencil. Ruler. Embroidery scissors. Embroidery and sewing needles. Tweezers. Penelope (or cross-stitch) canvas, 7 mesh-to-the-

---

☐ JUTE HEATHER (BEIGE) 1439 (3)
Ⓢ BLUE LOVAT HEATHER 1479
▯ LODEN HEATHER 1475
☒ JAMAICA GREEN HEATHER 1478
◪ DARTMOUTH (DARK GREEN) 1444
▷ SHAMROCK 1443
△ LIME 14271

⊞ MED. LIME 14272
⊟ LT. LIME 1427
⊡ MAROON 1425
◩ CHERRY SMASH HEATHER (DEEP ROSE)
⊡ PINK HEATHER 1415 (3)   1420 (3)
▽ ORANGE 1406
⊟ SAFFRON 14051

□ WHITE	⊞ ROYAL BLUE	☑ YELLOW-GREEN	☒ MED. BROWN
⊡ LT. GRAY	⊞ BR. SALMON	☒ LT. EMERALD	⊠ DP. BROWN
⊟ MED. GRAY	⊾ BR. RED	☑ DK. EMERALD	⊟ LT. BUTTERCUP
■ BLACK	◪ DK. RED	⊠ TURQUOISE	⊟ DK. BUTTERCUP
⊡ TAUPE	⊠ ROSE	⊠ PEACOCK BLUE	☒ LT. RUST
⊞ LT. WHEAT	⊟ DP. WINE ROSE	⫿ CORNFLOWER BLUE	☒ BR. ROSE RUST
⊠ WHEAT			⊠ DP. RUST

�W WHITE	⊘ LT. EMERALD	⊡ TAUPE
⊙ LT. GRAY	⊘ DK. EMERALD	⊞ LT. WHEAT
⊟ MED. GRAY	⊞ LEMON YELLOW	⊞ WHEAT
■ BLACK	⊟ LT. BUTTERCUP	⊘ MED. BROWN
⊠ TURQUOISE	⊟ DK. BUTTERCUP	⊙ DP. BROWN
⠿ CORNFLOWER BLUE	⊻ LT. RUST	⊟ ROSE
⠿ ROYAL BLUE	▼ BR. ROSE RUST	⊟ BR. RED
⊘ LT. YELLOW-GREEN	⊘ DP. RUST	■ DP. WINE ROSE

inch, approximately 18″ × 22″. Embroidery hoop and picture frame (optional). **For Blocking:** Sewing thread. Soft wooden surface. Brown wrapping paper. T-square. Thumbtacks.

MATERIALS: White or cream even-weave linen, at least 24″ × 28″. DMC six-strand embroidery floss: 1 skein each of white, light gray #318, medium gray #414, turquoise #518, cornflower blue #826, royal blue #820, light yellow-green #907, light emerald #913, dark emerald #911, lemon yellow #307, light buttercup #743, dark buttercup #741, light rust #922, bright rose rust #919, deep rust #918, light wheat #738, wheat #436, rose #335, bright red #326, and deep wine rose #815; 2 skeins of black #310, medium brown #435, and taupe #644; 3 skeins of deep brown #801. **For Mounting:** Stiff mounting cardboard (picture size). Small straight pins. Masking tape. Picture frame.

DIRECTIONS: See "Four Methods of Cross-Stitching." (See Contents for all General Directions.) Center canvas on linen and baste in place.

Following chart and color key, work cross-stitch design over canvas mesh and through linen. Work all cross-stitches using six strands of floss in needle. Each filled-in square on chart is equal to one cross-stitch.

When embroidery is complete, remove canvas threads carefully. Block and mount picture, following "Embroidery Basics." Frame as desired.

CROSS-POINT
Shown on pages 65 and 66

SIZES: Pillow, $12\frac{1}{2}″$ × $13\frac{1}{2}″$; Tote Bag, 10″ × 14″; Eyeglass Case, $3\frac{1}{4}″$ × 7″; Address Book Cover to fit 6″ × 7″ loose-leaf address book. Footstool and chair seat covers to fit furniture.

EQUIPMENT: Scissors. Tape measure. Tapestry and sewing needles. Masking tape. Dark sewing thread. Straight pins. Tailor's chalk. Embroidery hoop. Steam iron. Sewing machine. For footstool and chair seat covers: staple gun.

MATERIALS: Zweigart Pearl Aida cloth (Art. 1007), 42″ wide, 11 threads-to-the-inch, ecru: Pillow, $\frac{1}{2}$ yard; Tote Bag, $\frac{3}{8}$ yard; Eyeglass Case, $\frac{1}{4}$ yard; Address Book Cover, $\frac{1}{4}$ yard. To determine yardages for footstool and chair seat covers, measure area to be covered and add 6″ to each dimension. DMC pearl cotton #5; see color keys and illustrations; one ball each color in key, except for blue in tote, two balls; amounts for footstool and chair seat covers will vary. **Additional:** Pillow, fabric for back, $13\frac{1}{2}″$ × $14\frac{1}{2}″$ piece; green upholstery welting, $1\frac{1}{2}$ yards; polyester fiberfill; sewing thread to match fabric. Tote Bag, sturdy ecru canvas 45″ wide, 1 yard; pink upholstery welting, 3 yards; ecru sewing thread. Eyeglass Case, scrap of lining fabric; batting; ecru sewing thread. Address Book Cover, batting; green velvet cord, $1\frac{1}{2}$ yard; green sewing thread; white craft glue; scrap of fabric for lining.

DIRECTIONS: Read "Four Methods of Cross-Stitching." (See Contents for all General Directions.) Work each design with one strand of pearl cotton in tapestry needle, making each cross-stitch over one "square" of Aida cloth.

For Pillow: Cut 17″ × 18″ piece of Aida cloth. Mark $12\frac{1}{2}″$ × $13\frac{1}{2}″$ design area centered on cloth, leaving $2\frac{1}{4}″$ margin all around; baste. Fold cloth into quarters to find exact center and mark thread with pin. With long sides of cloth at top and bottom and following Zigzag chart, count three squares up from pin to make first pink stitch, indicated on chart by arrow. Following chart and working from center out to both right and left margins, complete pink row for five complete V's. Work adjacent green rows in same manner; continue working horizontal rows until design area is filled.

Trim margins around basting to $\frac{1}{2}″$. **To attach welting:** Begin in middle of one side; pin welting on right side of front inside basting, so that stitching of welting is close to basting line; overlap ends 1″ and cut away excess. Using zipper foot attachment and starting 2″ from beginning of welting, machine-stitch all around piece close to cord, rounding off corners slightly, to 2″ from end of welting. Snip out 1″ of cord from overlapping end. Turn under $\frac{1}{2}″$ of extra fabric and, butting ends of cord, fit it over the start of welting (see diagram). Finish stitching welting to piece. Place front and back pieces together, right sides facing and edges

PILLOW AND GLASSES CASE

☑	Green
⊡	Pink (Violet)

ZIGZAG

BOOK AND FOOTSTOOL

⊙	Blue (Gold)
⊟	Pink (Green)

TOTE AND CHAIR SEAT

⊙	Blue (Pink)
⊡	Pink (Violet)
Ⅱ	Violet (Blue)
☒	Green
Ⓢ	Gold

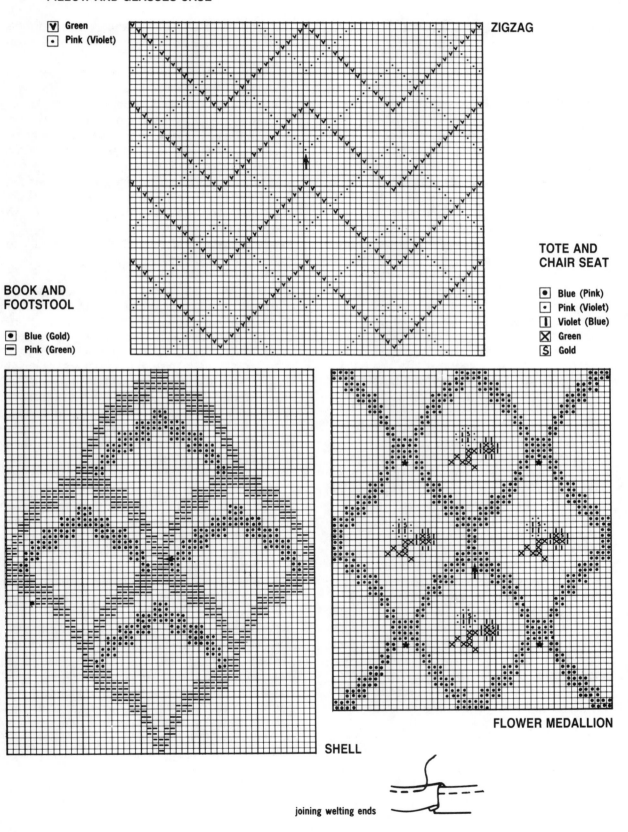

SHELL

FLOWER MEDALLION

joining welting ends

even. Stitch around piece close to stitching line of front, leaving an opening for turning. Clip corners, turn to right side, stuff with fiberfill, and slip-stitch opening closed.

For Tote Bag: Cut 13″ × 17″ piece of Aida cloth. Fold cloth into quarters to find exact center and mark thread with pin. With short sides of cloth at top and bottom and following Flower Medallion Chart, count 13 squares up from pin to make first blue stitch, indicated on chart by arrow. Working from center outward, repeat medallion pattern until there are five horizontal rows of five medallions each (about 10″ × 14″ in area); see illustration. Fill in each space with pink and violet flowers.

Cut 13″ × 17″ piece of canvas. Lay worked piece over canvas, wrong sides facing and raw edges even; pin. Baste a guideline along edge of embroidery through both thicknesses, using dark thread; trim margin around guideline to $\frac{1}{2}$″ for seam allowance. Cut same-size piece of canvas for back of tote and attach welting to outside edges of both pieces; see directions for pillow, above. For straps, cut two 3″ × 45″ canvas strips and fold each in half lengthwise. Stitch edges of long sides together, making $\frac{1}{2}$″ seam; turn; press. To attach straps, turn front and back tote pieces wrong side up. Along bottom of each, measure $2\frac{1}{4}$″ in from sides and mark. Pin one end of a strap outside each mark, so ends are even with bottom of piece and strap curves beyond top edge of piece to form handle; machine-stitch strap ends $\frac{1}{4}$″ from bottom edge; baste straps to piece along top edge. For sides and bottom of tote, cut $3\frac{1}{2}$″ × 39″ canvas strip and pin, with right sides facing and edges even, along sides and bottom of tote front, so that $\frac{1}{2}$″ extends beyond top edge; stitch close to cord. Stitch strip to tote back in same manner. Turn raw edge at top of tote to inside and slip-stitch.

For Eyeglass Case: Cut 9″ × $21\frac{1}{2}$″ piece of Aida cloth. Mark $3\frac{1}{2}$″ × 16″ design area centered on cloth, leaving $2\frac{3}{4}$″ margin all around; baste. With long sides of cloth at top and bottom and beginning at upper left corner of Zigzag Chart for first green stitch, work first green row across to right, repeating pattern for six V's (adjust margin at right if necessary, to align with last V). Work partial violet row across top. Continue working across,

following chart, until design area is filled, or until second complete violet row is worked (adjust bottom margin if necessary).

Trim margin outside basting to $\frac{1}{2}$″ for seam allowance. Cut same-size piece batting and baste to wrong side of worked piece. From lining fabric, cut two 7″ strips same width as worked piece. With right sides facing, edges even, and making $\frac{1}{2}$″ seams, stitch each short side of padded piece to one short side of a lining piece to form one long strip; press seams to one side. Fold strip in half widthwise, wrong side out, and stitch $\frac{1}{2}$″ seam along each long edge to form a "sack"; turn. Press raw edges at top of sack $\frac{1}{4}$″ to wrong side and topstitch closed. Push lining into padded piece with point of scissors.

For Address Book Cover: Remove pages and open address book so cover and spine lie flat; cut a layer of batting to fit and lightly glue to front of cover. Cut a piece of Aida cloth to fit cover, including spine, plus $1\frac{1}{2}$″ margin all around. Stretch cloth around cover and tape to inside. With tailor's chalk, lightly mark line around front leaf of cover only. Untape piece and set address book aside. Measure marked area and determine exact center; make first pink stitch on Shell Chart at center, indicated on chart by arrow. Working from center outward, work entire chart, completing all pink stitches, then blue stitches.

To complete cover, stretch piece over book, centering motif on front and gluing margins to inside; use point of scissors to push fabric at spine under ring section of binder. Cut piece of lining fabric to size of each inside cover; press edges under $\frac{1}{4}$″, then glue in place, overlapping edges of front piece. Using green thread and a needle, slip-stitch velvet cording to outside edge of cover as shown in illustration, butting and slip-stitching ends together.

For Footstool and Chair Seat Covers: Measure area to be covered, adding 6″ to each dimension, and cut Aida cloth to size. Fold cloth into quarters to determine exact center and mark with a pin. Following Shell Chart for footstool and Flower Medallion Chart for chair seat (or as desired), take first stitch at center, indicated on chart by arrow. Work desired pattern from center outwards, repeating pattern until desired-size cover is reached. For stool, work all green stitches, then gold stitches. For chair, complete pink medallions first, omitting starred rows if desired (see illustration for difference between chair and tote); then fill in with violet and blue flowers.

To cover stool or chair seat, center cross-stitch over upholstered cushion. Beginning at center on opposite sides and working toward corners, stretch fabric taut across cushion and staple fabric to cushion back, using staple gun.

CROSS-STITCH PILLOWS
Shown on page 67

SIZE: Each pillow, 16″ square.

EQUIPMENT: Pencil. Ruler. Masking tape. Scissors. Straight pins. Embroidery hoop. Embroidery needle. Steam iron. Padded surface. Sewing machine.

MATERIALS: For Each Pillow: Zweigart "Florina" fabric, 14 threads-to-the-inch, 20″ square. Paternayan Persian yarn, 3-strand: 3 skeins each Brown #402, Blue #501; 2 skeins each Red #840, Gold #701; 1 skein Camel #404. Off-white cotton

fabric 36″ wide, ½ yard. Sewing thread to match fabric. Fiberfill for stuffing.

DIRECTIONS: Read "Four Methods of Cross-Stitching" and see "Stitch Detail." (See Contents for all General Directions.) Chart is given for one quarter of design. To begin, measure 2″ in and 2″ down from upper right corner of fabric to locate position of first cross-stitch to be worked (upper right corner of chart); mark with a straight pin. Insert fabric in hoop to keep it taut.

To embroider, separate yarn and work with one strand in needle. Following "Four Methods of Cross-Stitching" "Stitch Detail," color key, and chart, work entire upper right corner of design; to work upper left quarter, reverse chart, omitting center vertical row marked by arrow. (Note that center blue row of crenelated border has one stitch rather than two.) To work bottom half of design, reverse stitched pattern, omitting center horizontal row.

Remove fabric from hoop and press. Trim fabric margins to ½″. Cut 16½″ square from cotton fabric; place fabric on right side of embroidery, matching raw edges; pin in place. Machine-stitch all around, ½″ from edges, leaving a 4″ opening for turning. Clip corners. Turn to right side. Stuff with fiberfill until plump; slip-stitch opening closed.

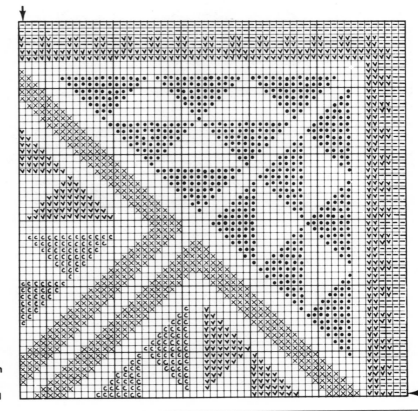

- ⊟ Gold
- V Blue
- ● Brown
- X Red
- C Camel

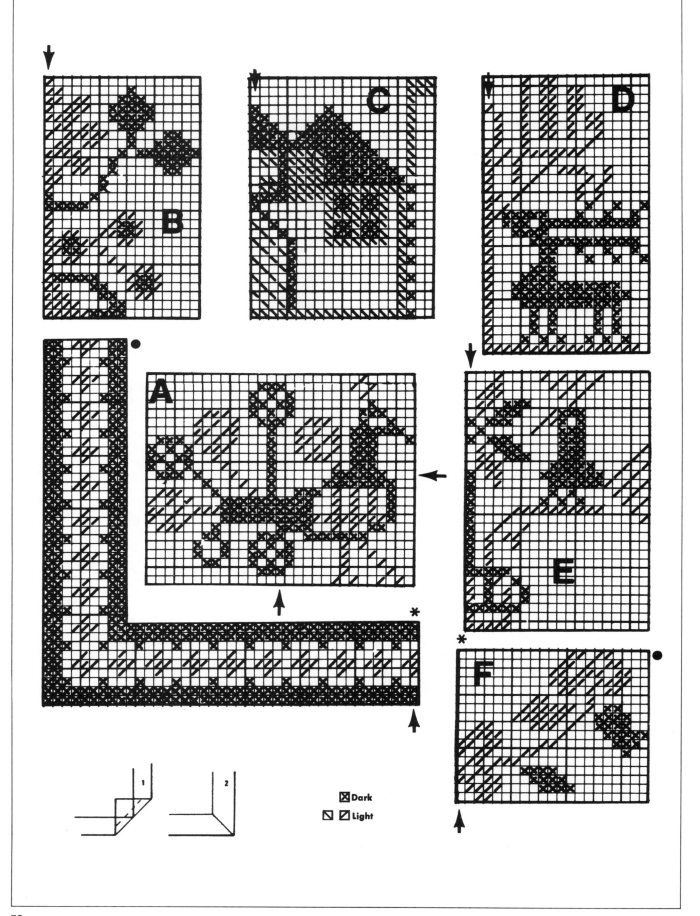

Dark
Light

DELFT MATS

Shown on pages 68–69

SIZE: Approximately 5″ square.

EQUIPMENT: Tailor's chalk. Straight pins. Scissors. Tape measure. Embroidery hoop (optional). Embroidery and sewing needles. Steam iron.

MATERIALS: (for each doily): Even-weave cream or white linen fabric with 32 threads-to-the-inch, 8″ square. DMC six-strand embroidery floss in light blue #334 and dark blue #311, or any light and dark shades of the same color, about 1 skein each. Sewing thread to match fabric.

DIRECTIONS: Overcast raw edges of linen to keep from raveling. With tailor's chalk, mark a line 1½″ in from each side. This is the outer line of border as well as edge of doily. Work border design first and then work center motif. To work cross-stitch, use two strands of floss in needle and work each cross-stitch over two threads of fabric (each square on chart represents one stitch over two threads horizontally and vertically). Work all underneath threads in one direction. Keep stitches as even as possible; be sure the ends of all crosses meet (see "Four Methods of Cross-Stitching.")

Find the center along one side of fabric at outer edge of border; mark with pin. Place fabric in hoop if desired. Follow border chart and color key. Begin working from chart at arrow, starting crosses at pin mark, one thread in from marked line.

Only one-quarter of the border is given. To complete one half, repeat chart in reverse omitting center row marked by star. Then repeat half border in reverse, omitting center rows (marked by dot).

For center motif, fold linen in half horizontally, then vertically to find the center. Mark point with a pin. Determine the center point of the chart and begin working cross-stitch from center. Follow chart and color key. Chart A is complete; B, C, D, E are half. To complete, repeat chart in reverse, omitting center vertical row marked by arrow. Chart F is one quarter of design. Follow border directions for the completion of design.

Steam-press the finished embroidery.

Fold each corner to the back (Fig. 1). Cut off corner ½″ from fold (dash line). Fold sides of doily to the back 1½″ all around, forming mitered corners (Fig. 2); fold ¼″ of raw edge under. Press. Slip-stitch hem to back and slip-stitch mitered corners.

GINGHAM SET

Shown on page 70

SIZES: Teacloth, 42″ × 44″; four place mats, each 13¾″ × 18″; pot holder, 6½″ × 7¼″; apron, adult size.

EQUIPMENT: Pencil. Ruler. Tailor's chalk. Sewing and embroidery needles. Embroidery hoop. Scissors. Sewing machine. Steam iron. Padded surface.

MATERIALS: Cotton or cotton-blend fabric 45″ wide: green gingham with ⅛″ checks; solid red, solid white. Rickrack ½″ wide, green, red. (See chart for all yardage amounts.) Susan Bates six-strand embroidery floss: white, 1 skein for each project; crimson, emerald, 4 skeins each for teacloth or place mats; 2 skeins each for apron; 1 skein each for pot holder. Green, red thread. Batting for pot holder. (**Note:** If making teacloth, apron and potholder, do not buy extra gingham fabric for apron and pot holder because pieces may be cut from teacloth scrap.)

	Tea-cloth	Mats	Apron	Pot Holder
Gingham	1¼	1⅛	⅓	scrap
Red	1¼	1⅝	¾	scrap
White	—	⅞	—	—
Green rickrack	4⅛	4½	1⅔	⅔
Red rickrack	4⅔	6½	1⅔	¼

GENERAL DIRECTIONS: Read "Embroidery Basics" for embroidery tips and "Stitch Details." Embroider design for each piece on gingham in cross-stitch, following chart and color key. Each square on chart represents one gingham check; each symbol on chart represents one cross-stitch worked over one check. Gingham checks are not perfectly square and usually run 8 checks per inch (cpi) in one direction and 7 checks per inch in the other on $\frac{1}{8}''$ check fabric. To begin embroidery, place gingham piece so that the 8 cpi edges are at top and bottom and 7 cpi edges are at sides. Mark top. Starting in upper right corner of piece, measure down and in as directed to nearest white check, for first cross-stitch; continue across to the left. Embroider all red and green cross-stitches on white checks and all white cross-stitches on green checks. Steam-press finished embroidery gently on a padded surface.

When embroidery is completed, cut out gingham piece as directed. Assemble piece with red fabric, trimming with rickrack. Make seams $\frac{1}{4}''$ wide (or two rows of squares), unless otherwise directed.

TEACLOTH: Measure $2\frac{1}{4}''$ down and 3″ in for first check; embroider with red cross-stitch for corner stitch. Complete corner motif from A to A (8 green stitches, 4 red stitches, 1 white stitch). Continuing across top, work section between A and C 12 times, then work A/B section once. Return to upper right corner. For right edge, work A/C section 11 times and A/B section once. Turn chart as necessary to work adjacent corners, then work border design along remaining two edges and fourth corner in same manner.

Cut out gingham piece, leaving 11 rows of checks around outer edge of embroidery and 6 rows of

checks around inner edge; piece will not be perfectly square. Measure $\frac{1}{2}''$ away from the outer edge of embroidery and pin red rickrack in place all around, easing at corners; there should be two rows of squares between embroidery and inner points of rickrack. Slip-stitch in place, turning raw ends under where they meet. Press inner edges of gingham $\frac{1}{4}''$ to wrong side, clipping fabric at corners.

With right side of gingham facing wrong side of red fabric, pin gingham border to red piece, trimming red fabric to size. Stitch pieces together around outer edges. Trim seams, clip corners at an angle, and turn gingham to right side; press so seam is not visible on right side. Pin green rickrack over inner pressed edges of gingham and slip-stitch in place, securing gingham to red piece.

PLACE MATS: Cut gingham fabric in half lengthwise and crosswise for four equal pieces. For each mat, measure $2\frac{3}{4}''$ down and $2\frac{3}{4}''$ in for first stitch. Work embroidery design around gingham in same manner as for teacloth; for top edges, work section between A and C four times and A/B section once; for side edges, work section A/C twice and A/B once. Cut out gingham piece and slip-stitch red rickrack in place as for teacloth; press raw inner edges $\frac{1}{4}''$ to wrong side. Make four.

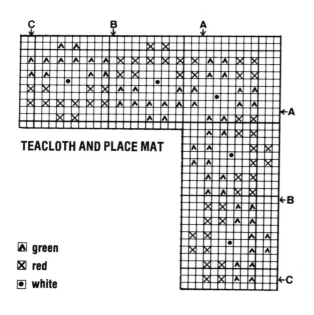

TEACLOTH AND PLACE MAT

⬛ green
☒ red
⊡ white

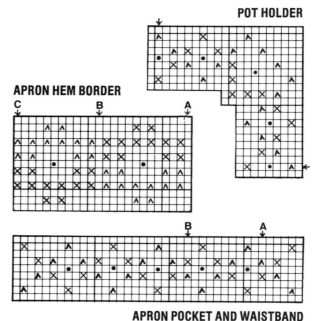

POT HOLDER

APRON HEM BORDER

APRON POCKET AND WAISTBAND

Cut eight pieces from solid red fabric, eac $14\frac{1}{4}''$ × $18\frac{1}{2}''$, or size of gingham pieces. Cut four pieces from white, each $13\frac{3}{4}''$ × $18''$. Sandwich each white piece, centered, between layers of red fabric and baste around edges, making four backings. Mark parallel lines across length of each backing, spacing lines about $2''$ apart. Stitch on marked lines to quilt. Assemble mats as for Teacloth.

POT HOLDER: Use scrap of gingham about $7''$ square. Measure $2''$ down and $1''$ in for first green cross-stitch (lower right in diagonal row). Complete corner motif and continue across top, to center of piece. Repeat chart in reverse to upper left, omitting center row marked with arrow. Returning to upper right, work right side in same manner. Complete border design along remaining two edges and fourth corner in same manner. Cut out gingham piece, leaving five rows of checks around outer edge of embroidery.

Cut one strip of gingham $1''$ × $4\frac{1}{2}''$ for hanger; cut two pieces from red fabric, each $7''$ × $7\frac{3}{4}''$; cut batting $6\frac{1}{2}''$ × $7\frac{1}{4}''$. Press long raw edges of gingham strip $\frac{1}{4}''$ to wrong side, then press strip in half lengthwise with raw edges inward; top-stitch pressed edges together. Fold strip in half crosswise, matching ends, then stitch to corner of one red piece on right side, matching raw edges. Baste batting, centered, to wrong side of one red piece. Stitch red pieces together with right sides facing and loop in between; leave opening for turning. Turn to right side; fold raw edges in; slip-stitch opening closed.

Press raw edges of gingham piece $\frac{1}{4}''$ to wrong side; pin to one side of red piece, leaving equal margins around edges. Count four rows of checks inside inner edge of embroidery and machine-stitch gingham to pot holder on this line, forming a square; remove basting from pot holder. Pin red rickrack over machine-stitched square and slip-stitch in place. Pin green rickrack over pressed edges of gingham and slip-stitch in place.

APRON: Mark the following strips on gingham so that 8 cpi are along the length of each strip: $3\frac{3}{4}''$ × $32''$ hem border, $5\frac{1}{2}''$ × $18\frac{3}{4}''$ waistband, and $3\frac{1}{4}''$ × $5\frac{3}{4}''$ pocket facing. Do not cut out pieces. With long edges of hem border as top and bottom, measure $1\frac{1}{4}''$ down and $\frac{3}{4}''$ in from upper right cor-

ner or marked strip to nearest white check; work first red cross-stitch at upper right of border motif. Continue working across gingham, embroidering section between A and C 10 times, then A/B section once. Slip-stitch red rickrack $1''$ above and parallel to bottom edge; there should be two rows of squares between embroidery and inner points of rickrack. Position pocket border and waistband with long edges as top and bottom. For pocket border, measure $1\frac{3}{4}''$ down and $\frac{3}{4}''$ in from upper right corner to nearest white check for first red cross-stitch; work pattern as shown. For waistband, measure $4''$ down and $\frac{5}{8}''$ in from upper right corner to nearest white check for first green cross-stitch at A; work in pattern from A to B across fabric to within 2 checks at opposite end. Measure $\frac{1}{2}''$ above embroidery on waistband and pocket border; slip-stitch red rickrack in place at this measurement, leaving two rows of checks between embroidery and rickrack. Cut out gingham pieces on marked lines; press long raw edges opposite rickrack under $\frac{1}{4}''$.

From red fabric, cut one skirt $32''$ × $20''$, one pocket $6''$ × $5\frac{3}{4}''$, and two ties, each $26''$ × $2\frac{3}{4}''$. For hem, stitch bottom long edge of gingham hem border to skirt with right side of gingham facing wrong side of skirt and raw edges even; press gingham to right side. Pin, then slip-stitch green rickrack over pressed edge of gingham border, attaching it to skirt. Press raw side edges of skirt $\frac{1}{4}''$ then again $\frac{1}{4}''$ to wrong side; topstitch in place. For pocket, with right side of gingham facing wrong side of pocket and raw edges even, stitch $5\frac{3}{4}''$ edges of pocket and top edge of border together. Fold border over to right side of pocket; slip-stitch green rickrack over pressed edge of gingham, attaching border to pocket. Press raw edges of pocket $\frac{1}{4}''$ to wrong side and pin to skirt so top of pocket is $6''$ below top of skirt and $7''$ away from left side edge; topstitch in place $\frac{1}{8}''$ away from pressed edges of pocket.

Baste across upper edge of skirt; gather to fit raw edge of gingham waistband. Stitch waistband to skirt with right sides facing, adjusting gathers to fit. Press long raw edges and one short edge of each tie $\frac{1}{8}''$ then again $\frac{1}{8}''$ to wrong side; stitch to secure. Fold finished end of each tie to the wrong side on a diagonal; slip-stitch to secure, making a pointed end. With right sides facing, stitch tie to each end of waistband so bottom edge of tie touches seamline of skirt and waistband; baste in place. With right side inward, fold waistband in half with ties in between; stitch side edges. Trim seams; clip corners; turn to right side and press. Slip-stitch pressed edge of waistband in place, covering seam allowance. On right side, pin, then slip-stitch green rickrack over seamline of waistband and skirt.

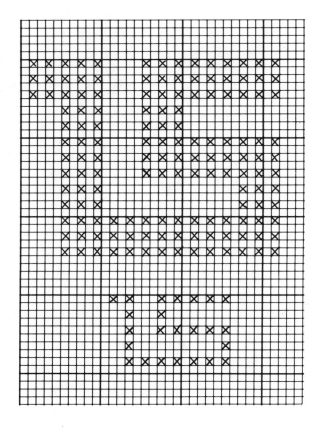

GINGHAM APRON
Shown on page 71

EQUIPMENT: Scissors. Embroidery needle. Tape measure.

MATERIALS: Blue-and-white checked gingham with 9 or 10 checks-to-the-inch, $\frac{3}{4}''$ yard, 36'' wide. Two skeins red six-strand embroidery floss. Sewing thread. Red rickrack, $1\frac{1}{2}$ yards.

DIRECTIONS: (See Contents for all General Directions.) From checked gingham, cut apron skirt 30'' wide and 21'' deep; cut two ties each $2\frac{1}{2}''$ wide and 25'' long, waistband 4'' wide and 16'' long and a pocket $5\frac{1}{2}''$ square.

Make narrow hems at 21'' sides of apron skirt and a $2\frac{1}{4}''$ hem at bottom. Sew rickrack on front along bottom hem line.

Read "Four Methods of Cross-Stitching." Using two strands of six-strand embroidery floss in needle, embroider wide Greek Key border design on skirt just above rickrack, following chart; work crosses in white checks of gingham only; repeat design across. Fold waistband in half lengthwise and embroider small border design on front half $\frac{1}{4}''$ up from edge; following chart, repeat across. Sew rickrack across front half of waistband above embroidery. Gather top edge of skirt in to $15\frac{1}{2}''$. Turn in long edges and ends of waistband. Insert gathered edge of skirt between front and back of waistband and stitch across. Hem both long edges of each tie to within 2'' of one end; fold one corner of unhemmed end diagonally over to side edge with right sides together; seam edges. Turn right side out. Insert raw end of each tie in ends of waistband and stitch.

Sew rickrack across pocket $1\frac{1}{4}''$ below one edge for top. Embroider narrow border across pocket below rickrack. Make $\frac{3}{4}''$ hem across top of pocket. Turn in $\frac{1}{4}''$ around sides and bottom of pocket; stitch pocket to apron $6\frac{1}{2}''$ from left side and $4\frac{1}{2}''$ below waistband of the apron.

SNOWFLAKE PLACE MATS
Shown on page 71

SIZE: 18'' × 12'' each.

EQUIPMENT: Pencil. Ruler. Scissors. Embroidery needle and small hoop. Straight pins. Zigzag sewing machine. Tailor's chalk. Iron.

MATERIALS: Zweigart's Hardanger cloth, 22 count (100% cotton even-weave fabric with 22 double-threads to the inch), red, 42'' wide, $\frac{1}{2}$ yard for two mats. Susan Bates six-strand cotton embroidery floss, one skein white. Red sewing thread.

DIRECTIONS: Read "Embroidery Basics" and see "Stitch Details." Cut fabric into two 21″ × 15″ pieces and press. Prepare raw edges as directed. Work counted cross-stitch corner motifs, following charts, "Embroidery Basics" and "Stitch Details".

Each square on charts represents two horizontal and two vertical double-threads on fabric; each symbol represents one cross-stitch. Work all stitches over two double-threads in each direction, yielding 11 stitches per inch. Separate floss and work with two strands in needle throughout.

For each mat, place fabric with long edges at top and bottom. For lower left corner motif (large snowflake), measure 4″ up from bottom and 4″ in from left edge; mark point with a pin to correspond with center stitch of motif on chart. Place area to be worked in hoop and stitch, counting cross-stitches from center out. Work upper right corner motif (two small snowflakes) in the same manner,

measuring $3\frac{3}{4}$″ down from top and $4\frac{1}{4}$″ in from right edge, for point to correspond with center stitch of top snowflake. Work bottom small flake, remembering to count two double-threads for each blank square on chart between flakes. Finish embroidery, following directions.

To complete mats, use tailor's chalk to mark a margin on wrong side of mat, 1″ in from all edges. Zigzag-stitch on marked line (through single thickness) all around. Place mat, wrong side up, on work surface. Following detail, measure and mark fabric edges 2″ (A) and then 3″ (B) away from each corner; draw a diagonal line between A's and B's as shown. Cut away corner between A's (shaded area); fold corner between B's to wrong side, then fold side edges in $1\frac{1}{2}$″. Pin fabric in place and press. Turn mat to right side and, using straight stitch, topstitch $\frac{1}{4}$″ in from folded edges all around. On wrong side, cut away excess fabric close to zigzag stitching.

UPPER RIGHT

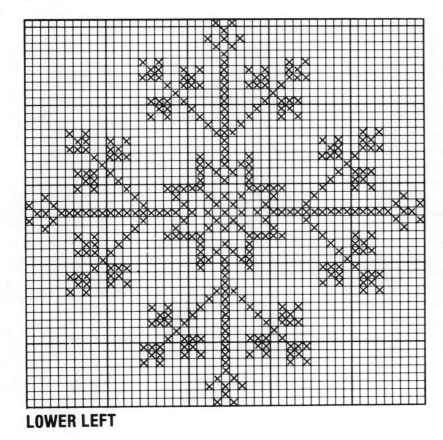

LOWER LEFT

fabric edge

zigzag stitching

fold line

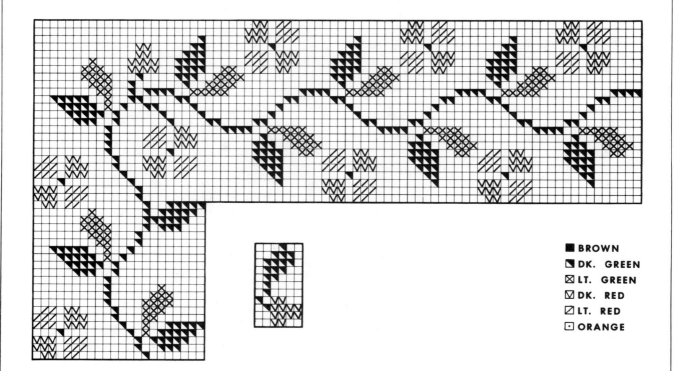

BROWN
DK. GREEN
LT. GREEN
DK. RED
LT. RED
ORANGE

"SAMPLER" MIRROR FRAME
Shown on page 72

EQUIPMENT: Embroidery or tapestry needle. Sewing needle. Scissors. Ruler. **For Framing:** Saw. Miter box. Backsaw. Hammer. Screwdriver. T-square. Nail set. Small flat paintbrush. Drill.

MATERIALS: Mirror with wooden frame about 1″ wide and ½″ thick, 22½″ × 19¼″ or desired size. Even-weave fabric (see Note), 33″ × 36″, or size to allow a 6″ border of fabric all around mirror. Six-strand embroidery floss: 3 skeins light red, 3 skeins medium red, 8 skeins dark blue-green, 3 skeins medium yellow-green. Black sewing thread. **For Framing:** Plywood ½″ thick 26½″ × 29¾″, or size to allow a 3½″ border all around mirror. Half-round molding ½″ wide, 10 ft., or sufficient amount to fit around plywood. Small finishing nails. Eight flat-head wood screws ¾″ long. Small can flat green paint. Walnut varnish-stain. Wood filler. Small screw eyes and wire. Tape.

Note: It is important to check carefully the count

of the threads both horizontally and vertically before starting work, as sometimes there is a slight variation in the count of the warp and weft threads to the inch. In this case, it is necessary to adjust design area.

DIRECTIONS: Cut even-weave fabric to a size that will allow a 3½″ border for embroidery and 2½″ for turning back all around mirror frame. To make a guide for embroidery, mark exact outline of mirror frame on the fabric with a line of running stitches, using black sewing thread; measure out 3½″ from this outline and make another line of black running stitches all around. The vine repeat border and corners (see large chart) will fit within this area if you make your crosses 8-to-the-inch and adjust the border design so it will fit a specific length, according to the size of your mirror. See "Four Methods of Cross-Stitching." Make crosses ⅛″ in size; count the number of threads of fabric in both directions to achieve this size. The full six strands of floss are used in the needle. Each square of chart is one stitch. Start embroidering the vine line only from each corner working toward center of each side. If the vine does not meet correctly at center, adjust the width of the middle curves, wider or narrower, to fit. Following chart, embroider the flowers and leaves along the vine curves. If an adjustment is made in the middle of a side, in place of the usual flower, embroider a bud or pair of buds on each side and single leaves, following small chart. Near corners, a flower may have to be omitted and a leaf added in its place, or a bud and leaves added on an outer corner curve, to fill an area. Stretch finished embroidery evenly and smoothly over plywood panel. Bring excess fabric to back; tape securely in place.

To frame, measure sides of plywood and with backsaw and miter box, cut half-round molding to fit. Paint molding pieces and mirror frame green. When dry, brush lightly and unevenly with walnut varnish-stain to give an antique look; let dry. Nail molding around plywood; countersink nails and fill holes with wood filler. When dry, touch nail holes with green paint. Center framed mirror on back of plywood and mark outline; remove mirror. Drill two holes at top, bottom, and sides of mirror outline, $\frac{1}{4}''$ inside line, through plywood. Mark corresponding places on back of mirror frame and drill starting holes in mirror frame. Place mirror on front of embroidered panel and insert screws from back of plywood. Hang with screw eyes and wire.

TASSEL PINCUSHION
Shown on page 76

SIZE: $5\frac{1}{2}''$ square.
MATERIALS: Knitting worsted, 2 ozs. turquoise (A); small amount contrasting color (B). Gold crochet cord (C). Afghan hook size F or 4. Piece of muslin, $6\frac{1}{2}'' \times 13''$. Nylon hose cut in small pieces for stuffing. Tapestry needle.
GAUGE: 5 sts = 1''.
CUSHION: BACK: With A and afghan hook, ch 29.
Row 1: Keeping all lps on hook, sk first ch, pull up a lp in next ch and in each ch across—29 lps.

To Work Lps Off: Yo hook, pull through first lp, * yo hook, pull through next 2 lps, repeat from * across until 1 lp remains. (Lp that remains on hook always counts as first st of next row.)
Row 2: Keeping all lps on hook, sk first vertical bar, pull up a lp under next vertical bar and each vertical bar across. Work off lps as before.
Rows 3–27: Repeat row 2. End off.
FRONT: Work same as for back.
FINISHING: Press pieces lightly.
Embroidery: Embroider front in cross-stitch, working 1 cross-stitch over vertical bar of 1 afghan st. Each square on chart represents 1 stitch. Use C double for embroidery.

Cut two pieces of muslin $6\frac{1}{2}''$ square; with right sides facing, sew together with $\frac{1}{2}''$ seams, leaving 3'' opening on one edge. Turn to right side. Stuff firmly; close opening.
Tassels (make 4): Cut four 3'' strands of A. Fold in half; wind and tie a strand of A $\frac{1}{4}''$ below folded end.

Pin pieces tog over pillow form. With 1 strand of B and C held tog, sc around edge working through both pieces and catching a tassel at each corner as follows: Insert hook through both pieces, pull yarn through, put 4 loops of tassel on hook, complete sc.

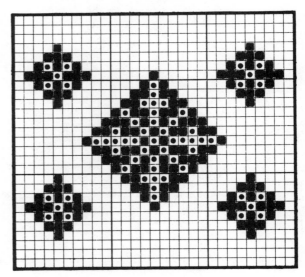

■ B
◨ C

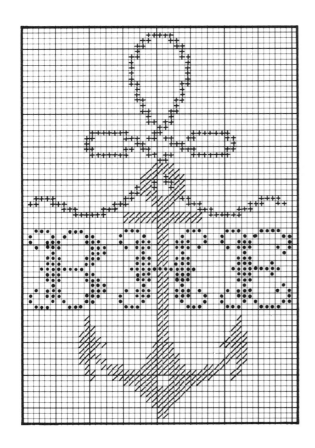

CROSS-STITCH TOWELS
Shown on page 73

EQUIPMENT: Penelope (cross-stitch) canvas, 10 mesh-to-the-inch, about 15″ × 12″ for dolphin; 9″ × 6″ for the others. Ruler. Pencil. Scissors. Large-eyed embroidery needle. Waterproof felt-tipped pens: red, blue and yellow. Tweezers. Basting thread.

MATERIALS: White terry cloth hand or bath towels. DMC six-strand embroidery floss: for smaller motifs, one skein each of deep coral #350, yellow ochre #782 and navy #823; for dolphin, one skein deep coral #350 and nine skeins navy #823.

DIRECTIONS: With felt-tipped pens, mark designs centered on canvas, following chart and color key. Each square on chart represents one mesh of canvas and one cross-stitch. Indicate stitches on canvas by marking across intersecting threads. Using alphabet charts as a guide, mark your own monogram around anchor motifs.

Center the marked canvas near one end of towel, leaving a reasonable margin of towel at sides and bottom. Baste canvas to towel horizontally and vertically through the center of the canvas. Then

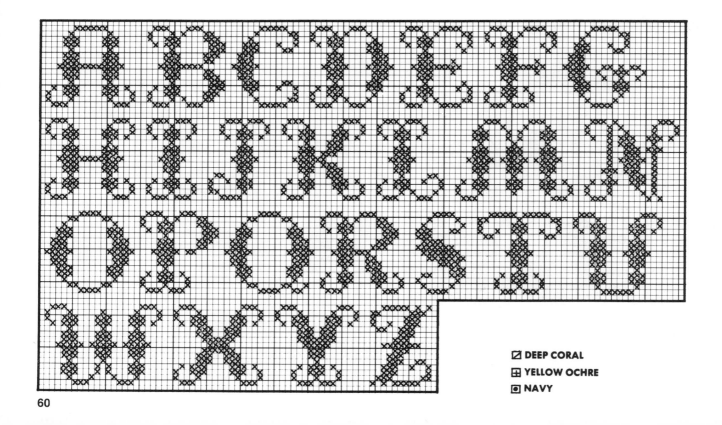

- ◪ **DEEP CORAL**
- ⊞ **YELLOW OCHRE**
- ◉ **NAVY**

baste diagonally in both directions and around sides of canvas.

Using six strands of floss, make cross-stitches following color key, taking each stitch diagonally over the double mesh of canvas and through the towel (see "Stitch Details.") Work all underneath threads in one direction and all the top threads in the opposite direction. Keep stitches as even as possible and make all crosses touch by using same holes for adjacent stitches.

When design is completed, remove basting threads. Cut away excess canvas around edges of design. With tweezers, carefully draw out canvas threads, leaving the finished cross-stitch design on towel.

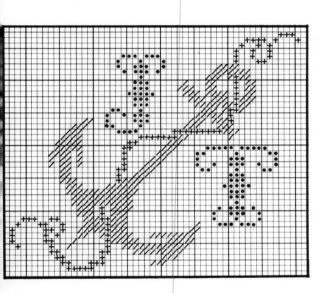

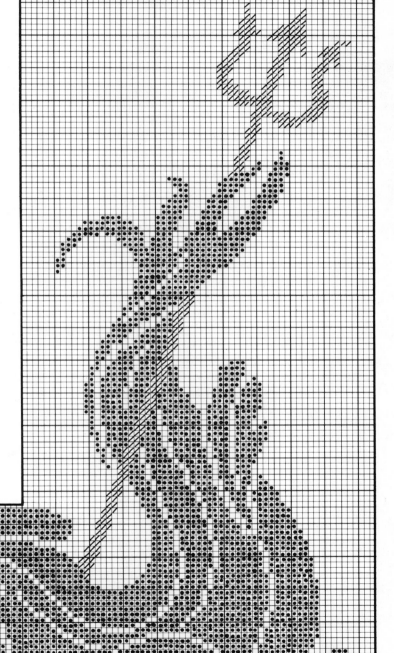

ORANGE-BLOSSOM TABLECLOTH

Shown on page 74

SIZE: Embroidered area is 23″ × 47″ and is designed for rectangular table.

EQUIPMENT: Embroidery and sewing needles. Scissors. Pencil. Ruler. Straight pins. Embroidery hoop (optional). Basting thread.

MATERIALS: Royal blue Zweigart Lugano even-weave fabric Article 3835 in length to fit your table.

To determine yardage needed, measure length and width of table, being sure to include enough fabric for overhang. If desired, purchased table-cloth may be used and embroidery worked over penelope canvas. See DMC six-strand embroidery floss in colors listed on color key; number of skeins needed is indicated in parentheses next to each color.

DIRECTIONS: (See Contents for all General Directions.) Center of fabric must be determined

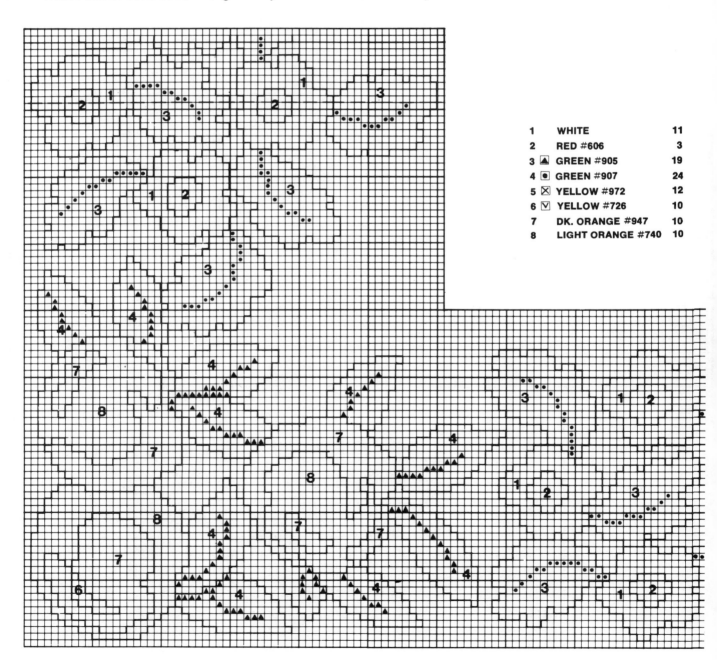

1		WHITE	11
2		RED #606	3
3	▲	GREEN #905	19
4	◉	GREEN #907	24
5	⊠	YELLOW #972	12
6	⊻	YELLOW #726	10
7		DK. ORANGE #947	10
8		LIGHT ORANGE #740	10

before beginning embroidery. To find center, fold fabric in half vertically and then horizontally. Mark center point with straight pin. To determine placement of short side of design, use pencil and ruler to mark a dot 23½" down from center point of cloth. You will begin stitching at this point. Refer to "Four Methods of Cross-Stitching," paying special attention to "On Even-Weave Fabric." Using full six strands of floss in needle, work each cross-stitch over four threads of fabric; each square on chart represents one stitch taken over four threads horizontally and vertically.

Begin stitching at row A, marked by arrow on chart. Chart given is for one quarter of design. To complete, work entire chart to row marked B; reverse chart to complete other quarters.

To make cloth, fold up ¼" all around fabric; baste. Turn up ¼" again; hem.

GIANT POT HOLDERS

Shown on page 75

SIZE: 10" square.

MATERIALS: Rayon and cotton rug yarn, 6 70-yard skeins white (W), 1 skein each of dark green (DG), light green (LG), olive green (OG), dark red (DR) and scarlet (S). Aluminum afghan hook size 10. Large-eyed yarn needle.

GAUGE: 7 sts = 2"; 3 rows = 1".

POT HOLDER (make 4): With W and afghan hook, ch 30.

AFGHAN STITCH: Row 1: Keeping all lps on hook, pull up a lp in 2nd ch from hook and in each ch across—30 lps.

To Work Lps Off: Yo hook, pull through first lp, * yo hook, pull through next 2 lps, repeat from * across until 1 lp remains. (Lp that remains always counts as first st of next row.)

Row 2: Keeping all lps on hook, sk first vertical bar, pull up a lp under next vertical bar and under each vertical bar across. Work lps off as before.

Rows 3–28: Repeat row 2. End off W.

Edging: Join DG, work 1 rnd sc around pot holder, working 1 sc in each st, 3 sc in each corner. Sl st in each sc around.

Hanger: Join DG in one top corner of pot holder, ch 33, join with sl st to top corner opposite. Ch 1,

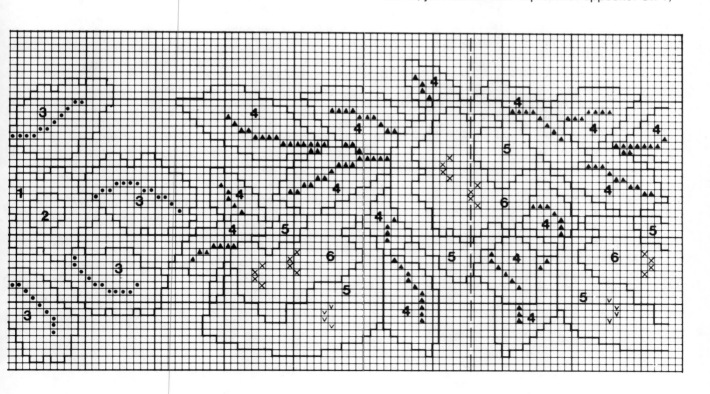

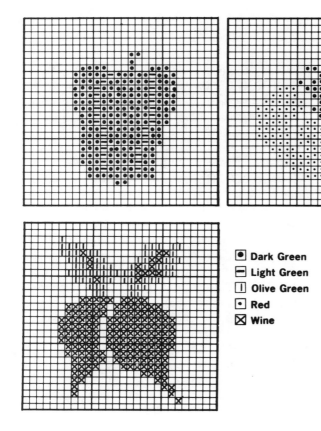

Dark Green ⊙
Light Green ⊟
Olive Green ☐
Red ⊡
Wine ☒

turn; sl st in each ch across. End off. Weave in ends.

FINISHING: Pin out to square shape. Block, using wet cloth and hot iron. Let dry. Embroider designs in cross-stitch, working 1 cross-stitch over 1 vertical bar, following charts. To finish bean embroidery, split a length of DG in half. With split strand, embroider stems and leaf veins in outline st; make two lazy daisy sts at top of each bean. See "Stitch Details."

MAT-AND-RING SETS
Shown on page 77

EQUIPMENT: Needle. Ruler. Scissors. Iron.
MATERIALS: Even-weave linen, 27 threads-to-the-inch, in color desired, $13\frac{3}{4}'' \times 22\frac{1}{4}''$ for each mat; about $3'' \times 6''$ for each napkin holder. Six-strand embroidery floss in color desired; contrasting color for eyes and other details. Sewing thread to match linen. Small matchbox for each napkin holder. All-purpose glue.

DIRECTIONS: (See Contents for all General Directions.) **Place Mats:** See "Stitch Details." Use two strands of floss in needle to work cross-stitch. Use three strands to work buttonhole-stitch borders. Work each stitch over two threads of linen (each square on chart represents one stitch over two threads horizontally and vertically).

For each mat, cut fabric $13\frac{3}{4}'' \times 22\frac{1}{4}''$ (this is enough for largest mat). Measure in $1\frac{1}{4}''$ from edges and mark a line across each side. Starting at upper left, work buttonhole stitch along marked line for a few inches across top and down left side. Following chart on page 80 for design, start working motifs across top and down each side in cross-stitch. For all designs except octopus reverse direction of animals after passing center of longer sides (see illustration). Finish cross-stitch motifs, making number across top, bottom and sides as shown in illustration. Work eyes in cross-stitch in contrasting color of floss. Using three strands of floss in needle, work ear and leg definitions on elephant and kangaroo in backstitch; work elephant tail in straight stitch. Continue buttonhole-stitch border outside motifs around all sides. Trim fabric around all sides to $1\frac{1}{4}''$ if necessary. Work second row of buttonhole stitch around inside of cross-stitch motifs.

For hems, turn under $\frac{1}{4}''$ around all sides and

Continued on page 80

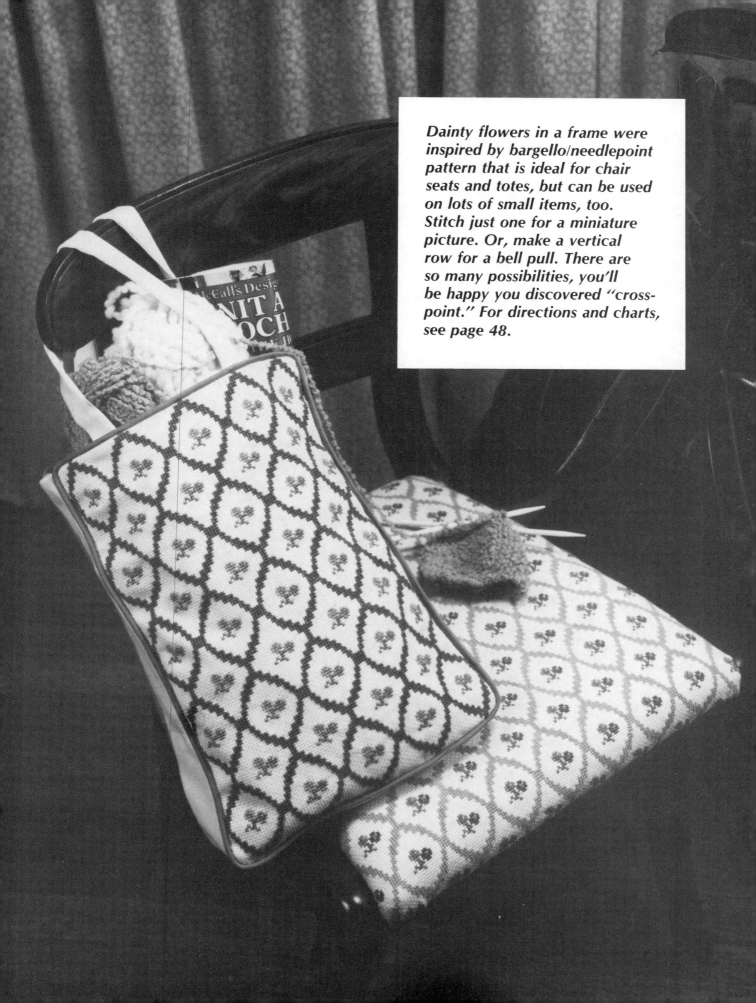

Dainty flowers in a frame were inspired by bargello/needlepoint pattern that is ideal for chair seats and totes, but can be used on lots of small items, too. Stitch just one for a miniature picture. Or, make a vertical row for a bell pull. There are so many possibilities, you'll be happy you discovered "cross-point." For directions and charts, see page 48.

Two favorites—cross-stitch and needlepoint—combine here for "cross-point." Needlepoint inspired the patterns, cross-stitch is the technique. Open-air argyles pattern a pillow and eyeglass case. Cross-stitch zigzags across the fabric in two colors. Elegant shells are reminiscent of a favorite bargello pattern. Here, they decorate an address book and are used for upholstery. Use two shades of one color for a subtler effect.
Directions begin on page 48.

*Geometric motifs in
rich earth colors pattern
two counted cross-stitch
pillows. Each is 16"
square. See page 51
for directions.*

Patterns from across the sea, worked in thread-count stitchery and delft blue tones. Two shades of blue DMC embroidery floss are cross-stitched on a counted-thread fabric (32 threads to the inch). Each is 5" square—a delightful little touch for country dining. For larger mats, use fabric with fewer threads per inch. Delft Mats directions on page 53.

Counted cross-stitch on crisp gingham—it is as easy as 1, 2, 3, counting the checks as you work. Use gingham borders on bright red place mats and tablecloth; trim with perky rickrack. For a festive look, stitch an apron and pot holders to match. Gingham Set, page 53.

White snowflakes are cross-stitched on red even-weave fabric for bright holiday place mats; page 56.

Classic Greek Key design decorates this gingham apron, then rickrack adds the finishing touch. See page 56.

A border motif from an Early American sampler is embroidered in cheery reds and greens to frame a mirror. Cross-stitches are worked on an even-weave fabric by counting threads— two threads each way on our fabric. Our framed mirror measures 27" × 30¼". Directions include instructions for framing and for adjusting the size of the frame; see page 58.

*Embroidery magic transforms plain towels into
seafaring beauties! Dolphin/anchor/monogram motifs
are worked with six strands of DMC floss.
Directions for Cross-Stitch Towels, page 60.*

A rectangular frame of oranges and orange blossoms enhances a tablecloth. This design is an easy cross-stitch on even-weave fabric. Orange Blossom Cloth, directions on page 62.

Cross-stitch vegetables
decorate 10"-square
afghan crochet pot holders in
rayon, cotton rug yarn.
Giant Pot Holders,
page 63.

Perk up everyday accessories with colorful cross-stitch. Tassels and cross-stitch adorn a $5\frac{1}{2}''$-square pincushion made in afghan crochet of knitting worsted. Work embroidery with knitting worsted, too. Tassel Pincushion, page 59.

A familiar sampler motif becomes a bold, modern design by working 8-to-the-inch crosses over even-weave fabric. Cover turns an inexpensive scrap basket into a stylish bedroom accessory. About $12\frac{1}{2}''$ high. Directions, page 80.

Cross-stitch creatures parade around the edges of easy-to-stitch, fun-to-use place mats. Napkin holder is made on a matchbox form; adjust one motif to fit center. Mat-and-Ring Sets, see page 64.

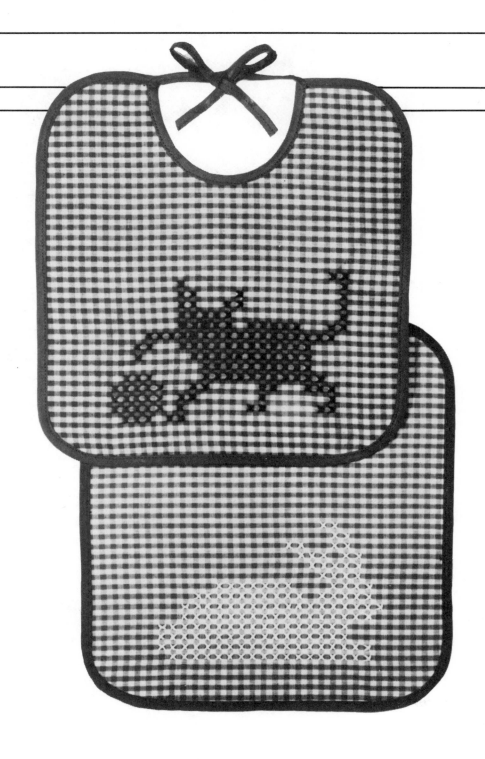

Frisky kitten with a red ball and a white bunny are embroidered on gingham fabric. Bibs, in three thicknesses, are bound with bias tape. Directions for Cross-Stitch Bibs, page 83.

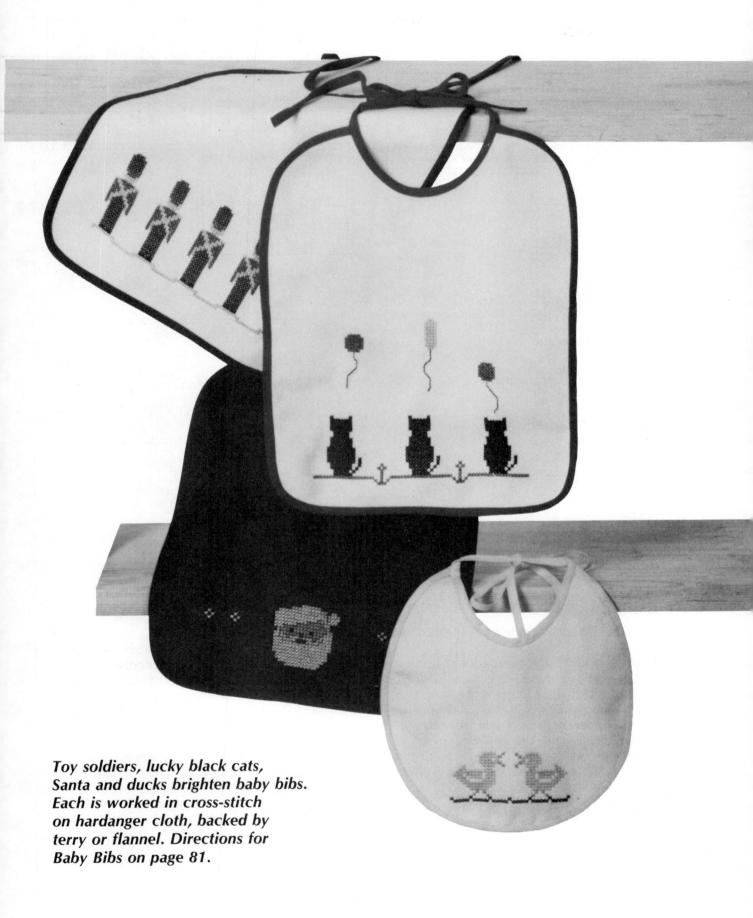

*Toy soldiers, lucky black cats,
Santa and ducks brighten baby bibs.
Each is worked in cross-stitch
on hardanger cloth, backed by
terry or flannel. Directions for
Baby Bibs on page 81.*

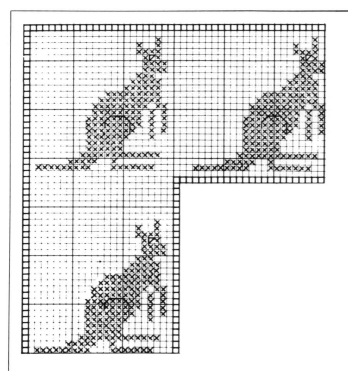

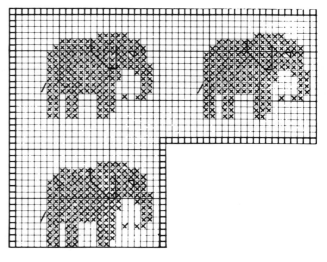

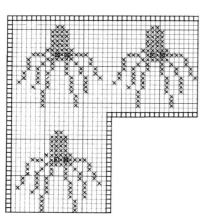

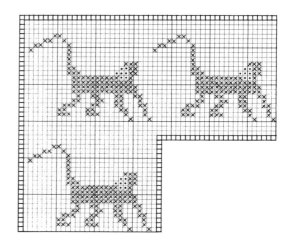

Continued from page 64

press. Fold $\frac{1}{2}''$ to wrong side and slip-stitch hem; press.

Napkin Holders: Remove matches from match box and inner box, using just outside frame. Cut a piece of linen large enough to fit around frame plus $\frac{3}{8}''$ all around. Place linen around frame with ends overlapping on bottom side; mark outline of top side. Remove linen and embroider motif, centering in outlined area. Turn under $\frac{3}{8}''$ around one end and both longer sides; press. Glue embroidered piece around frame with turned-under end overlapping raw end.

CROSS-STITCH WASTEBASKET
Shown on page 76

EQUIPMENT: Scissors. Embroidery needle. Straight pins. Embroidery hoop optional.

MATERIALS: Even-weave ecru fabric $13\frac{1}{2}'' \times 30''$, to fit an oval metal basket $12\frac{1}{2}''$ high, $\times$ 11" wide, $\times$ 7" deep. Six-strand embroidery floss, one skein each of light red, medium red, medium orange, brown, medium yellow-green; two skeins dark blue-green. Olive-green grosgrain ribbon $\frac{5}{8}''$ wide, 2 yards. For lining basket, rust red or other contrasting color of adhesive-backed plastic, felt, or paper. Masking tape. Sewing thread.

DIRECTIONS: Read "Four Methods of Cross-

Stitching." Work design following chart; each square of the chart is one stitch. Make cross-stitches $\frac{1}{8}''$ in size; count the number of threads of fabric in both directions to achieve this size. The full six strands of floss are used in the needle. Use either a regular long-eyed embroidery needle, or a blunt-tipped needle, such as a tapestry needle, which you may find easier to work with.

Tape fabric edges to prevent raveling. To center design on the background fabric, fold fabric in half both ways, mark center with a pin. Find center of design on chart, start working from center out. Embroider half of design given in chart, then embroider other half, reversing chart. Turn in $\frac{1}{2}''$ on each long edge of fabric and slip-stitch. Slip-stitch a ribbon along each long edge of fabric, with outer edges even. If wastebasket is not plain white, cover outside with white fabric or paper first. Place embroidered fabric around basket, turn one end in and overlap on back to fit snugly; pin in place. Slip-stitch back seam. Adhere plastic, or glue paper or felt lining on inside.

PARTY-TIME BABY BIBS
Shown on page 79

EQUIPMENT: Fine tapestry needle. Sewing needle. Scissors. Pencil. Colored pencil. Paper for patterns. Tracing paper. Straight pins. Embroidery hoop. Sewing machine.

MATERIALS: Zweigart Hardanger (even-weave) fabric, 22 threads-to-the-inch in colors desired: For each large bib, 11″ × 13″ piece; for small bib, 9″ × 9″ piece. Double-fold bias tape in contrasting or matching colors. Terry cloth or flannel in matching colors for backing. Six-strand embroidery floss, one skein of each color in key. Matching thread.

DIRECTIONS: (See Contents for all General Directions.) Using sharp colored pencil, draw lines across patterns, connecting grid lines. Enlarge patterns by copying on paper ruled in $\frac{1}{2}''$ squares. Complete half-patterns indicated by dash lines. Trace enlarged patterns. Center traced pattern on bib fabric; pin in place. With contrasting sewing thread, make long basting stitches around outline and down vertical center. Remove pins and carefully remove paper pattern, leaving basting stitches on fabric. You will need the pattern later for cutting out backing.

To prevent raveling, whip edges by hand or zig-zag with sewing machine. Work designs in cross-stitch, following charts and color key. Each symbol of chart represents one cross-stitch worked over two vertical and two horizontal threads. Short dash lines represent backstitch (see "Stitch Details.")

- ■ **Brown**
- ◣ **Dk. Green**
- ☒ **Lt. Green**
- ◪ **Dk. Red**
- ◿ **Lt. Red**
- ◉ **Orange**

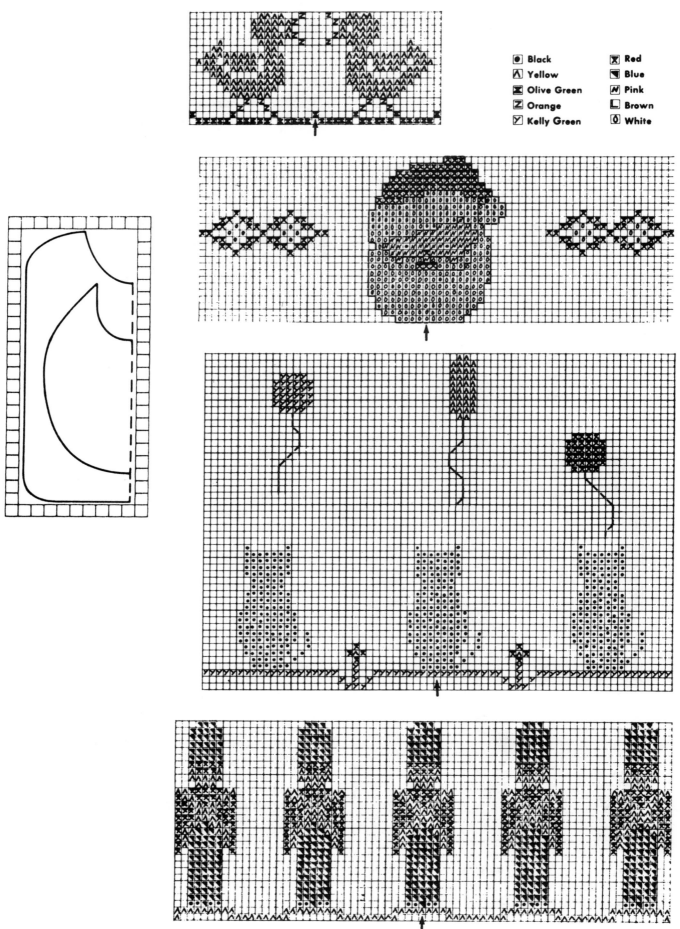

Black · ⊙
Yellow · ⋀
Olive Green · ⊠
Orange · ⊡
Kelly Green · ⋎
Red · ⊗
Blue · ◄
Pink · ⋈
Brown · ⌴
White · ⊙

To begin a length of floss, have end on back and work over it to secure; to end, run needle under four or five stitches on back. Do not use knots. When working cross-stitches, keep all crosses in the same direction; work all underneath stitches in one direction and all top stitches in opposite direction. Make all crosses touch by inserting your needle in the same hole used for the adjacent stitch.

To begin, count 25 horizontal threads up from bottom of basted outline; start with center stitch indicated by arrow. Place fabric in hoop and continue embroidering design. Work all cross-stitches and the balloon strings on cat bib with two strands of floss in needle. Work backstitches outlining Santa with one strand of floss in needle.

Backing: Pin paper pattern to terry cloth or flannel; cut out. Pin backing to wrong side of bib; stitch in place all around. Encase raw edges, omitting neck edge, in double-fold tape; pin in place; stitch all around. Cut piece of tape 30″ long for neck edge and ties. Pin so that middle of tape is at neck edge center, then stitch in place, beginning at one end of tie, around neck edge and out to other end of tie.

CROSS-STITCH BIBS
Shown on page 78

EQUIPMENT: Paper for pattern. Pencil. Ruler. Scissors. Embroidery and sewing needles.

MATERIALS: Gingham with 8 checks-to-the-inch, $\frac{1}{4}$ yard. Matching double-fold bias tape. Matching sewing thread. Six-strand embroidery floss. Cotton flannelette, 9″ × 10″.

DIRECTIONS: (See Contents for all General Directions.) Enlarge pattern for bib, given below, by copying on paper ruled in 1″ squares; complete half-pattern indicated by long dash line. Using pattern, cut two bib pieces of gingham; cut one bib piece of flannelette.

On one gingham piece for front, work design in cross-stitch (see "Stitch Detail,"), following charts; start embroidery 1″ above bottom of bib. Work underneath stitch of crosses all in one direction, then complete crosses with top stitches all in opposite direction. Using four strands of floss in needle, embroider cat in black with red ball and blue eyes, working in light checks of gingham; work rabbit with white floss, working in dark checks, or as desired.

Place flannelette piece between gingham pieces with embroidered piece up; baste together. Bind top, sides, and bottom with bias tape. Bind neck edge with tape, leaving 9″ ends for ties. Stitch long edges of ties together.

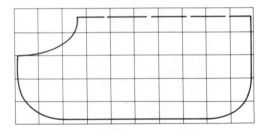

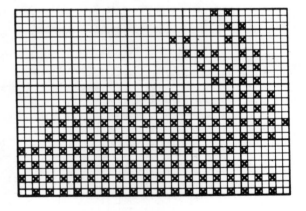

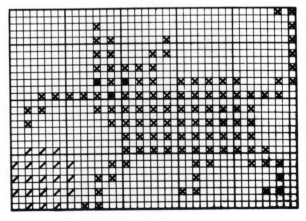

ALBUM COVER

Shown on page 105

EQUIPMENT: Pencil. Ruler. Scissors. Sewing and embroidery needles. Embroidery hoop (optional). Penelope (cross-stitch) canvas, 10 mesh-to-the-inch, same size as album cover. Tweezers.

For Blocking: Brown paper. Soft wooden surface. T-square. Hammer. Thumbtacks.

MATERIALS: Photo album, approximately 13″ × 14″, with removable covers. **(Note:** Covers attached with screws are recommended; if covers are tied, you will need grommets for the eyelets.) Blue denim fabric (see Directions for estimating

☒ Pink	◪ Purple
◳ Dk. Green	⊡ Lt. Green
⊟ Red-Orange	

amounts for your album). DMC six-strand embroidery floss (8.7-yard skeins): 1 skein each purple #552, red-orange #809, light green #906, dark green #469; 3 skeins pink #605. All-purpose glue.

DIRECTIONS: (See Contents for all General Directions.) Remove screws or ties from album cover. Measure front and back covers. Adding 2″ to width and doubling height, cut out denim for each cover. **(Note:** If album pages have a separate binding, cut fabric same measurement as width, $\frac{1}{2}$″ longer at top and bottom.)

Using basting thread, outline size of album front on denim, having equal amounts of fabric at top and bottom, $\frac{1}{2}$″ at center binding, $1\frac{1}{2}$″ at outer edge. Center canvas within cover outline. Baste canvas to fabric.

See "Four Methods of Cross-Stitching" for working cross-stitch over Penelope canvas. Using four strands of floss in needle, follow chart and color key to work design. Add or subtract pink background crosses to enlarge or reduce design area to fit your album. When embroidery is finished, remove basting threads and use tweezers to remove Penelope canvas.

Block embroidered piece following directions in "Embroidery Basics."

To cover album, center back album cover on wrong side of corresponding denim. Bring excess at top and bottom to center of inside cover; glue firmly. Mitering corners and trimming at fold, bring fabric at outer edge to inside cover; glue in place. Turn excess fabric at center binding to inside cover; glue firmly in place. Repeat for front cover, being sure embroidery is positioned as desired. For binding on pages, glue fabric on original binding from edge to edge; turn $\frac{1}{2}$″ at top and bottom to inside and glue firmly in place.

Using point of scissors, pierce fabric to accommodate screws. Use grommets to reinforce holes if necessary. Reassemble album.

TULIP TRIO
Shown on page 107

SIZE: Mirror, $9\frac{3}{4}$″ × $13\frac{3}{4}$″. Pillow: $12\frac{1}{2}$″ × $11\frac{3}{4}$″.
EQUIPMENT: Tape measure. Ruler. Straight pins. Scissors. Pencil. Masking tape. Sewing and embroidery needles. Embroidery hoop (optional). Paintbrush for box. Compass. Steam iron. Tailor's chalk.

MATERIALS: White or off-white linen fabric 22 threads-to-the-inch, 36″ wide, $\frac{5}{8}$ yard (enough fabric for all three items). Matching sewing thread. DMC six-strand embroidery floss in colors listed in color key, one skein of each for mirror and lid cover and two skeins of each for pillow. All-purpose glue. **For Mirror:** Mirror, $9\frac{3}{4}$″ × $13\frac{3}{4}$″; heavy buckram, $9\frac{3}{4}$″ × $19\frac{3}{4}$″; corrugated cardboard 9″ × 13″; picture hanging wire; narrow velvet ribbon, $1\frac{1}{4}$ yds; small beads in same colors as tulips, 28. **For Pillow:** Cotton fabric for back in desired color $13\frac{1}{2}$″ × $12\frac{3}{4}$″; muslin, two $14\frac{1}{2}$″ × $13\frac{3}{4}$″ pieces; polyester fiberfill for stuffing. **For Box:** Round wooden box with lid, 5″ diameter; acrylic paint in color desired; one small glass button; ball fringe to match linen with $\frac{3}{4}$″ pompons, $15\frac{3}{4}$″.

GENERAL DIRECTIONS: Cut linen to size given in individual directions. Tape edges to prevent raveling.

Complete charts are given for mirror and lid cover; quarter chart is given for pillow. Find center of linen as directed in individual directions; mark with pin. Place fabric tautly and evenly in hoop with pin in center.

Thread embroidery needle with three strands of the six-strand floss. Follow color key and chart for design; begin embroidery at center. Each square of chart represents two threads horizontally and two threads vertically. Work crosses over two threads with all underneath stitches going in one direction and all top stitches going in opposite direction (see "Stitch Detail."). Be sure the ends of crosses meet in same hole of cloth; keep stitches even. Do not make knots. To start, leave 1″ end of floss on underside of cloth and work over it to secure. Begin and end successive strands by running ends under stitches on back of work. Remove tape and carefully steam-press embroidery.

MIRROR: Cut linen $11\frac{1}{4}$″ × $20\frac{3}{4}$″. Place linen flat on table, wrong side up. Place mirror in center of linen, with longer edges of mirror and linen parallel; fold extended sides of linen over mirror. Indicate side edges of mirror on linen by creasing along folds and marking lightly with tailor's chalk on right side. Remove mirror and turn linen to right

side. Mark a line $\frac{1}{2}''$ from each end, parallel to first lines. Using long running stitches, baste along the four lines, thus marking off the two side panels to be embroidered. Embroider mirror's left-side panel first, which is now at your right. Fold and crease fabric in half lengthwise to indicate horizontal center line; mark center point on the line $1\frac{1}{2}''$ from vertical line at far right. Begin working design at center point, indicated on chart by arrow. Sew a bead above each tulip, as indicated on chart by black squares. To embroider remaining panel, work design in reverse.

After steam-pressing linen, center buckram on wrong side; pin in place. At sides, fold $\frac{1}{2}''$ linen

⊠ PALE GREEN #912
⊡ DARK ROSE #326
· MEDIUM ROSE #961
⧄ BLUE #797
☑ LILAC #208

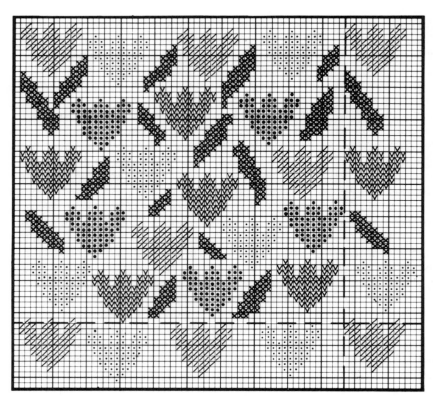

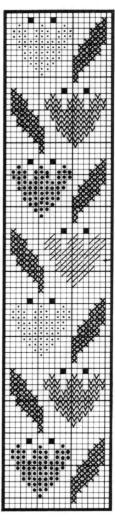

margins over buckram; press. With right sides facing, fold each side of fabric along inner basted lines. Press. Stitch top and bottom edges of pockets with $\frac{3}{4}''$ seams. Turn to right side; remove basting; press. At center areas of top and bottom, fold $\frac{3}{4}''$ linen margins over buckram and press. Slip mirror into frame.

To hang mirror, mark vertical center of flat surface of cardboard (make sure long edges of cardboard are at top and bottom). Mark a point at each side 5″ from center and 1″ above center. Make holes at each point. Cut long length of wire; insert wire end in one hole; twist wire to secure, then tape over the hole. Repeat with other end at other hole, pulling wire through holes to adjust length of hang. Glue cardboard to mirror back and let glue dry thoroughly. Hang mirror. Glue velvet ribbon over wire to cover. Make velvet bow and glue to cover point of hanging. Cut two lengths of velvet ribbon and glue along exposed mirror edges at top and bottom.

PILLOW: Cut linen fabric $13\frac{1}{2}'' \times 12\frac{3}{4}''$. Find center of fabric by folding in half horizontally and then vertically. Turn so that longer edges are vertical. Larger area of chart, marked off by dash lines, indicates one-quarter of entire design. Work this quarter in upper left corner, starting from center of fabric (indicated on chart by intersection of dash lines).

Repeat three times to complete entire design. Additional vertical and horizontal rows (marked by dashes) are given to indicate beginning of repeat pattern.

Pin steam-pressed embroidered linen to cotton fabric, right sides together. Stitch all around with $\frac{1}{2}''$ seams, leaving $10\frac{1}{2}''$ open along one side. Turn to right side.

To Make Inner Pillow: Sew muslin rectangles together with $\frac{1}{2}''$ seams, leaving 6″ opening along one side. Turn to right side and stuff fully. Turn raw edges in and slip-stitch closed.

Insert inner pillow in pillow cover. Turn raw edges in; slip-stitch closed.

BOX COVER: Paint box with acrylic paint in desired color.

While box is drying, cut linen $8\frac{3}{4}''$ square. Find the center of linen in the same manner as for pillow. Work center and embroider outward following color key. Sew button to motif center.

With a pencil and compass, mark a $7\frac{1}{4}''$-diameter circle around embroidery. Cut out circle. Turn edge under $\frac{1}{4}''$; steam press. Make long running stitch $\frac{1}{8}''$ from edge of circle; place linen over lid and pull running stitch thread to gather. Ease fabric puckers evenly around lid; knot thread to secure. Glue edge of linen to lid; then glue ball fringe around linen edges.

FOUR SEASONS SET
Shown on page 108

EQUIPMENT: Tape measure. Ruler. Straight pins. Scissors. Pencil. Sewing needle. Embroidery needle. Embroidery hoop.

MATERIALS: Gingham with seven checks-per-inch, $\frac{3}{4}$ yd, 45″ width, in each color: pink for summer; yellow for autumn; blue for winter; light green for spring. Coordinating broad-cloth, two 7″ squares in each color. Matching sewing threads. Rickrack, 24″ long, in red, green, white or yellow. "Bone" ring, 1″ in diameter, one for each pot holder. Small amount of polyester batting for each pot holder. Six-strand embroidery floss one skein each in colors indicated below (less will be needed if making all seasons):

Summer: Medium green, dark green, red, white, medium brown, dark brown, dark gray, light gray, bright yellow, blue, dark gold, light brown, black.

Autumn: Red, medium green, dark green, chartreuse, blue-green, dark brown, medium brown, bright yellow, orange-gold, orange, white, black, dark gray, light gray, blue, peach.

Winter: Red, black, white, dark gray, light gray, medium green, dark green, blue, medium brown.

Spring: Chartreuse, medium green, dark green, black, dark brown, light brown, white, dark gray, light gray, bright yellow, peach, lavender, orange, blue, pale yellow.

DIRECTIONS: (See Contents for all General Directions.) For apron skirt, cut one piece $32\frac{1}{2}''$ wide, $20\frac{1}{2}''$ long. Cut waistband 18″ long, $3\frac{1}{2}''$ wide.

SPRING

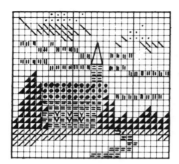

SUMMER

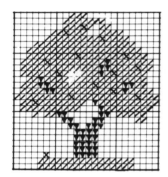

AUTUMN

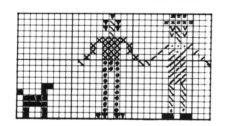

WINTER

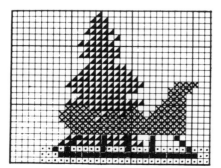

⊠ RED 666	⬓ DK. GOLD 350
■ BLACK 41	◎ DK. GRAY 225
· WHITE 25A	Ⅱ LT. GRAY 224
▼ DK. BROWN 409D	◉ BLUE 444
⊟ MED. BROWN 409C	⊟ CHARTREUSE 236
⊞ LT. BROWN 409B	◣ LAVENDER 493
◪ DK. GREEN 414C	◸ PEACH 916
◿ MED. GREEN 899	☐ ORANGE-GOLD 254
☑ BRIGHT YELLOW 153	▣ ORANGE 466
Ⅲ PALE YELLOW 151	⊞ BLUE-GREEN 271

Cut two ties each 17" long, 3¾" wide. Mark piece for pot holder 5¼" square in center of excess material; do not cut out until embroidery is completed.

See "Four Methods of Cross-Stitching," especially "on Gingham." Thread needle with three strands of six-strand floss. Following charts and color key, embroider cross-stitch design on apron skirt, placing bottom row of design 5" up from lower edge of apron fabric. Embroider pot holder front in center of marked square.

Satin-stitch steeple in blue floss on Spring pot holder and bells in black on Spring and Autumn aprons. See "Stitch Details."

To make birch markings on tree at right side of Spring apron, work straight stitches with black floss on white cross-stitches, using wiggly lines on chart as a guide for placement.

To Assemble Apron: Stitch ¼" hems along sides of apron skirt. Stitch 2¼" hem across bottom edge. Gather waist of apron skirt to 17½" to fit waistband, leaving ¼" seam allowance at each side. Place right sides of apron and waistband together with raw edges even. Stitch band onto apron, easing in gathers. Turn waistband right side up; do not fold.

Stitch ⅛" hem along lower edge of both ties. To make diagonal ends of ties, fold hemmed edge of each diagonally to upper edge. Stitch ⅛" hem along upper edge, being sure to catch folded end. At unhemmed ends, pleat ties to fit half of waistband width. With right sides facing and raw edges even, lay pleated ends on lower half of band. Fold upper half of band down over lower half, right sides in. Stitch across ends ⅛" from edges through all thicknesses. Turn waistband, bringing ties out to sides; press along fold. Turn raw edges of band under; slip-stitch to back.

Pot Holder: When embroidery is complete, cut away excess material, leaving 5¼" square. Turn gingham edges under ¼", center and topstitch onto one square of broadcloth. Carefully cut away broadcloth under the gingham to within ½" of stitching; this allows batting to puff out embroidery. Place second square of broadcloth over gingham, right sides together. Stitch around three sides making ¼" seams; turn right side out. Insert two layers of batting out to all edges, and one more under gingham area only. Turn under raw edges and slip-stitch fourth side closed. Topstitch rick-rack over edges of gingham square, stitching through all thicknesses. Tack ring on top corner.

SERVIETTE SET
Shown on page 109

SIZE: 13" × 19".
EQUIPMENT: Scissors. Sewing and embroidery needles. Ruler. Straight pins. Pencil.
MATERIALS: Even-weave yellow linen, 20 threads-to-the-inch, 14½" × 23¼" for place mat, 8" square for doily. DMC six-strand embroidery floss: one skein each of aqua #992, lilac #209; red #309. Yellow sewing thread.
DIRECTIONS: (See Contents for All General Directions.) **Place Mat:** Overcast raw edges of 14¼" × 23¼" linen to keep from raveling. Measure 4¼" in from left along both long edges and mark a line across linen for area A; see diagram. Measure 7¾" in from left and mark a second line; the area between the two lines is B. The remaining area is C. Embroidery will be worked around edges of A and C only, as indicated by wavy lines on diagram; work area C on right side and area A (pocket) on wrong side.

To work cross-stitch, use three strands of aqua floss in needle and work crosses over two threads

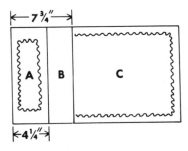

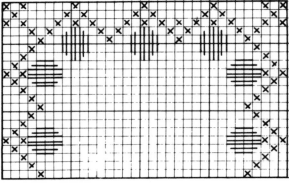

PLACE MAT

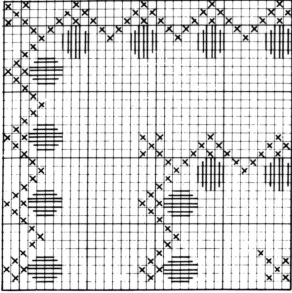

DOILY

of linen (each X on chart is to be worked over two horizontal and two vertical threads of linen). To embroider large dots, use four strands of floss in needle and work in satin stitch, taking stitches between threads of linen and on top of threads to make solid dots. See "Stitch Details." Alternate colors of dots in red and lilac. Mark $\frac{3}{4}$" around each side for hems. Start embroidery two threads in from hem lines.

Starting at top left of area C, embroider zigzag cross-stitch border and 18 large dots, following outer border of place mat chart to right and working to right corner as indicated on chart. Embroider zigzag cross-stitch and 15 large dots down right side; repeat corner at bottom. Embroider bottom border same as for top border.

Turn mat to wrong side and embroider border around area A, two threads in from hem lines and following the same chart. Slash into hem allow-ance at line between A and C at top and bottom. Turn in edges of A to right side on hem line. Fold $\frac{1}{4}$" in on all edges and slip-stitch hem. Make hem around B and C, turning allowance over to wrong side. Fold A over to front of mat for pocket. Slip-stitch A to B and C along top and bottom edges. Slip-stitch long edge of pocket to C, leaving a 6" opening for napkin $1\frac{1}{2}$" from top.

Doily: Mark $\frac{3}{4}$" hem line all around 8" square linen. Starting two threads in from hem line, embroider border and inner square following chart for doily; work seven large dots along each side between corners. Turn hems to wrong side; slip-stitch as for mat.

BREAKFAST SET
Shown on page 109

EQUIPMENT: Scissors. Embroidery needle. Tape measure. Tracing paper. Pencil.

MATERIAL: Even-weave cream or white linen fabric, 27 threads-to-the-inch: 14" × 18" for place mat; 5" × 10" for egg cozy; 5" × 19" for napkin holder. Sewing thread to match linen. DMC six-strand embroidery floss, 1 skein each orange #740 and yellow #725. **For Egg Cozy:** cotton flannel or batting and thin lining fabric, each 5" × 10". **For Napkin Holder:** cardboard box approximately $6\frac{1}{2}$" long, $2\frac{1}{2}$" wide and at least $3\frac{1}{2}$" high. All-purpose glue.

DIRECTIONS: Mat: (See Contents for all General Directions.) Cut linen 14" × 18". Measure $1\frac{1}{4}$" in from all edges and pull a thread out at this point on each side (this is hemming line). For embroidery, use two strands of six-strand floss in needle, and work in cross-stitch (see "Four Methods of Cross-Stitching.") Following color illustration and chart, work from left to right, starting $\frac{1}{4}$" in from pulled threads; repeat cross-stitch pattern at each end of mat.

To make mitered corners for hems, fold two adjacent sides over to right side of mat $\frac{3}{4}$" in from edges. Pull up corner and stitch diagonally across corner. Repeat for each corner. Turn hem to wrong side; turn in $\frac{1}{4}$" on all edges; baste hem. Hemstitch by hand or by machine over edges and through pulled thread lines.

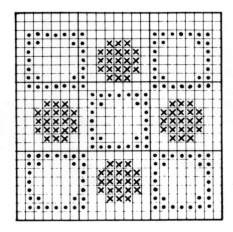

Egg Cozy: Trace the actual-size pattern; complete half-pattern indicated by long dash line. Using pattern, cut two pieces of linen and two of lining fabric. Mark an outline $\frac{1}{4}''$ in from cut line for seams. Cut two pieces of flannel or batting following seam size.

Work cross-stitch pattern as for mat, repeating chart to fill entire area within seam lines on both linen pieces.

With right sides facing, stitch the two linen pieces together on seam lines around curved sides. Turn to right side. Using six strands of floss in needle, embroider a row of chain stitches across top of cozy, following the seam line. Stitch a flannel piece to wrong side of each lining piece. With right sides of lining pieces facing, stitch together around curved sides. Insert lining in linen cover. Turn in bottom edges of linen cover and lining and slip-stitch all around.

Napkin Holder: If box is higher than $3\frac{1}{2}''$, cut down each side evenly to this measurement. Cut a strip of linen 5" wide and 19" long (or length to fit around box plus 1"). Measure $1\frac{1}{4}''$ in from each long edge and pull a thread from linen at these points. Starting $\frac{1}{4}''$ down from top pulled thread and $\frac{1}{2}''$ from one end, work cross-stitch pattern, repeating chart along length of linen strip to within $\frac{1}{2}''$ of opposite end.

For top and bottom hems, fold $\frac{3}{4}''$ on each long edge over to back. Turn in $\frac{1}{4}''$ at edge and baste. Hemstitch by hand or machine over edge and through pulled thread line. Fold strip in half crosswise, right sides facing. Stitch ends together with $\frac{1}{2}''$ seams (measure piece to fit snugly over box first). Slip linen cover over box; glue top and bottom edges of cover all around box to complete.

FLOWER PILLOWS
Shown on page 106

SIZE: 16" square.

MATERIALS: Knitting worsted weight yarn, 2 4-oz. skeins white. Afghan hook size 10. For embroidery, small amounts of yarn of knitting worsted weight or finer yarn used double, in the following colors: For Rose: pink, bright red, cardinal red, maroon, yellow, gold, light rust, light green, apple green, olive, bottle green; For Violets: violet, purple, red purple, dark yellow, light green, medium green, dark green, light pink, dark pink. Tapestry needles. 16" foam pillow

GAUGE: 11 sts = 3"; 13 rows = 4".

PILLOW TOP (make 2): Ch 60. **Row 1:** Pull up a lp in 2nd ch from hook and in each ch across.

To Work Lps Off: Yo hook, pull through first lp, * yo hook and through next 2 lps, repeat from * across. Lp that remains on hook counts as first st of next row.

Row 2: Keeping all lps on hook, pull up a lp under 2nd vertical bar and under each vertical bar across. Work lps off as before. Repeat row 2 for 51 rows or until piece is square. Sl st in each

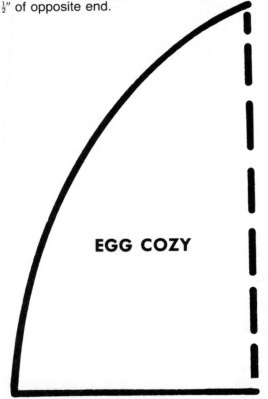

EGG COZY

vertical bar across. End off. Block pieces square to same size.

EMBROIDERY: Following charts, embroider designs in cross-stitch, large design centered on front, small design centered on back. Large rose begins on 7th row from bottom, the 2 olive sts on 21st and 22nd sts from left edge. Violets begin on 3rd row from bottom, the first dark pink cross on 20th st from right edge. Embroider dark green stems in couching stitch, little leaves in lazy daisy stitch. Embroider dark pink flowers in lazy daisy stitch with yellow French knot centers. See "Stitch Details."

FINISHING: Sc pillow pieces tog, inserting foam pillow before closing last seam.

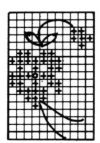

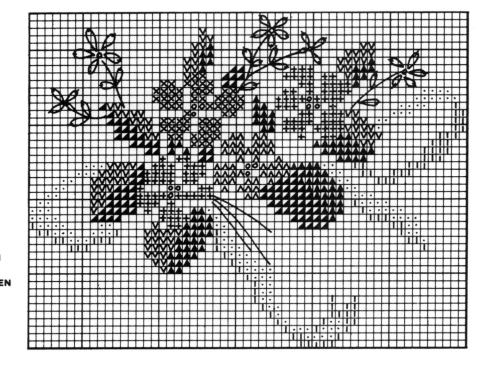

- ⊡ LIGHT PINK
- ☑ LIGHT GREEN
- ◩ RED PURPLE
- ▣ MEDIUM GREEN
- ⊞ YELLOW
- ⊞ DARK PINK
- ⊞ VIOLET
- ⊠ PURPLE
- ◪ DARK GREEN

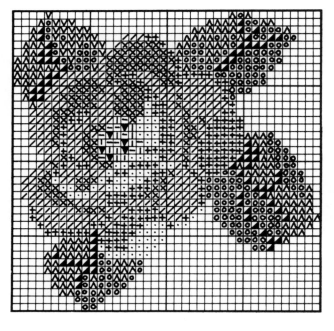

- ⊡ PINK
- ◪ CARDINAL
- ⊠ MAROON
- ⊞ YELLOW
- ⊟ GOLD
- ◪ BOTTLE GREEN
- ◙ OLIVE
- ◪ RUST
- ◪ APPLE GREEN
- ◪ LIGHT GREEN
- ⊞ RED

FLOOR CUSHIONS AND RUGS

Shown on pages 110–111

SIZE: Cushions, 24″ square. Rugs, 24″ × 34″.

MATERIALS: Heavy rug yarn, 10 4-oz. skeins of Yellow for one pillow and rug set. For set with large flower design, 2 skeins each of deep rose and scarlet, 1 skein each of blue, emerald green and brown. For set with small flower design, 1 skein each of deep rose, scarlet, emerald green, brown and dark turquoise. Crochet hook size K. Rug needles. For each pillow, ¾ yd. 60″ heavy fabric. Two 1 lb. bags of polyester fiberfill.

GAUGE: 2 sc = 1″; 2 rows = 1″ (double strand).

LARGE FLOWER CUSHION: With double strand of yellow, ch 50. **Row 1:** Sc in 2nd ch from hook and in each ch across—49 sc. Ch 1, turn each row.

Row 2: Sc in each sc across. Repeat row 2 until there are 52 rows. Work 1 rnd sc around entire pillow top, working 3 sc in each corner. Join; end off.

Following chart, using yarn double in rug needle, embroider design in cross-stitch, working 1 cross-stitch over 1 sc. Row 1 of chart is row 1 of crochet.

Make pillow same size as cushion top; sew cushion top to pillow with matching sewing thread.

LARGE FLOWER RUG: Work as for cushion until there are 73 rows. Work 1 row sc on each side edge of rug.

Following chart, using yarn double in rug needle, embroider design in cross-stitch, working 1 cross-stitch over 1 sc. Work to B on chart; then repeat from A to top of chart.

SMALL FLOWER CUSHION: With double strand of yellow, ch 50. **Row 1:** Sc in 2nd ch from hook and in each ch across—49 sc. Ch 1, turn each row.

Row 2: Sc in each sc across. Repeat row 2 until there are 49 rows. Work 1 rnd sc around entire pillow top, working 3 sc in each corner. Join; end off.

Following chart, using yarn double in rug needle, embroider design in cross-stitch, working 1 cross-stitch over 1 sc. Row 1 of chart is row 1 of crochet.

Make pillow same size as cushion top; sew cushion top to pillow with matching sewing thread.

SMALL FLOWER RUG: Work as for cushion until there are 70 rows. Following chart, using yarn double in rug needle, embroider design in cross-stitch, working 1 cross-stitch over 1 sc. On center flower design, leave 2 rows free before, after and between flowers instead of 1 row as on cushion, but work border design as shown. Work to B on chart, then repeat from A to top of chart. If desired, work 1 rnd sc around entire rug, working 3 sc in each corner. Join; end off.

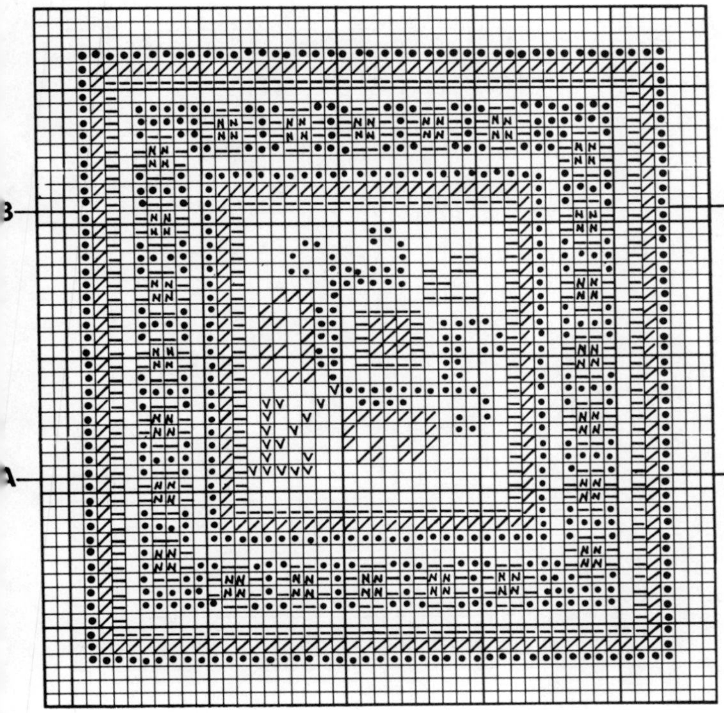

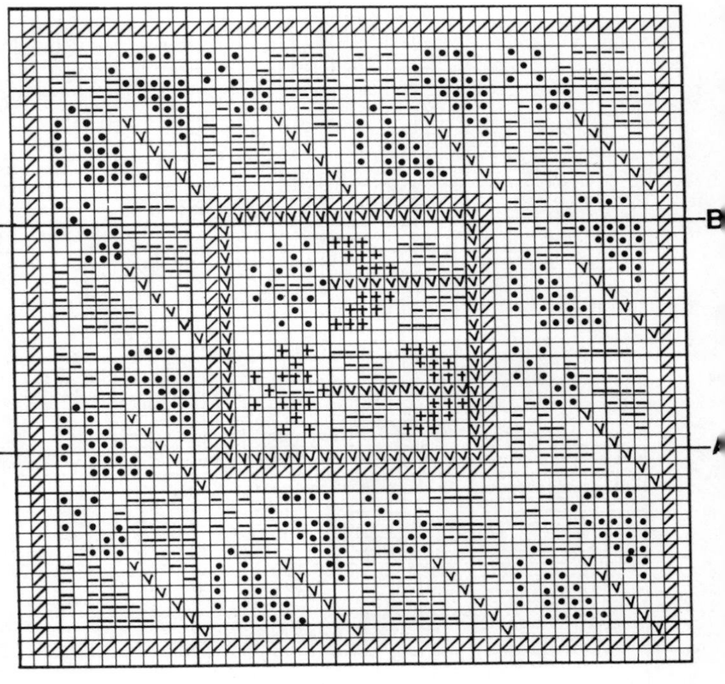

● RED ╱ BROWN ▭ DEEP ROSE N BLUE V GREEN ✝ TURQUOISE

RING OF ROSES TABLECLOTH

Shown on page 112

SIZE: Embroidered area is approximately 19″ in diameter. Although shown on a round table, embroidery would be equally effective on a square or rectangle.

EQUIPMENT: Embroidery and sewing needles. Scissors. Pencil. Ruler. Basting thread. Tweezers.

MATERIALS: Readymade linen or linen-like cloth with smooth finish in size desired. Penelope (cross-stitch) canvas, 10 mesh-to-the-inch, about 22″ square. DMC six-strand embroidery floss, one skein of each color listed in Color Key, unless otherwise indicated in parentheses.

DIRECTIONS: (See Contents for all General Directions.) Center of fabric must be determined before beginning embroidery. To find center, fold cloth horizontally and vertically into quarters and mark center point with a pin. Find center of penelope canvas; lightly mark center mesh with pencil. Matching center points, place Penelope canvas on top of tablecloth. Pin and baste canvas in place.

Center of cloth is indicated by X at center of chart. Counting off one mesh of canvas for every square on chart, determine your own starting point for embroidering design.

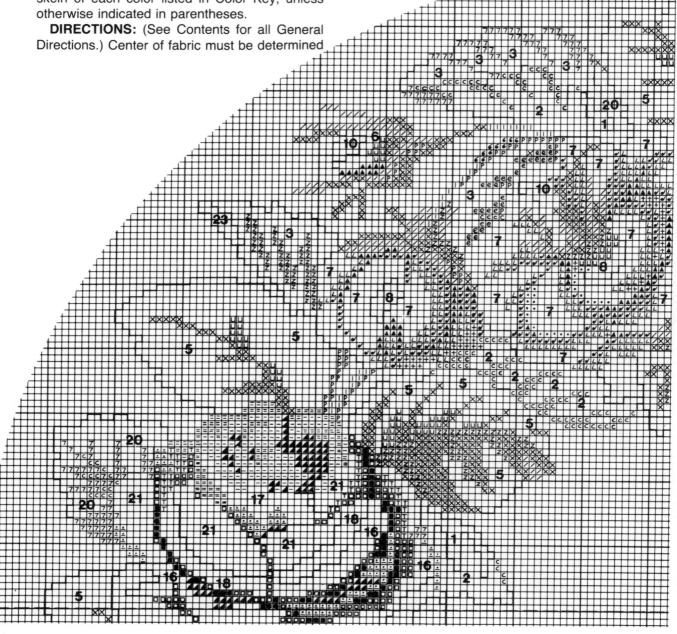

Refer to "Four Methods of Cross-Stitching," paying special attention to "On Penelope Canvas." Using four strands of floss in needle, cross-stitch entire cloth. Each stitch is made over one mesh of canvas. **(Note:** To make chart easier to read, we have marked off large areas of the same color and designated them by number; these numbers appear in the color key.)

If desired, single roses may be scattered on overhang as illustrated. Additional floss and can-

C	1	DEEP GREEN 367		15	DEEP PINK 326
e	2	MEDIUM GREEN 320		16	PINK 776
6	3	LIGHT GREEN 368		17	PALE PINK 818
7	20	PALE GREEN 369		18	ICE PINK 819
Z	23	DEEP OLIVE 937		6	CINNAMON RED 347 (2)
X	4	MEDIUM OLIVE 469	V		DEEP GARNET 814
/	5	LIGHT OLIVE 470 (3)		9	GARNET 815 (2)
U		PALE OLIVE 471		11	FLAG RED 304 (2)
P		YELLOW GREEN 732			WATERMELON 891
I		LIGHT YELLOW GREEN 734			TAUPE 223
Y		PALE YELLOW GREEN 472			TOAST 760
H	7	PEACH 353 (2)		12	MAHOGANY 902
.	8	PALE PEACH 754	Z	25	DEEP GOLD 782
L	10	ROSEY PEACH 351	Y		GOLD 783
/		DEEP ROSE 326	N	22	LIGHT GOLD 725
III	13	MEDIUM ROSE 309	O	19	YELLOW 726
X	14	ROSE 899	..	24	GRAY 646
				21	WHITE (2)

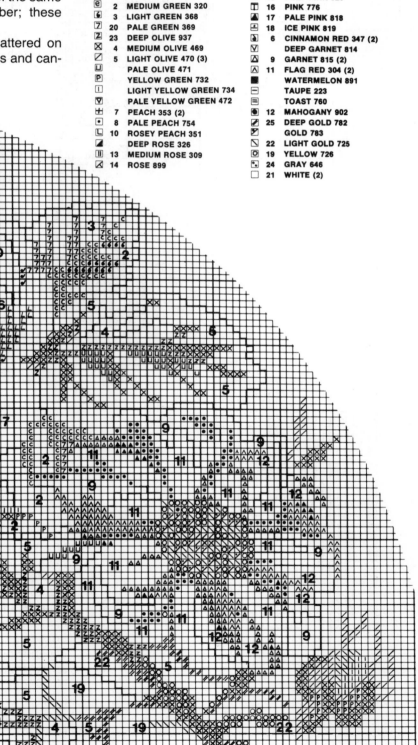

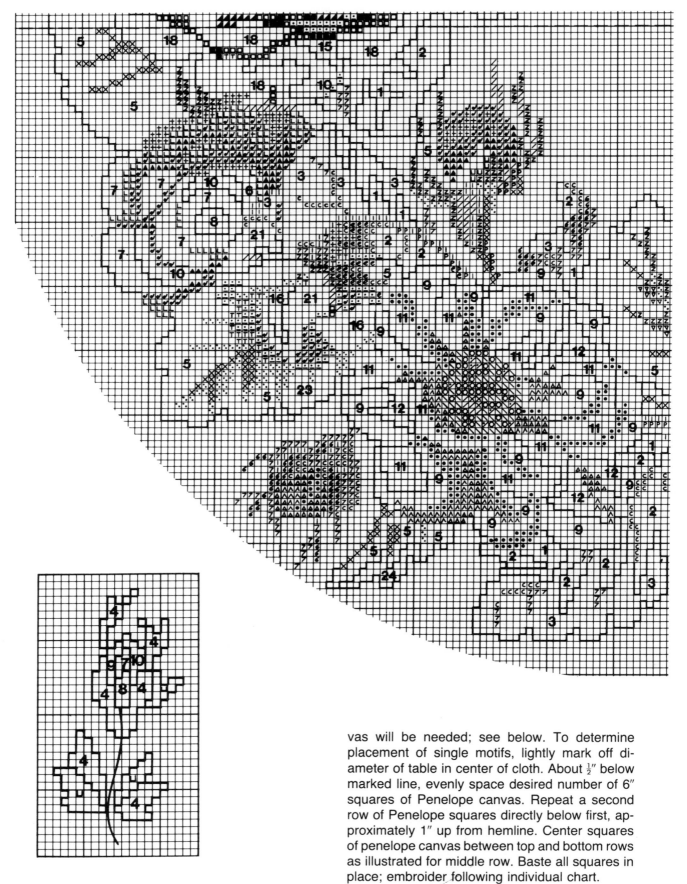

vas will be needed; see below. To determine placement of single motifs, lightly mark off diameter of table in center of cloth. About $\frac{1}{2}''$ below marked line, evenly space desired number of 6″ squares of Penelope canvas. Repeat a second row of Penelope squares directly below first, approximately 1″ up from hemline. Center squares of penelope canvas between top and bottom rows as illustrated for middle row. Baste all squares in place; embroider following individual chart.

When embroidery is complete, remove threads from Penelope canvas following directions in "Four Methods of Cross-Stitching." Steam-press if necessary.

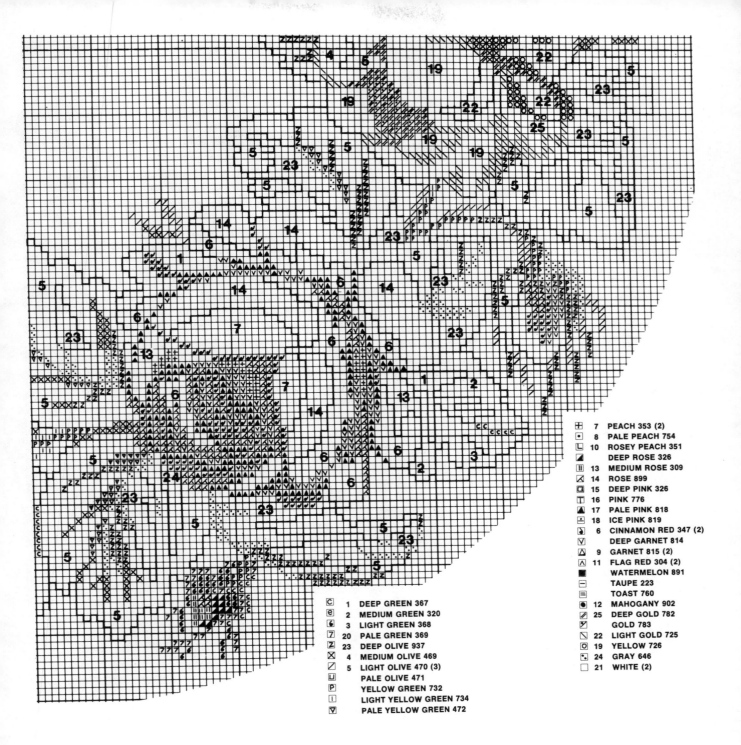

	7	PEACH 353 (2)
⊡	8	PALE PEACH 754
L	10	ROSEY PEACH 351
◢		DEEP ROSE 326
▥	13	MEDIUM ROSE 309
⊠	14	ROSE 899
▣	15	DEEP PINK 326
⏧	16	PINK 776
▲	17	PALE PINK 818
▨	18	ICE PINK 819
⬙	6	CINNAMON RED 347 (2)
▽		DEEP GARNET 814
△	9	GARNET 815 (2)
⋀	11	FLAG RED 304 (2)
■		WATERMELON 891
⊟		TAUPE 223
⊟		TOAST 760
◉	12	MAHOGANY 902
⊘	25	DEEP GOLD 782
⊠		GOLD 783
⟍	22	LIGHT GOLD 725
○	19	YELLOW 726
⊡	24	GRAY 646
☐	21	WHITE (2)

C	1	DEEP GREEN 367
℮	2	MEDIUM GREEN 320
ⓒ	3	LIGHT GREEN 368
⊿	20	PALE GREEN 369
Z	23	DEEP OLIVE 937
X	4	MEDIUM OLIVE 469
⊿	5	LIGHT OLIVE 470 (3)
Ⓤ		PALE OLIVE 471
P		YELLOW GREEN 732
Ⓘ		LIGHT YELLOW GREEN 734
▽		PALE YELLOW GREEN 472

ANTIQUE SAMPLER

Shown on page 147

SIZE: 16″ × 20″, as shown.

EQUIPMENT: Tape measure. Pencil. Scissors. Embroidery hoop or stretcher frame, 16″ × 20″. Sewing and embroidery needles. Steam iron. Padded surface. Zigzag sewing machine (optional). Tack hammer.

MATERIALS: Zweigart "hardanger" cloth, 22 threads-to-the-inch, #264 ivory, 20″ × 24″; DMC six-strand embroidery floss, one skein of each color listed in color key unless otherwise indicated in parentheses. Stiff white cardboard for mounting, 16″ × 20″. Short straight pins. Spray adhesive. Wooden frame with 16″ × 20″ rabbet opening. Brown wrapping paper.

DIRECTIONS: (See Contents for all General Directions.) Press hardanger cloth carefully; zigzag or whipstitch raw edges to prevent raveling. Find exact center of fabric by basting a line from center of one edge to center of opposite edge, making sure to follow one row of threads across; then baste a line from center of third edge to center of fourth edge in same manner; basting threads will cross in center.

Work major portion of design in cross-stitch, following chart on pages 100–101, color key and "Stitch Details". Each symbol on chart represents one cross-stitch worked over two vertical and two horizontal double threads, except where noted below.

Separate the six strands of embroidery floss; use two strands in needle to embroider design. Insert area to be embroidered in hoop, or thumbtack fabric securely to stretcher frame, keeping

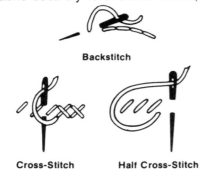

Backstitch

Cross-Stitch   **Half Cross-Stitch**

fabric taut and grain straight. When working cross-stitches, work all underneath stitches in a row in one direction, then all top stitches in opposite direction. Make all crosses touch by inserting needle each time in same hole used for an adjacent stitch. Begin stitching by leaving end of floss on back and working over it to secure. To end strand or begin a new one, weave floss under stitches on back of work; do not make knots.

To begin, place fabric with short edges at top and bottom; measure 3½″ in from one long raw edge along marked horizontal center line and mark point with pin; match point with arrow on chart. Begin working border design, keeping in mind that two double threads are counted as one square on chart. Work border around to where you began. Work house and landscape, following chart and leaving outlined areas for animals, birds and one tree blank. Fill in outlined areas with half cross-stitch, following letters given in color key; work each half cross-stitch over one set of horizontal and vertical double threads. For yellow animal to the right of the path, work nose, eye and collar in gold. For tree, work all single lines (branches and bird's beak) in dark brown backstitch; see "Stitch Details." Work bottom tips of flowers in yellow(D), middle sections in gold(B), and black sections in dark brown. Note that some flower sections divide the graph in half; keep in mind that each square of the graph represents two sets of threads, and that the outlined areas are worked over one set of threads. Work trunk in dark brown. Work bird in gold with light brown tail, dark brown eye, and yellow beak tips. Work angels following chart.

Work personalized section as follows: Using pencil and following upper and lower-case alphabets, lightly chart desired name and date onto separate graph (Fig. 1, page 102), being sure to center your design within the space given. Note that Figure 1 is an actual depiction of the border, with stitches worked over two sets of horizontal and vertical double threads. Upper-case letters are worked in same manner; chart each stitch over four spaces as shown in upper-case alphabet. Lower-case letters are worked in cross-stitch over one set of horizontal and vertical double threads; chart each stitch in one space as shown

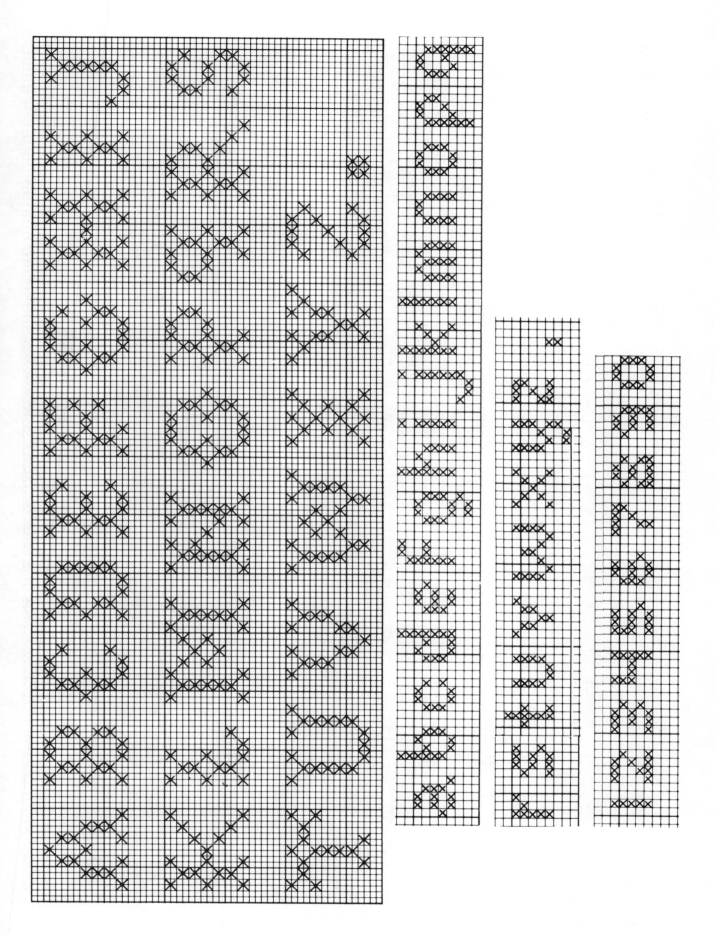

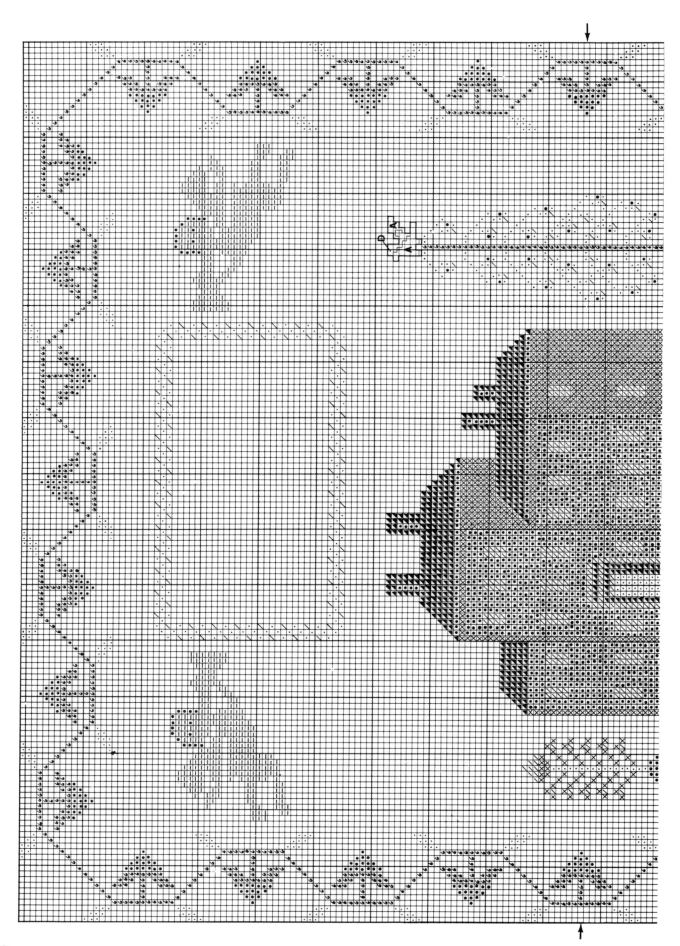

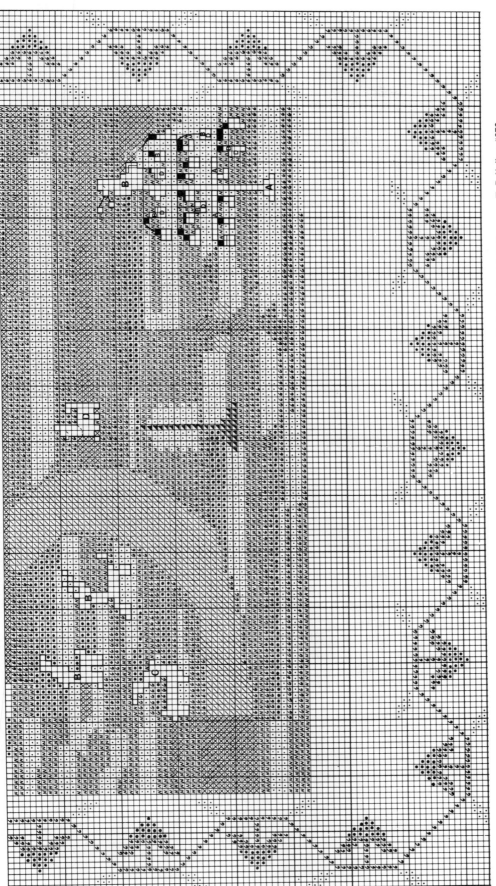

A Dark Brown #801
Light Brown #780 (2)
B Gold #680
C Light Gold #729

D Yellow #676
Dark Green #890 (2)
Medium Green #367 (2)
Light Green #3347 (2)

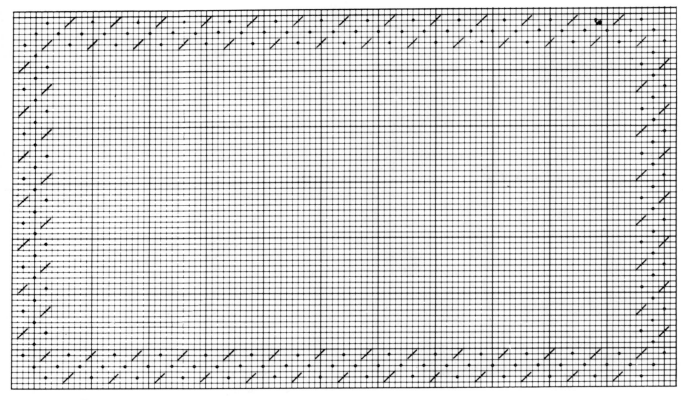

FIGURE 1

in lower-case alphabet. Should your name be longer than the alloted space, try to shorten it by using initials or by writing your entire name in lower case. After your chart is drawn, work name section on sampler in cross-stitch to complete the design.

After embroidery is complete, steam-press gently on padded surface. Stretch pressed fabric right side up over mounting cardboard. Be sure threads of fabric are straight horizontally and vertically, and that embroidery is centered. Push pins through fabric margins partway into sides of board; pin corners first, then work from center of each side toward corners, spacing pins about ¼" apart all around mounting board. When design is even, drive pins into edge of board with tack hammer. If a pin does not go in straight, it should be removed and reinserted. Trim away excess fabric, leaving ½" for turning; fold to wrong side of cardboard and adhere with spray adhesive. Frame mounted embroidery; cover back with brown paper.

CHILD'S PRAYER
Shown on page 149

SIZE: Design area, 9¾" × 12¾."
EQUIPMENT: Embroidery needle. Embroidery frame (optional). Penelope (cross-stitch) canvas, 10 mesh-to-the-inch, about 10" × 13". Sewing needle. Basting thread. Tweezers. Tracing paper. Pencil. Dressmaker's carbon (tracing) paper. **For Blocking:** Soft wooden surface. Brown wrapping paper. Ruler. T-square. Thumbtacks.

MATERIALS: White medium-weight linen, linen-like cotton, or quality muslin, 18" × 21". DMC six-strand embroidery floss: One skein of each of the following: turquoise #995, light turquoise #996, light green #907, dark green #904, pink #604, orange #971, light gold #742, purple #552, brown #434.

DIRECTIONS: Read "Four Methods of Cross-Stitching." (See Contents for all General Direc-

NOW I LAY ME DOWN TO SLEEP
I PRAY THEE LORD MY SOUL TO KEEP

IF I SHOULD DIE BEFORE I WAKE
I PRAY THEE LORD MY SOUL TO TAKE

	DK. GREEN 904		LT. TURQUOISE 996
	PURPLE 552		PINK 604
	LT. GOLD 742		TURQUOISE 995
	ORANGE 971		LT. GREEN 907

tions.) Center canvas on right side of fabric; baste in place.

Using three strands of floss in needle and referring to chart and color key, work all cross-stitches of border and prayer as indicated. Each filled-in square represents a cross-stitch.

Remove Penelope canvas as indicated. Connect cross-stitch flowers with dark green stems worked in outline stitch ("see Stitch Details.") Work dark green leaves as indicated in lazy daisy stitch.

Using tracing paper, trace actual-size pattern below for center panel. Center traced design in panel; insert dressmaker's carbon underneath tracing. Using dry ball-point pen, carefully trace around entire design to transfer to fabric.

Using two strands of floss in needle and following illustration for color, embroider panel as follows: Work outlines of star, curtains, bed, bedposts, little girl's feet and nightgown, and teddy bear in outline stitch. Work teddy bear's body, little girl's hair and nightgown in short straight stitches. Work moon crescent and bows on teddy and little girl in satin stitch. Work windowpane dividers and sash in chain stitch. Flowers on curtains have French knot centers; work radiating straight stitches from knot for flower shape. Outline entire flower with outline stitch. Work cross-stitches where indicated.

When embroidery is finished, block and mount following directions under "Embroidery Basics." Frame as desired.

Graceful cross-stitch letters from an antique sampler spell out the title, while flowers add to the old-fashioned look. Scattered cross-stitches make a modern "dotted swiss" on the denim background. Design is worked over Penelope canvas. Directions include how to cover standard album; see page 84.

Afghan-stitch crochet makes a perfect pair of pillows, beautifully embroidered in cross-stitch.
Full-blown rose and nosegay of violets decorate the pillow fronts; a rosebud and single violet, the backs.
Directions begin on page 91.

*Cross-stitch tulips
by the bunch enhance
a pillow, mirror frame and
box lid. Embroidery
is worked in six-strand
floss on linen.
Directions for Tulip Trio
are on page 85.*

Celebrate the seasons with four colorful apron/pot holder sets. Charming Americana scenes from the days when young needleworkers learned their ABCs on a sampler are created in cross-stitch on gingham. Spring, worked on fresh leaf green, shows a quaint New England church. Summer, on soft pink, depicts a picket-fenced barn. Autumn, on yellow to echo the autumn leaves, shows a little red schoolhouse—the students are on the pot holder! Winter, on cool blue, boasts a delightful covered bridge in snow. Four Seasons Set, page 87.

A napkin pocket makes this place mat ideal for outdoor dining: when breezes blow, the napkin won't. A lovely doily complements set. Simple repeat design is satin stitch, cross-stitch. Serviette Set directions on page 89.

Circles in squares pattern a pretty breakfast set—egg cozy, napkin holder, and mat. Drawn thread creates a "beaded" edging on the cloth. Breakfast Set directions on page 90.

Keep out the cold and warm your heart with bright colors and patterns. Folk art florals and geometrics enhance a pair of floor cushions and matching rugs. All in single crochet, worked with double strand of rug yarn and embroidered in cross-stitch with glowing colors of the same yarn, pillows and rugs are easy to make, great to own. Floor Cushions and Rugs directions on page 93.

*Count the threads, take a stitch,
and watch your garden grow! This fabulous
tablecloth can be dotted throughout
with rosebuds or left plain.
Directions on page 94.*

KING-SIZE SAMPLER

Shown on page 146

SIZE: 41″ × 62″.

EQUIPMENT: Paper for patterns. Large sheets of tissue paper. Pencil. Scissors. Tapestry needles. White sewing thread. Sewing needle. Straight pins. Tape measure.

MATERIALS: Green burlap 52″ wide, 2 yards. DMC Laine Tapisserie (tapestry yarn) 8.8-yard skeins: 10 skeins pink #7121; 12 skeins medium coral #7104; 7 skeins dark coral #7106; 3 skeins red #7107; 19 skeins yellow #7431; 9 skeins gold #7725; 7 skeins rust-brown #7446; 9 skeins pale blue #7599; 9 skeins medium blue #7597; 5 skeins pumpkin #7922; 4 skeins black; 14 skeins white; 34 skeins yellow-green #7771. **For Mounting:** Fiberboard, 41″ × 62″. Large straight pins. Masking tape.

DIRECTIONS: (See Contents for all General Directions.) Before doing embroidered borders, work all the lettering in center panel, following Large Chart. See "Four Methods of Cross-Stitching" for how to cross-stitch. All crosses are worked over two horizontal and two vertical threads of burlap. Crosses are indicated on charts by symbols which represent different colors (see color key). Each square of chart represents two horizontal and two vertical threads of burlap. Other stitches are worked as shown on chart.

To do the star-stitch squares that make up the letters at top of chart, work each stitch from center space out over two threads of burlap, making eight stitches to complete each square. The other stitches are straight vertical stitches worked over four or more threads of burlap. Use single strands of yarn in tapestry needle throughout.

To start, measure in from top left corner of burlap 10″, then measure 10″ down; this is top left corner of Large Chart. Following chart, work row of pink cross-stitch border across and down both sides for some distance; continue cross-stitch border as work progresses. Starting two threads down and four threads in from top left corner of border, work star-stitch letter in pink yarn, following chart. Make first three letters pink, next three medium coral, next three dark coral, last letter red. Skip two horizontal threads of burlap and

work row of cross-stitch in pale blue. Skip one thread of burlap and make next row of letters: first three medium blue, next three pale blue, next three yellow-green, last two yellow.

Work the cross-stitch bands following chart. On row of pointed motifs, first make outline of stars across in rust-brown. Then make straight stitches within outline: first three motifs yellow, next three yellow-green, next three pink, next three medium coral, next two dark coral, next three yellow-green, last three yellow.

On next row, make letters with straight stitches, each over four threads of burlap. Make first two letters medium coral, next two white, next two yellow-green, next two pale blue, last two yellow. Make cross-stitch row across. On next row of straight-stitch letters, make first two pale blue, next letter pink, next letter medium coral, next two yellow, next letter gold, last three orange. Work cross-stitch motif row across. On next row of straight-stitch letters, make first three pale blue, last two white.

Following chart and color key, work remainder of chart in cross-stitch to bottom row of pointed motifs. Work cross-stitch outlines first. Fill in straight vertical stitches, making first two motifs medium coral, next motif dark coral, next two motifs medium coral, next motif white, next medium blue, next medium coral, next medium blue, next white, next two medium coral, next motif dark coral, last two medium coral.

Using letters already worked as a guide, plan name, date, and place to give sampler your personal signature.

Following Tree Chart, work tree panel below row of pointed motifs. Start at bottom center of panel and work tree chart out to right. Work complete half chart; then work chart in reverse to left to finish tree design. Make all trees and flowers in cross-stitch, all mounds along bottom in a combination of cross-stitch and straight vertical stitches. Where indicated on chart, work a tiny bird in half

⊟ PINK	⊡ WHITE	◥ ORANGE
☑ MEDIUM CORAL	◺ PALE BLUE	⊠ YELLOW-GREEN
☑ DARK CORAL	⊞ MEDIUM BLUE	☑ GOLD
⑤ RED	⊡ YELLOW	▭ RUST-BROWN
■ BLACK		

LARGE CHART FOR ALPHABET SAMPLER

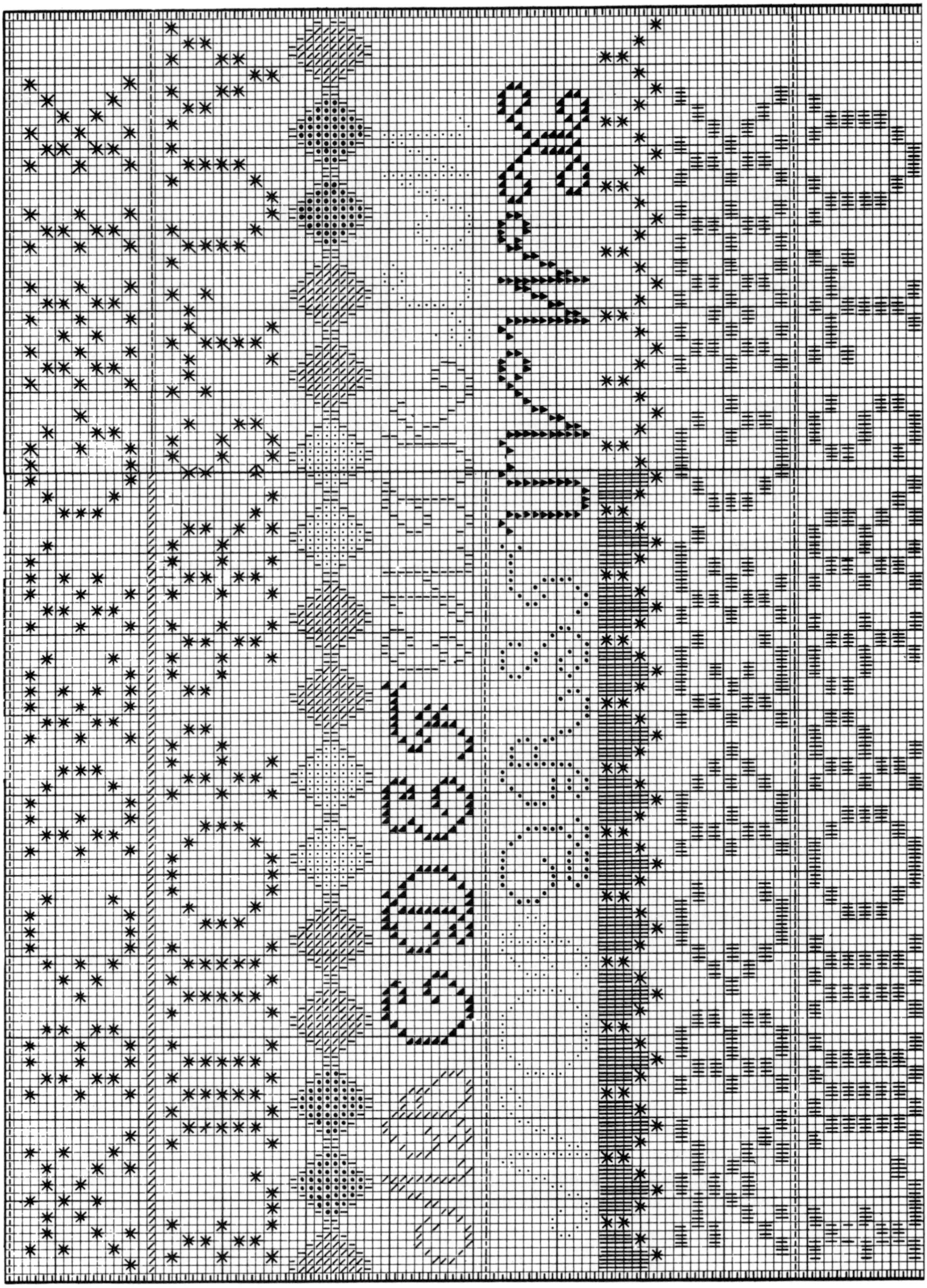

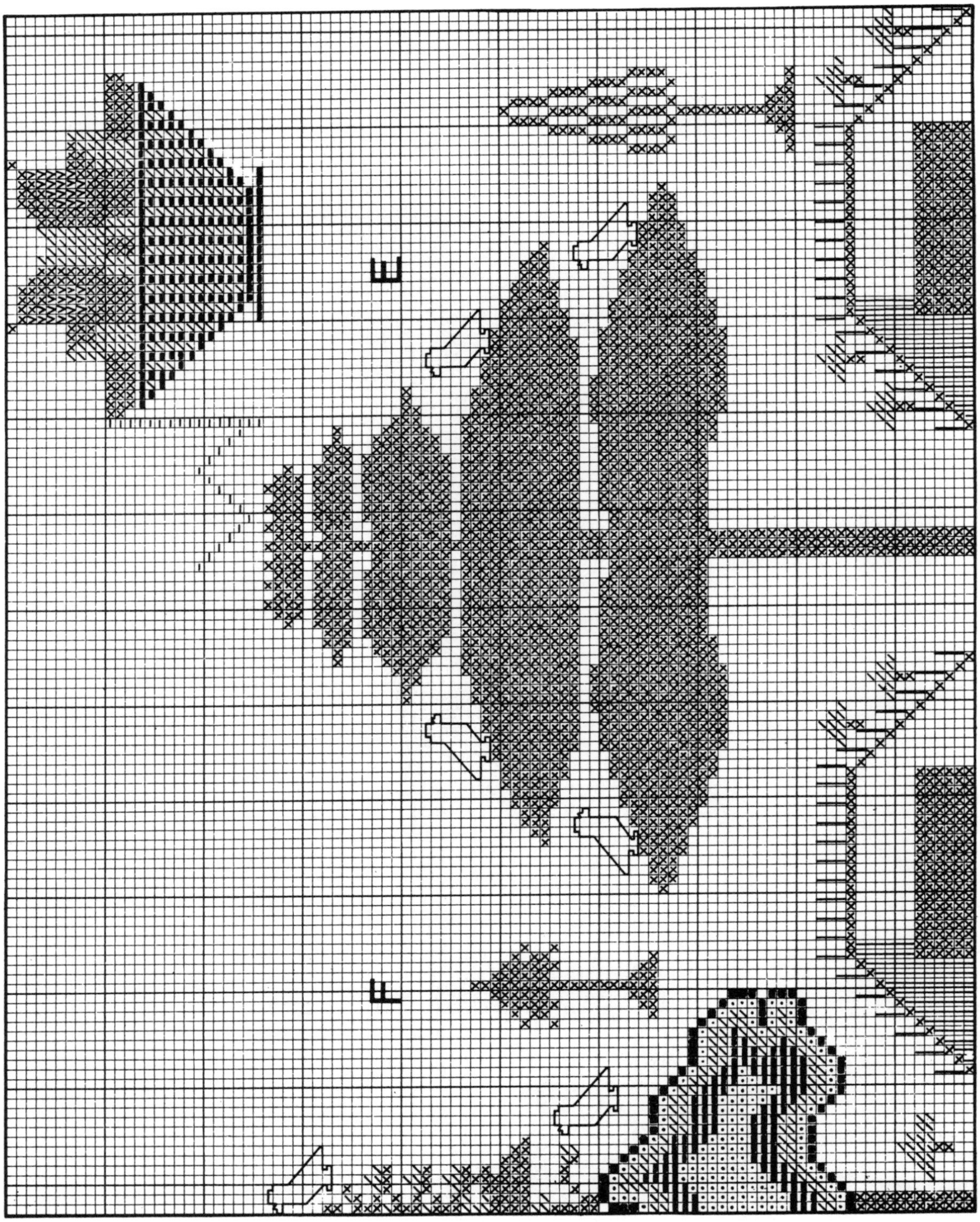

E

F

TREE CHART

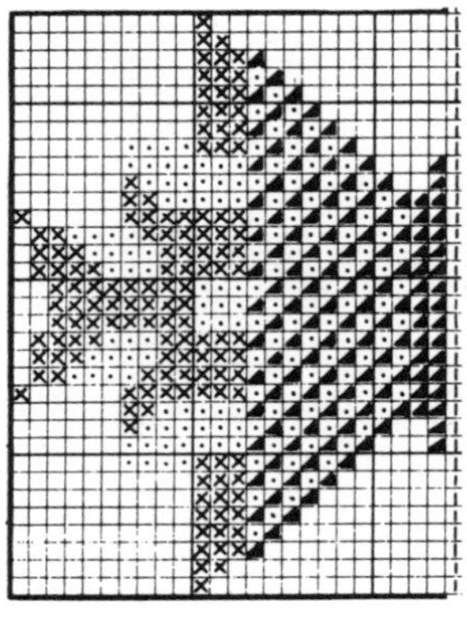

BASKET CHART

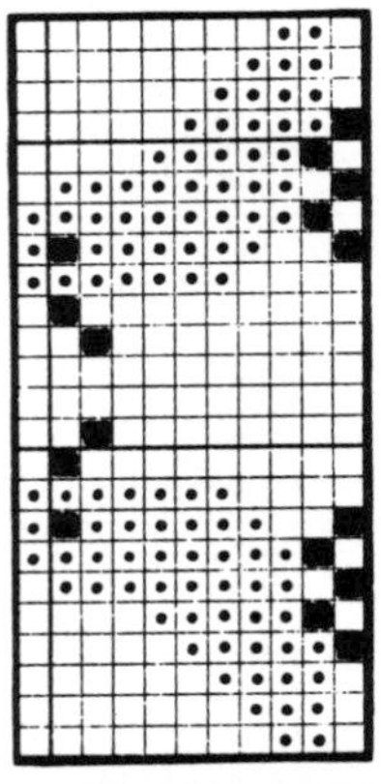

TINY BIRDS CHART

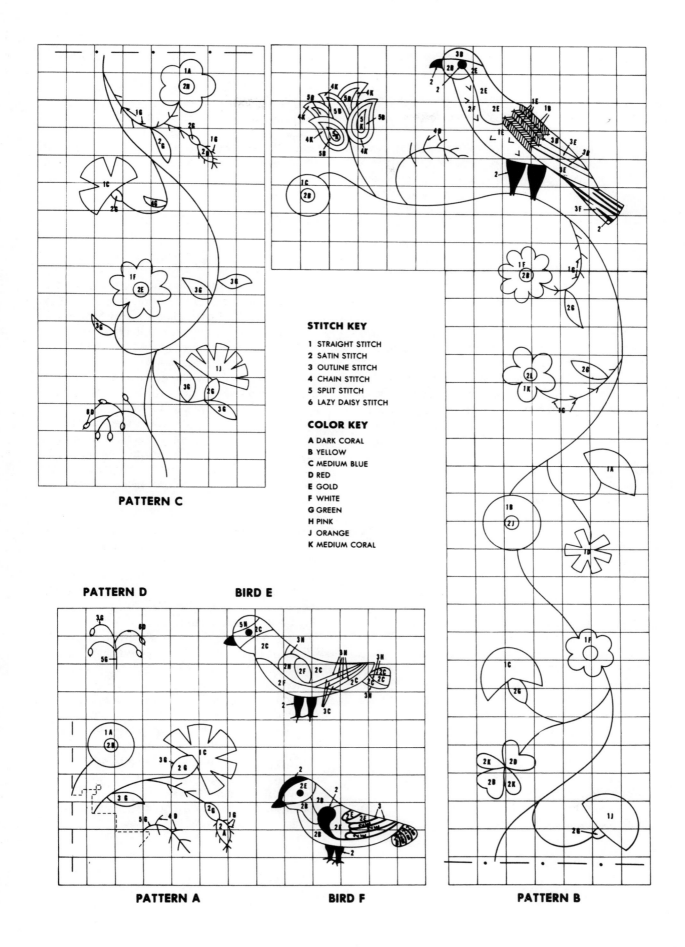

PATTERN C

STITCH KEY

1 STRAIGHT STITCH
2 SATIN STITCH
3 OUTLINE STITCH
4 CHAIN STITCH
5 SPLIT STITCH
6 LAZY DAISY STITCH

COLOR KEY

A DARK CORAL
B YELLOW
C MEDIUM BLUE
D RED
E GOLD
F WHITE
G GREEN
H PINK
J ORANGE
K MEDIUM CORAL

PATTERN D

BIRD E

PATTERN A

BIRD F

PATTERN B

crosses over one thread of burlap, following chart for Tiny Birds.

Work basket at top center of cross-stitch panel on Large Chart; then work Tree Chart baskets at each side at bottom of panel (bottom of basket lines up with last stitch of border on Large Chart).

Embroidered Border: The remainder of sampler is worked in various embroidery stitches. See "Stitch Details." Enlarge patterns on paper ruled in 1" squares. Trace patterns on tissue paper.

Starting at top of panel above right side of basket, pin Pattern A, matching short dash lines to edges of basket. With long white thread in sewing needle, make running stitches through tissue and burlap on all lines of pattern. Carefully pull away tissue, leaving running stitches as embroidery guide. Pin Pattern B around right top corner of panel and down side. Match dot-dash lines of Pattern C to B and pin C in place down side of panel to bottom basket. Stitch running stitch on all lines of patterns as before and pull away tissue.

Trace all patterns again. Turn each pattern over and retrace on back for left side of panel. Place patterns on left side and outline as before with white thread.

Trace Pattern D four times. Pin one Pattern D at center top of each mound at bottom of panel and outline with white thread. Trace Birds E and F as given and make two reverse tracings. At points indicated by letters E and F on Tree Chart, pin the four birds in position all facing to center; outline with white thread as for other patterns.

Embroider all stems in green, using single strand of yarn in needle. Embroider main continuous stems in chain stitch; make off-shooting stems in split stitch. Following numbers for stitches and letters for colors, embroider flowers and leaves, using single strand of yarn in needle. Work straight stitches radiating out from center point. Where outline stitch, split stitch, or chain stitch is indicated to fill an area, make rows of stitches close together, conforming to shape of area.

On birds, work satin stitch across areas in narrowest direction. Solid black areas are done with black yarn.

Finishing: When embroidery is complete, stretch burlap over fiberboard, placing bottom of mounds along bottom edge of fiberboard. Push pins through burlap into edges of board, starting at center of each side and working toward corners. Stretch burlap smoothly and be sure threads of burlap are straight. Turn excess burlap to back of fiberboard; tape.

HAPPY HEARTS SAMPLER
Shown on page 145

SIZE: $9\frac{7}{8}'' \times 15\frac{3}{8}''$, design area.

EQUIPMENT: Tape measure. Scissors. Pencil. Masking tape. Embroidery hoop (optional). Embroidery needle. **For Blocking and Mounting:** Soft wooden board. Brown wrapping paper. Rust-proof thumbtacks. Turkish towel. T-square. Ruler. Sewing and darning needles.

MATERIALS: Off-white, even-weave linen with 23–24 threads-to-the-inch, 16" × 22". Six-strand embroidery floss, 7-yd. skeins: 1 each light green, rose, champagne, medium brown, black, light blue, gold; 2 skeins dark green; 3 skeins each of brick red and dark blue. **For Mounting:** Sewing thread to match linen. Heavy mounting cardboard. Frame.

DIRECTIONS: Charts are given exactly as sampler is worked. Each square on chart represents one thread of fabric. Large crosses are worked over two threads; small crosses are worked over one. Use two strands of floss for small crosses; use three strands for large crosses.

Place linen on a smooth, hard surface. Using pencil, lightly mark on linen a $9\frac{7}{8}'' \times 15\frac{3}{8}''$ rectangle (area for embroidery). To prevent raveling, tape edges with masking tape.

Thread embroidery needle with 18" to 20" length of floss, using number of strands indicated above. Read "Four Methods of Cross-Stitching" for working cross-stitch on even-weave fabric. Follow color key and charts to work cross-stitch sampler. Large chart is half-pattern of sampler; repeat in reverse for second half. Follow separate charts to complete alphabets and to work poem.

To personalize sampler, use letters in saying to chart your name. Letters not used are in separate chart below.

Block and mount following directions in "Embroidery Basics." Frame as desired.

clocks, crocks, ladderback chairs
tieback curtains, patchwork squares
samplers, quilts, pewter and pine
friends for dinner·hot mulled wine
pot roast, potatoes, cherry tarts
love, happiness, happy hearts

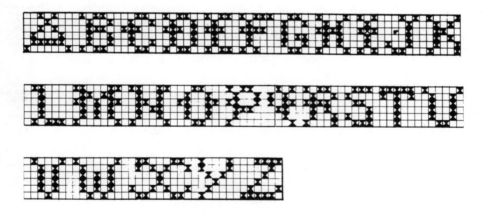

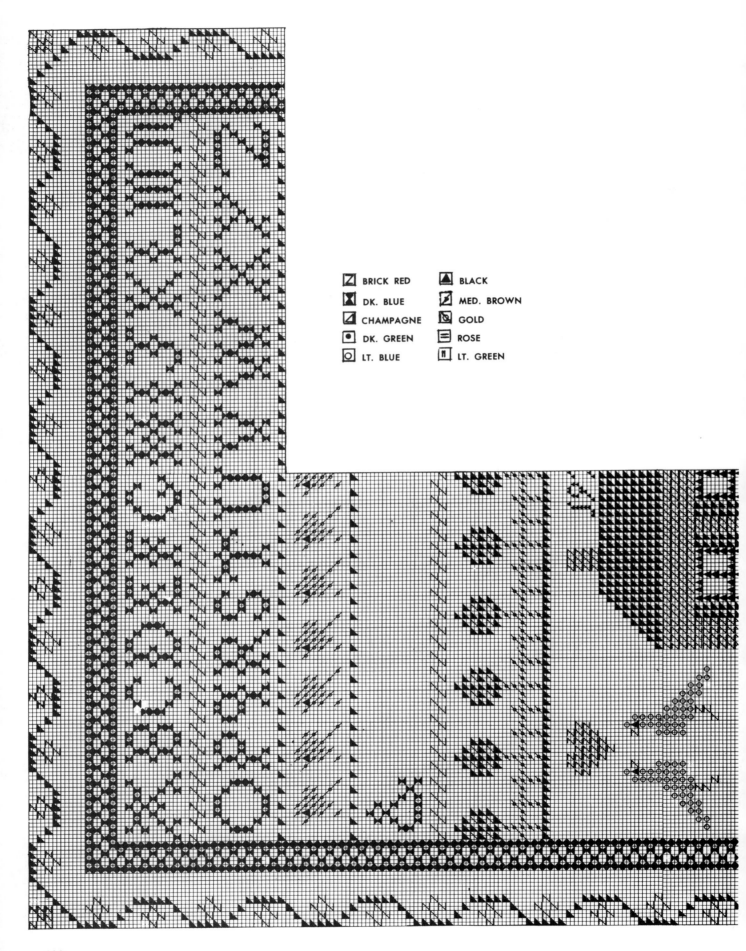

BRICK RED BLACK
DK. BLUE MED. BROWN
CHAMPAGNE GOLD
DK. GREEN ROSE
LT. BLUE LT. GREEN

COLONIAL HOUSE SAMPLER

Shown on page 148

DESIGN SIZE: About 16″ × 21½″.
EQUIPMENT: Embroidery needle. Scissors. Sewing thread. Penelope (cross-stitch) canvas, 12 mesh-to-the-inch, about 19″ × 25″. Embroidery hoop (optional). Tweezers. **For Blocking:** Brown paper. Soft wooden surface. T-square. Hammer. Thumbtacks.

MATERIALS: White or off-white linen, 25″ × 30″. Six-strand embroidery floss: 2 skeins each of gold, yellow, light green, medium green; 1 skein each of baby blue, cornflower blue, dark green, old gold, dark brown, white. **For Mounting:** Heavy white cardboard 19″ × 25″. Straight pins. Masking tape. Frame, 19″ × 25″ rabbet size.

DIRECTIONS: (See Contents for all General Directions.) Fold piece of linen in half horizontally, then vertically to find center. Mark point with pin. Carefully center canvas over center point of linen and baste in place to linen (see directions for cross-stitching over Penelope canvas, under "Four Methods of Cross-Stitching" and charts.)

For embroidery, use two strands of floss throughout, except three strands for white only. Arrows on chart indicate center lines; find center point and begin working cross-stitches from this point, following chart for placement of colors. Each square on chart represents one stitch. Work crosses over mesh of canvas as shown in "Stitch Details," being careful to work all stitches in the same direction, with ends of stitches touching; do not catch canvas thread. Solid line on chart indicates backstitch; outline spaces on windows, steps, and awning are satin stitch. To work these

after cross-stitch is completed, see Finishing below.

Chart is for a little more than one-half of the design with center motifs given complete. Repeat other motifs on second half (see illustration). Border design is slightly more than one-quarter; repeat around all sides, making corners as shown in illustration.

When cross-stitch design is complete, remove basting threads and carefully draw out canvas threads with tweezers following directions under "Stitch Details."

FINISHING: With white, work three rows of satin stitch steps; with yellow, work satin stitch windows and awning; with baby blue, work back-stitch around steps, and around swan. See "Stitch Details."

Block and mount finished embroidery following directions under "Embroidery Basics."

☒ GOLD
⊞ YELLOW
☑ LIGHT GREEN
◉ MEDIUM GREEN
◪ BABY BLUE
◙ CORNFLOWER BLUE
◪ DARK GREEN
⊠ OLD GOLD
◪ DARK BROWN
◪ WHITE

WEDDING/ANNIVERSARY SAMPLERS

Shown on pages 150 and 151

SIZE: design area, 10″ × 13″.

EQUIPMENT: Sewing and embroidery needles. Basting thread. Embroidery frame (optional). Tweezers. Dressmaker's tracing (carbon) paper. Tracing paper. **For Blocking:** Soft wooden surface. Brown wrapping paper. Thumbtacks. Ruler. T-square. Pencil.

MATERIALS: Medium-weight linen or linen-like cotton in color desired, 16″ × 19″. Penelope (cross-stitch) canvas, 10 mesh-to-the-inch, approximately 10″ × 13″, for main design. Needlepoint canvas, 16 mesh-to-the-inch, 6″ × 8″ for lettering. DMC six-strand embroidery floss (8.7-yd. skeins): "Wedding Day": 1 skein each of green #3346, yellow #307, dark blue #823; 2 skeins white, rose #603, blue #793. "25 Years Wed": 1 skein each orange #608, pink #605, brown #300, olive green #580; two skeins yellow #745, three skeins white (blanc).

DIRECTIONS: Baste Penelope canvas to fabric as directed in "Four Methods of Cross-Stitching." (See Contents for all General Directions.) Following chart and color key, at right, use three strands of floss in needle to work cross-stitch border and center design. When embroidery is complete, use tweezers to remove Penelope canvas.

To personalize sampler, baste needlepoint canvas in place: top of letters in date will be 1½″ above center design; top of letters in name begin ½″ below center design. Using two strands of floss in needle, work names and dates in cross-stitch, following alphabet and number chart below.

When embroidery is complete, use tweezers to remove canvas.

Trace patterns for facial features on both, ferns on "Wedding Day," and ball of yarn, logs, fire, and hurricane lamps on "25 Years Wed." Place tracing on fabric in correct position; insert dressmaker's carbon in between and trace around entire design to transfer.

Following "Stitch Details", and illustrations for colors, complete embroidery on sampler as follows: "Wedding Day:" Work orange blossom leaves in lazy daisy stitch. Work fern stems, facial features, bouquet streamers in outline stitch. Work fern leaves and bell top in straight stitch. "25 Years Wed:" Work hurricane lamps, fire's flames, clock top, and yarn in outline stitch. Work andirons, clock's hands in straight stitch. Work flowers on her chair with lazy daisy petals and French knot centers. Work French knots in squares on his chair and at top of clock. Work fireplace logs in satin stitch.

When all embroidery is finished, block and mount following directions under "Embroidery Basics." Frame as desired.

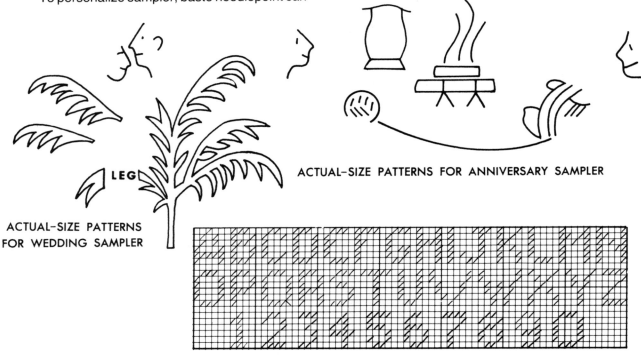

ACTUAL-SIZE PATTERNS FOR ANNIVERSARY SAMPLER

LEG

ACTUAL-SIZE PATTERNS FOR WEDDING SAMPLER

◉ WHITE   ⊠ DK. BLUE #823

◣ YELLOW #307   ⊿ BLUE #793

⊟ ROSE #603

☑ PINK #605 ⊟ OLIVE GREEN #580
🅱 BROWN #300 ⊞ YELLOW #745

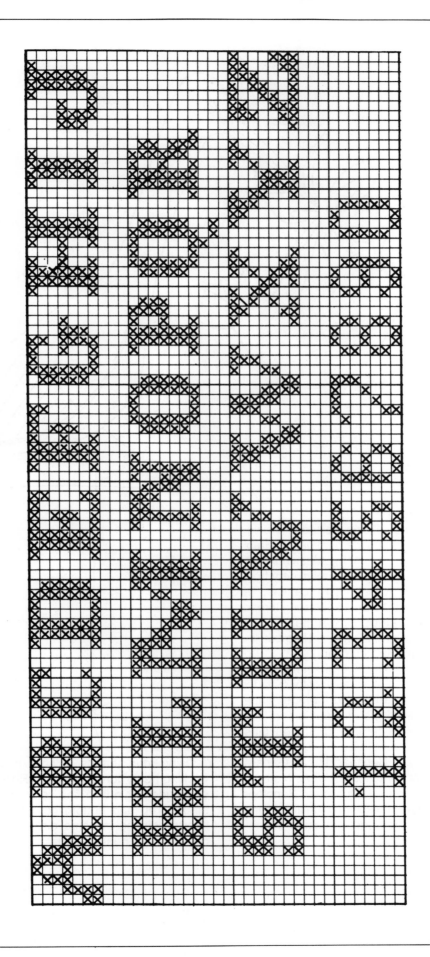

BIRTH SAMPLER
Shown on page 152

SIZE: Design area, 14″ × 15¾″.

EQUIPMENT: Pencil. Ruler. Scissors. Tracing paper. Dressmaker's tracing (carbon) paper. Graph paper (10 squares to the inch). Masking tape. Embroidery and sewing needles. Embroidery hoop (optional). Penelope (cross-stitch) canvas, 10 mesh-to-the-inch, about 15″ × 16″. Basting thread. Tweezers. **For Blocking:** Brown paper. Soft wooden surface. T-square. Hammer. Thumbtacks.

MATERIALS: Light blue linen fabric, 20″ × 22″. Six-strand embroidery floss (8-yd. skeins): 3 skeins red; 2 skeins dark blue; 1 skein each of four shades of gray (from light to dark), ecru, orange, white, pale pink, yellow, light green, dark green. **For Mounting:** Heavy white cardboard. Straight pins. Frame, 14½″ × 15¾″ rabbet size.

DIRECTIONS: (See Contents for all General Directions.) Following directions in "Four Methods of Cross-Stitching," cross-stitch over Penelope canvas. Baste canvas in place on blue linen. Only corner of border is given; repeat design as indicated in directions below.

Using four strands of floss in needle, begin working heart border. **(NOTE:** Rows of hearts on each side begin with one color and end with another.) Top and bottom borders each have 14 hearts pointing in same direction; side borders consist of 18 hearts each.

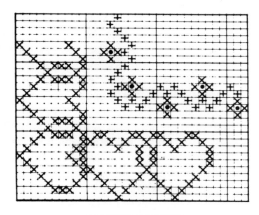

HEART BORDER

To Personalize: On graph paper, mark outline of area within inside border; each mesh of canvas is one square on graph. Using the alphabet and numbers furnished, make a chart for lettering as follows: Measure $\frac{3}{8}''$ down from top of ruled-off area, and center the child's name. Measure $\frac{3}{8}''$ up from bottom of ruled-off area, and center the birthdate.

When design is complete, remove basting. Cut away excess canvas around edges of design. Using tweezers, carefully draw out canvas threads following directions under "Four Methods of Cross-Stitching."

Using three strands of red floss in needle, center a French knot in each "diamond" formed by cross-stitches on inner border.

Trace actual-size pattern for stork and baby. Having carbon paper between, center design within borders and tape pattern to fabric. Go over lines of pattern with a pencil to transfer design to fabric. Remove pattern and carbon.

Using three strands of white in needle, work clouds in outline or stem stitch (see "Stitch Details." Using two strands of ecru, work body of stork in split stitch. Using four shades of gray to shade wing as illustrated, work wing in satin stitch with two strands of floss in needle. Using three strands of dark gray, outline wing in outline or stem stitch. Clouds and grass are to be done freehand, following illustration.

Using two strands of orange in needle, work beak in satin stitch. Using three strands of orange, work stork's feet in outline or stem stitch.

Baby's hands, face, and feet are worked in split stitch, using two strands of pink. Using three strands of yellow, work French knots for hair. Using two strands of blue, work eyes in French knots. Using two strands of orange, work mouth in outline stitch, nose in straight stitch.

Using three strands of white, work outline of diaper in outline or stem stitch. Using three strands of floss in needle, work grass in outline stitch, alternating green and dark green to give a shaded effect.

When embroidery is finished, block and mount following directions under "Embroidery Basics." Frame as desired.

GOD BLESS OUR HOME SAMPLER

Shown on page 176

EQUIPMENT: Scissors. Tape measure. Embroidery needle. Embroidery frame (optional). Masking tape.

MATERIALS: Even-weave white or cream-color fabric (see Note below). Six-strand embroidery floss: 1 skein each of medium yellow, gold, light yellow-green, dark emerald green, royal blue, lavender, purple, dark brown, medium gray, and black; 2 skeins each of light scarlet, rose-pink, medium turquoise, and russet brown; 5 skeins of medium green.

Note: The fabric to be used must be evenly woven, so the threads can be counted individually. It is important that the count of threads be the same horizontally and vertically. The number of threads-to-the-inch and the number of threads over which you stitch will determine the finished size of your sampler. For example, if the fabric has about 30 threads-to-the-inch and crosses are worked over three threads, the design area will be about 11″ × 15″. To calculate the size, multiply the number of crosses horizontally (109) and the number vertically (150) by the number of threads over which the crosses will be worked (3, 4, etc.); then divide the total of each side by thread count of fabric to obtain the dimensions. Many fabrics have slightly different number of threads-to-the-inch horizontally compared to vertically. Check your fabric for which way you want to work design.

DIRECTIONS: See "Four Methods of Cross-Stitching." (See Contents for all General Directions.) Cut even-weave fabric 3″ larger all around than finished design size. To center the embroidery, fold the fabric in half lengthwise, then fold again crosswise; mark the center point with a pin.

To Embroider: Use four or six strands of floss in the needle, depending upon the size of crosses, for all colors except black. Use four strands of black if working the colors with six strands; use three strands of black if working colors with four. Use six strands for larger crosses, four strands or less for smaller crosses.

Determine the center point of the chart and begin working cross-stitch from the center, following the chart for colors and placement of design. Work each stitch over the same number of threads across and down, being careful to work all stitches in the same direction, with stitch ends touching.

Complete the sampler, if desired, by adding your initials and the date in block letters in positions indicated. Use two strands of black floss in the needle; make smaller crosses than in sampler.

Block and mount (see "Embroidery Basics.") Frame as desired.

☑ LT. SCARLET
⊞ ROSE PINK
⊡ MED. YELLOW
⧅ GOLD
⧄ LT. YELLOW-GREEN
◪ DK. EMERALD GREEN
⊠ MED. GREEN
⧈ MED. TURQUOISE
⬚⬚ ROYAL BLUE
⊟ LAVENDER
⬚ PURPLE
⧄ RUSSET BROWN
⬛ DK. BROWN
⧅ MED. GREY
■ BLACK

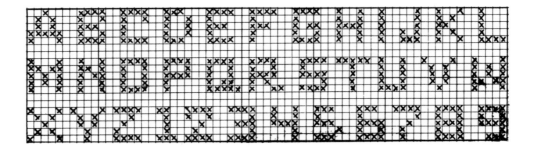

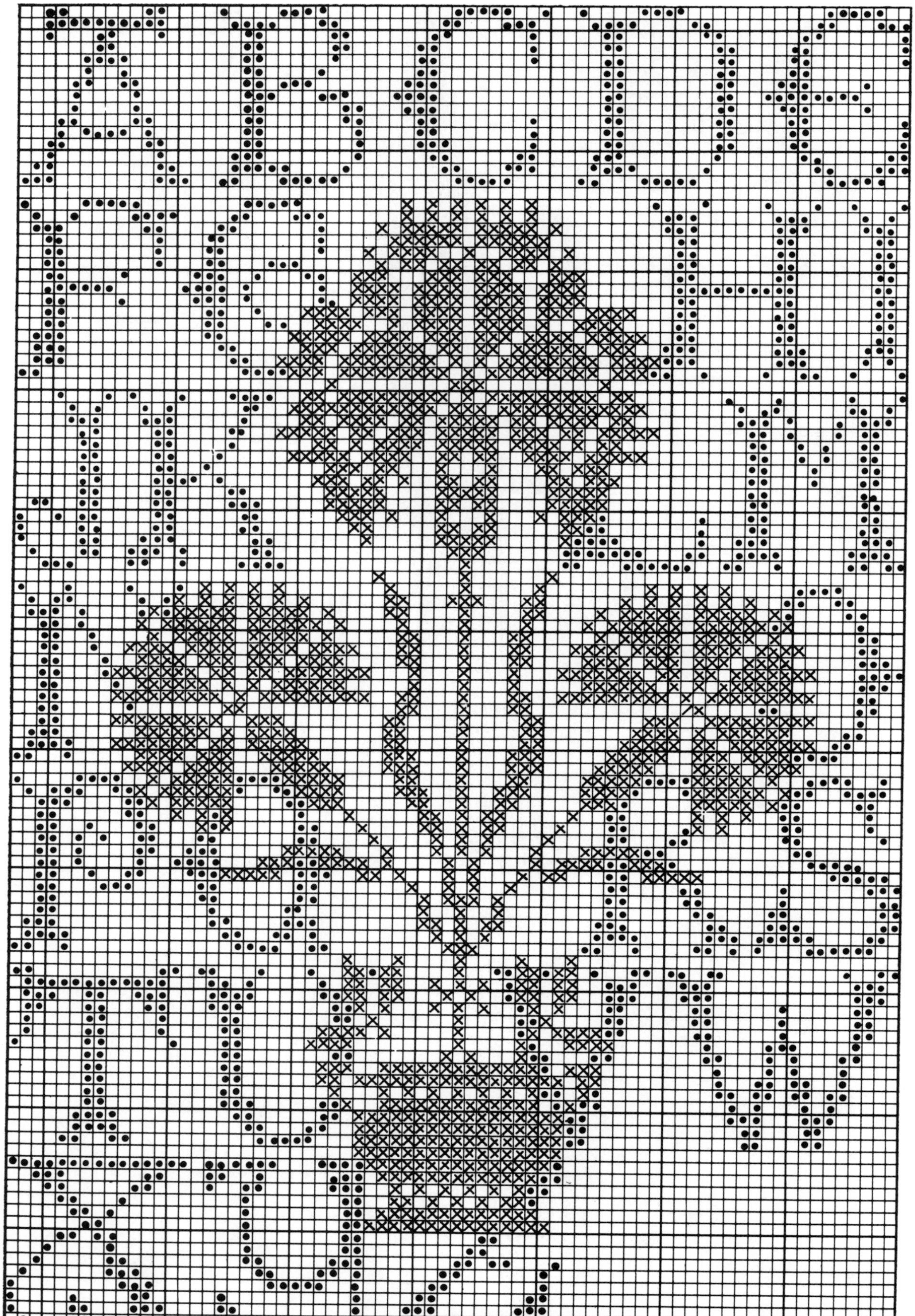

ALPHABET SAMPLER
Shown on page 177

FINISHED SIZE: $11\frac{3}{4}'' \times 17\frac{3}{4}''$.

EQUIPMENT: Ruler. Pencil. Scissors. Embroidery hoop and needle. Straight pins. Steam iron. Sewing machine (optional).

MATERIALS: Zweigart "Florina" (ecru-colored, even-weave fabric, 14 threads-to-the-inch) $14'' \times 20\frac{1}{2}''$. Paternayan Persian yarn in 8-yard skeins: Medium Blue #503, two skeins; Navy Blue #571, three skeins. Illustration board $11\frac{1}{2}'' \times 17\frac{1}{2}''$. Masking tape.

DIRECTIONS: (See Contents for all General Directions.) To prevent fabric from raveling, whip-stitch edges by hand, or machine-stitch $\frac{1}{8}''$ in from all edges. Cut floss or yarn into 18" strands. To begin a strand, leave an end on back and work over it to secure; to end, run needle under four or five stitches on back. Do not use knots. When working cross-stitches, keep all crosses in the same direction; work underneath stitches in one direction and top stitches in the opposite direction, making sure that strands lie smooth and flat. Make all crosses touch by inserting needle in same hole used for adjacent stitch (see "Stitch Details.")

Place fabric in hoop, making sure horizontal and vertical threads are straight and even; move hoop as needed. Work design, following chart and color key.

Each square on chart represents two horizontal and two vertical threads on fabric; each symbol represents one cross-stitch. Separate yarn and work with single strand in needle throughout. Work all letters (dots) in Navy Blue and entire flower motif (Xs) in Medium Blue. Work all stitches over two threads in each direction.

To Stitch: With short fabric edges at top and bottom, measure 2" down and in from upper left corner to correspond with upper left corner of chart; mark with a pin. Following chart, begin top of letter A by counting two threads down and four threads to the right, for first stitch. Work first row of alphabet. Work second row of alphabet, including top of central flower. Continue working letters and flower motif to end of chart. Work one or two of your own initials in the center of blank space at lower right corner. (It is best to plot out initial(s) in pencil on chart before embroidering.) Place finished embroidery, face down, on padded surface and steam-press lightly from center outward.

To Finish: Center illustration board on wrong side of stitched fabric; fold raw edges over board and tape in place. Frame as desired.

KINDNESS SAMPLER
Shown on page 178

SIZE: Design, $16'' \times 20\frac{1}{8}''$.

EQUIPMENT: Ruler. Pencil. Scissors. Embroidery and sewing needles. Embroidery hoop or wood picture frame, $19'' \times 23''$. Thumbtacks. Basting and pastel-colored thread. Penelope (cross-stitch) canvas, 10 mesh-to-the-inch, about $19'' \times 23''$. Felt-tipped pens: pink and green. Tweezers. **For Blocking:** Brown paper. Soft wooden surface. T-square. Hammer. Ruler.

MATERIALS: White or off-white linen fabric, $25'' \times 29''$. DMC six-strand embroidery floss (8.7-yd. skeins): 9 skeins pink #899, 5 skeins green #699. **For Mounting:** Heavy white cardboard, $19'' \times 23''$. Straight pins. Frame, $19'' \times 23''$ rabbet size.

DIRECTIONS: (See Contents for all General Directions.) With pink and green felt-tipped pens, mark design on canvas. Each chart square represents one mesh of canvas; mark stitch placement in center of mesh. Starting $1\frac{1}{2}''$ from top of canvas, mark flower and heart designs in pink and motto in green. Making sure that horizontal and vertical threads of canvas and linen match, center canvas on linen. Make lines of basting horizontally and vertically through the center of the canvas. Working from the center to each edge of the canvas, make additional lines of basting parallel to and 2" away from these center lines. If using frame, stretch linen over it. Secure margins to back of frame with thumbtacks.

Follow directions under "Four Methods of Cross-Stitching" for working cross-stitch on Penelope canvas. Use four strands of floss in needle

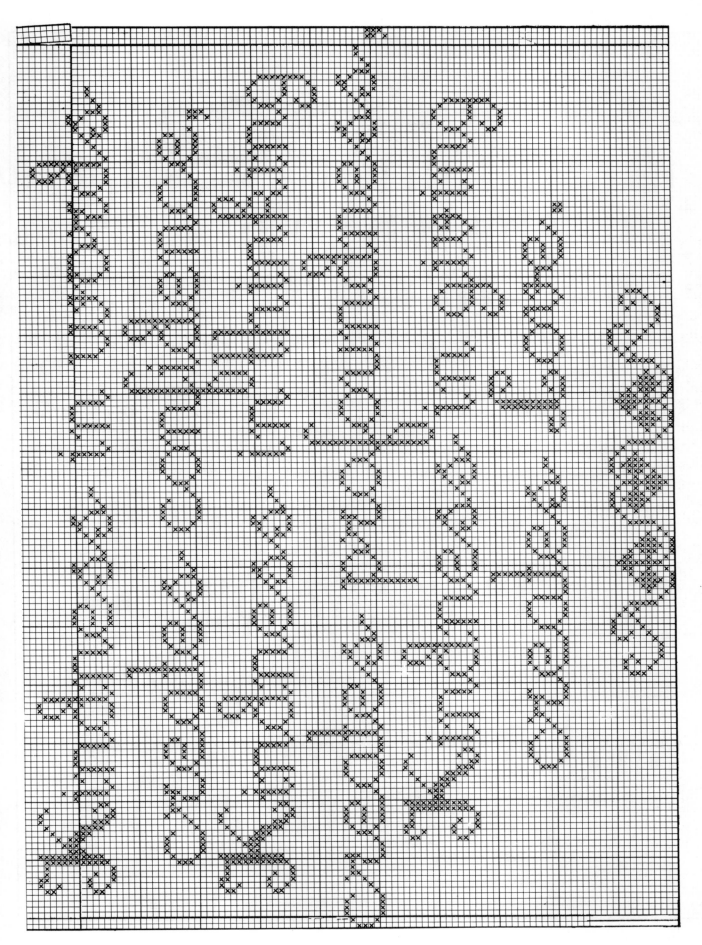

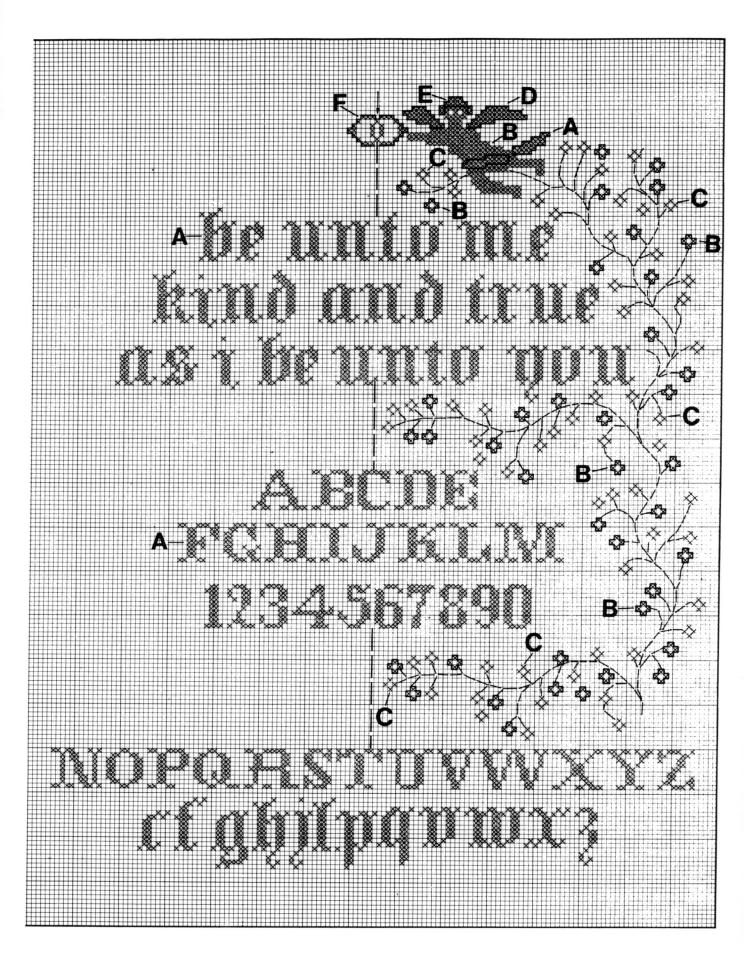

throughout. Work the motto in green and the flower and heart designs in pink. Each X on the chart represents one cross-stitch. Taking each stitch diagonally over the double mesh of canvas and through the fabric, make crosses as shown in diagram. Be careful not to catch canvas. When design is completed, remove basting. Cut away excess canvas around edges of design. With tweezers, carefully draw out canvas thread (see "Four Methods of Cross-Stitching").

When embroidery is finished, block and mount following directions under "Embroidery Basics." Frame as desired.

WEDDING SAMPLER
Shown on page 179

SIZE: 18″ × 18″.

EQUIPMENT: Fine tapestry needle. Scissors. Pencil. Graph paper. Embroidery hoop or frame. Masking tape. **For Blocking:** Softwood surface. Rustproof thumbtacks. T- or carpenter's square.

MATERIALS: Cream-color "Davos" Zweigart even-weave linen, 18 threads-to-the-inch, 22″ × 22″. DMC six-strand embroidery floss (8.7-yard skeins); see color key for colors and number of skeins required. Sewing thread. Heavy cardboard for mounting, 18″ × 18″.

DIRECTIONS: (See Contents for all General Directions.) To keep fabric from raveling, whip-stitch around edges with sewing thread. Fold fabric in half for vertical center; mark line with long basting stitches. Also mark 18″ × 18″ area for picture centered on fabric, leaving 2″ margins all around.

Work cupid and vine design and "be unto me" motto, following chart and color key. Each X symbol of chart represents one cross-stitch worked over two horizontal and two vertical threads. Each empty square of chart represents two horizontal and two vertical threads of fabric. Solid lines of vines represent long backstitches. See "Stitch Details." For flowers, use six strands of floss in needle; for all other cross-stitches, use four of the six strands. Work backstitches with four strands. To begin a length of floss, leave end on back and

work over it to secure; to end, run needle under four or five stitches on the back. Do not use knots.

To begin design, work first stitch (indicated on chart by arrow) across basted center line, counting 30 horizontal threads down from upper marked line. Place fabric in frame and continue embroidering design, following chart. Repeat in reverse for left side.

To complete embroidery with your own names and date, work out design first on graph paper. Using the alphabet and numbers given on chart, plan your lettering to fit within the lower area, referring to illustration for help in spacing letters. Following your graph chart, work lettering and date in green.

When embroidery is complete, block the piece; see "Embroidery Basics." Remove basting.

To mount, center heavy cardboard on wrong side of sampler. Wrap excess fabric to back, neatly mitering corners; tape securely in place. Check that sampler is centered and square; adjust if necessary. Frame as desired.

RINGBEARER'S PILLOW
Shown on page 179

SIZE: 9″ × 11½″.

EQUIPMENT: See Wedding Sampler, at left.

MATERIALS: Cream-color "Davos" Zweigart even-weave linen, 18 threads-to-the-inch, 13″ × 15½″. DMC Six-Strand Embroidery Floss (8.7-yard skeins): 2 skeins each pale peach #754 and green #320. For backing and cording, peach fabric 36″ wide, ½ yard. Peach sewing thread. Cable cord ¼″ diameter, ¾ yards. Unbleached muslin 36″ wide, ⅓ yard. Polyester fiberfill. Masking tape.

DIRECTIONS: (See Contents for all General Directions.) To keep fabric from raveling, whip-stitch around edges with sewing thread or bind edges with masking tape. Mark 9″ × 11½″ area, centered on fabric, for pillow design, leaving 2″ margins all around.

Place fabric in hoop or frame. Starting in upper right corner of marked outline, work peach background and flowers and green stems, following

A GREEN #320 (4)	D TURQUOISE #807 (small amount)
B LIGHT PEACH #353 (3)	E BROWN #433 (small amount)
C DARK PEACH #352 (2)	F DEEP YELLOW #742 (small amount)

chart. Each X symbol of chart represents one cross-stitch worked over two horizontal and two vertical threads. Each empty square of chart represents two horizontal and two vertical threads of fabric. Solid lines of vine represent long back-stitches. See "Stitch Details." Work entire design with three strands of the six-strand floss in needle. To begin a length of floss, leave end on back and work over it to secure; to end, run needle under four or five stitches on the back. Do not use knots. When right half has been completed, repeat design in reverse on left side, omitting center row of motifs; center of design is marked by dash lines on chart.

To complete embroidery with your own initials, work out design first on graph paper. Using the alphabet given on separate chart, plan your lettering to fit within the center space; refer to illustration for help in spacing letters. Following your graph chart, work lettering in green.

When embroidery is complete, turn to "Embroidery Basics." to block the piece; after blocking, trim fabric margins to $\frac{1}{2}''$. Cut backing fabric same size as trimmed front piece. With right sides facing, stitch back and front pieces together, making $\frac{1}{2}''$ seams; leave opening in center of one side. Turn pillow right side out and stuff; turn raw edges $\frac{1}{2}''$ to inside, then slip-stitch opening closed.

$\boxed{\vee}$ LT. OLIVE GREEN 470
$\boxed{\blacktriangle}$ DK. AQUA 992
$\boxed{\blacktriangledown}$ DK. CORAL 891
$\boxed{\blacksquare}$ CORNFLOWER BLUE 793
$\boxed{\bullet}$ DK. OLIVE GREEN 937
$\boxed{\times}$ LT. AQUA 993
$\boxed{|}$ LT. CORAL 892

GINGHAM SAMPLER

Shown on page 180

SIZE: design area, 12″ × 14″.
EQUIPMENT: Scissors. Sewing and embroidery needles. Basting thread. Embroidery hoop (optional). **For Blocking:** Soft wooden surface. Brown wrapping paper. Ruler. T-square. Thumbtacks.
MATERIALS: Gold-checked gingham, 8 squares-to-the inch, 16″ × 18″. DMC six-strand embroidery floss (8.7-yard skeins): 1 skein each of light olive green #470, dark aqua #992, dark coral #891, cornflower blue #793; 2 skeins each of dark olive green #937, light aqua #993, light coral #892. **For Mounting:** Stiff mounting cardboard. Masking tape.
DIRECTIONS: Using sewing needle and basting thread, baste ¼″ hems all around fabric to prevent raveling. See "Four Methods of Cross-Stitching," reading "On Gingham." Using four strands of floss in needle, work cross-stitches following chart and color key on this page. When embroidery is finished, remove basting threads; block and mount as directed in "Embroidery Basics." Frame as desired.

GINGHAM SAMPLERS

Shown on page 181

FINISHED SIZES: "House" 12″ × 16″, **"Home Sweet Home"** (p. 75) 10″ square.
EQUIPMENT: Ruler. Pencil. Scissors. Embroidery hoop and needle. Straight pins. Steam iron. Sewing machine (optional).
MATERIALS: Gingham fabric with ⅛″ checks, orange and yellow, ½ yard each. **Note:** In some gingham fabrics, the checks are not perfectly square; cut gingham and work samplers so that the greater number of checks-per-inch run horizontally. Cut orange 21½″ × 17⅜″ (21½″ is horizontal measurement) for "House." Cut yellow 16⅛″ square for "Home Sweet Home." DMC six-strand embroidery floss, one skein of each color in color key. Artist's stretcher strips 12″ × 16″ for "House"

and 10″ square for "Home Sweet Home." White cotton duck fabric 45″ wide, ½ yard (for both). Deep color grosgrain ribbon ¾″ wide, 2 yards for "House"; 1½ yards for "Home Sweet Home." Staple gun and staples. All purpose glue.
DIRECTIONS: (See Contents for all General Directions.) To prevent fabric from raveling, whip-stitch edges by hand, or machine-stitch ⅛″ in from all edges. Cut floss into 18″ strands. To begin a strand, leave an end on back and work over it to secure; to end, run needle under four or five stitches on back. Do not use knots. When working cross-stitches, keep all crosses in the same direction; work underneath stitches in one direction and top stitches in the opposite direction, making sure that strands lie smooth and flat. Make all crosses touch by inserting needle in same hole used for adjacent stitch (see "Stitch Details.")

Each symbol on chart represents one stitch on fabric. Work stitches over checks, so that one complete cross-stitch covers one check. Place orange gingham with short edges at sides. Fold each piece in half to find vertical center; mark at top edge with a pin. Measure down 3½″ to correspond with arrow on chart. Place fabric in hoop, making sure horizontal and vertical threads are straight and even; move hoop as needed. **To stitch "House,"** count four checks down from arrow to begin purple border; complete, following chart and color key. **To stitch "Home Sweet Home,"** count two checks down from arrow to begin blue border; complete, following chart and color key. Place finished embroidery, face down, on padded surface and steam-press lightly from center outward.

To Finish: Assemble frame, following manufacturer's directions. Cut duck fabric 2½″ larger all around than outside frame dimensions. Center frame on duck; stretch fabric around frame edges, folding excess to back. Making neat mitered corners, staple fabric edges to frame back. Repeat with embroidered gingham, centering design carefully; pin excess gingham to duck at frame edge before stapling, and check that stitched borders are parallel to frame edges; adjust if necessary. Staple as for duck. Glue ribbon, cut to fit, around frame edges; overlap ends at bottom corner.

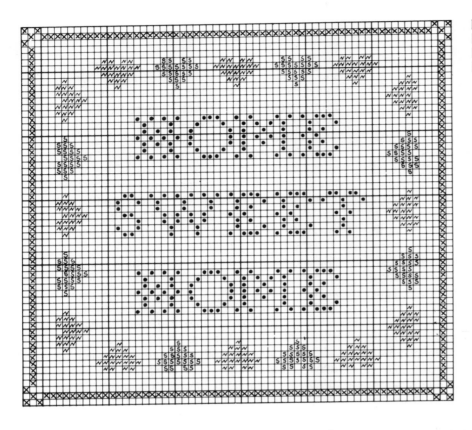

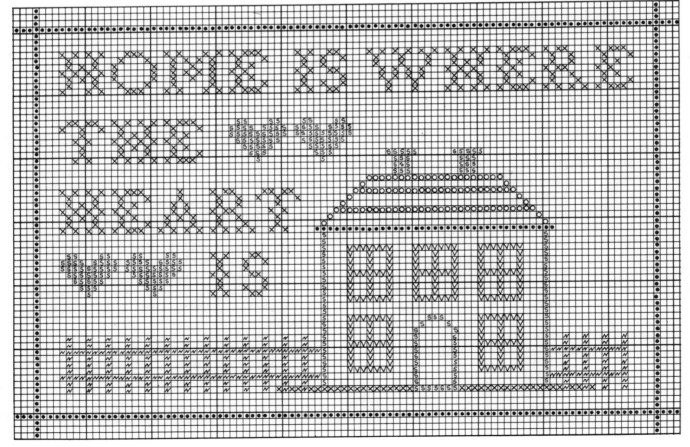

- ◨ RED #666
- ☑ DARK BLUE #797
- ◩ GRAY #318
- ◼ BLACK #310
- ⊡ YELLOW #743

MERRIMENT EXPRESS

Shown on pages 182–183

SIZE: 12″ × 14″ × 2″, each pillow.

EQUIPMENT: Ruler. Scissors. Embroidery needle. Embroidery hoop. Straight pins. Sewing needle. Iron.

MATERIALS: Even-weave white or off-white linen fabric 20 threads-to-the-inch, 1¼ yards, 56″ wide, for four. DMC six-strand embroidery floss: 4 skeins red #666; 5 skeins gray #318; two skeins each of dark blue #797, light green #912, and purple #208; one skein each of black #310, yel-

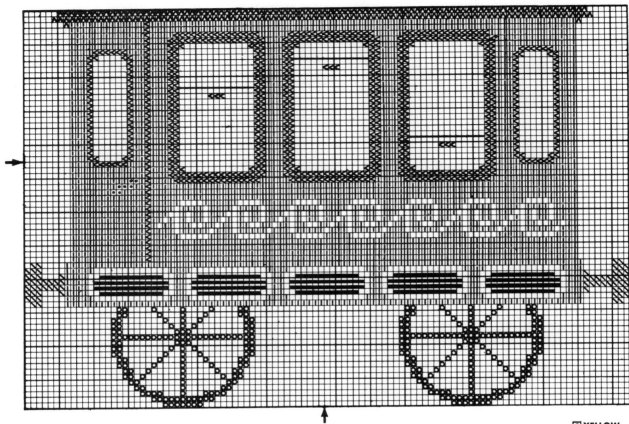

low #743, medium green #701, dark green #909, rust #922, gray blue #931, gray beige #642, brown #400, tan #436. Foam rubber cushion forms, 12″ × 14″, 2″ thick. White sewing thread.

DIRECTIONS: (See Contents for all General Directions.) For the boxing, cut four 3″-wide strips across width of fabric for four pillows. From the rest of fabric, cut eight pieces, each 14″ × 16″. Stay-stitch along edges of fabric to prevent raveling.

To Embroider: For each pillow, embroider one piece of fabric and reserve one piece for back. To work embroidery, place fabric in hoop, keeping it taut. Use three strands of floss in needle and

Continued on page 153

⊡	YELLOW
▣	DK. GREEN
⊞	LT. GREEN
◳	GRAY
◙	RED
◸	RUST
◹	PURPLE

Traditional motifs are brightened with a delightful verse, a humorous touch of today. Sampler is worked completely in cross-stitch on a counted thread fabric, 24 threads-to-the-inch. Variation in stitch size is achieved by making some crosses over two threads (alphabets, house) and some over one thread (verses). Happy Hearts Sampler, about 10″ × 15 ½″; directions on page 118.

clocks, crocks, ladderback chairs
tieback curtains, patchwork squares
samplers, quilts, pewter and pine
friends for dinner-hot mulled wine
pot roast, potatoes, cherry tarts
love, happiness, happy hearts

m. beams

145

Elaborate alphabets and border designs create a delightful center panel inspired by an antique piece. Missing letters were not unusual—J and U were often omitted and so was Z. We kept these variations in our wall-sized version to maintain the original charm. Worked with DMC tapestry yarn on burlap in a variety of stitches, the sampler measures 41" × 62", framed. King-Size Sampler, page 113.

This charming sampler is a faithful reproduction of an antique stitched by a young girl in 1831. The border and tree motifs are traditional, while the building may have been the stitcher's home. Turn to page 98 for modern-day directions.

Eliza Carr

August 22, 1831

*Cross-stitch sampler in subtle tones is a charming
adaptation of one made in 1849 by an 11-year-old girl.
Stitches are worked over 12 to-the-inch Penelope
canvas on linen, following chart supplied.
Colonial House Sampler; directions on page 121.*

*Sweet and familiar to generations of tots, this
nightly prayer makes a charming cross-stitch picture
for the nursery. Stitches are worked 10 to-the-inch
over Penelope canvas with DMC embroidery floss.
Bedtime scene, worked in a few simple stitches,
is traced. Directions on page 102.*

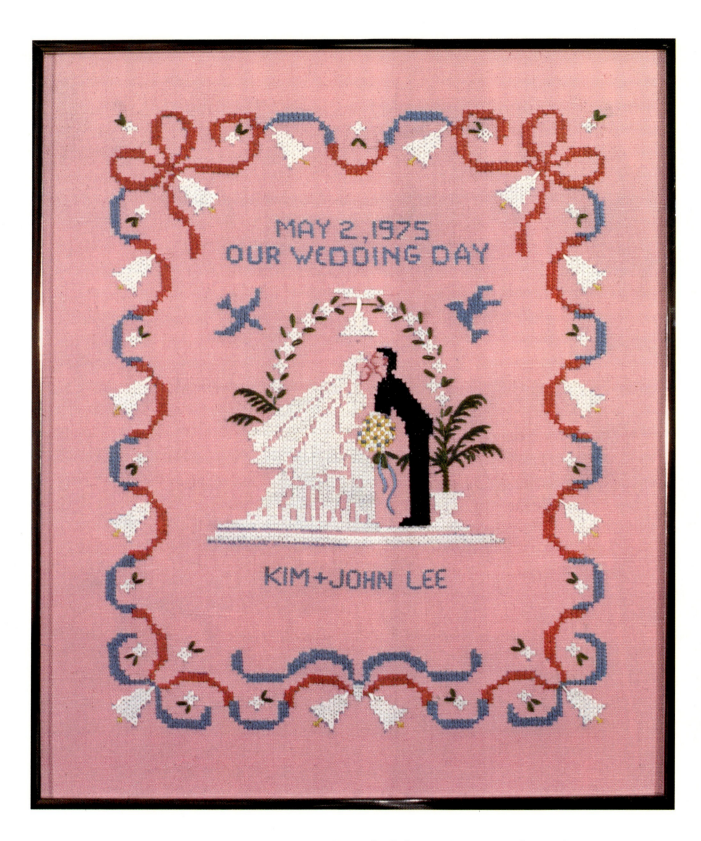

*Wonderful ways to remember a happy occasion,
two samplers that could become the
most cherished pictures in a home.
"Wedding Day" makes a perfect wedding gift;*

"25 Years Wed" is a charming remembrance for the silver anniversary. Both are worked mainly in cross-stitch, with a few other simple stitches. Directions for both begin on page 124.

*Red, white, and blue—fresh, sprightly colors
for the nursery of a tiny girl or boy—predominate in
this birth sampler that is the perfect "welcome" gift for baby.
Border is worked in cross-stitch; the stork and
his precious bundle are in other simple stitches.
Directions for Birth Sampler on page 128.*

Continued from page 144

work over two threads vertically and two threads
horizontally to make cross-stitches (see "Stitch
Details."). To work cross-stitch, make all underneath threads in one direction and all the top
threads in the opposite direction. Keep the stitches
as even as possible and make all crosses touch
by inserting needle in the same hole as used for
the adjacent stitch. Be careful not to pull stitches
too tightly. Each square on chart represents one
stitch. Solid lines on chart indicate backstitch. Work
backstitches after cross-stitch is completed.

Mark pillow outline 12″ × 14″ on each piece of
fabric, leaving equal margins. Arrows on charts
indicate center lines. Find center on each side of
fabric and mark at edge of outline. Begin working

- RED
- GRAY BLUE
- GRAY
- GRAY BEIGE
- BROWN
- MED. GREEN
- TAN

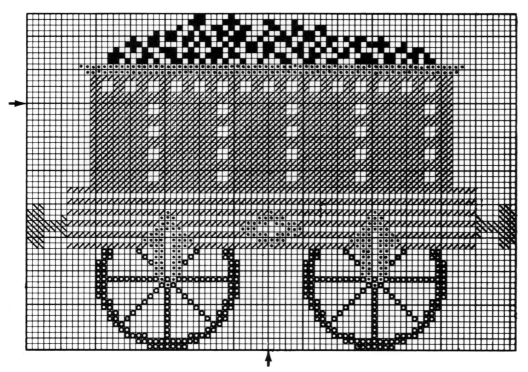

⊡ RED #666
⊠ PURPLE #208
⊞ GREEN #701
◼ BLACK #310
⊠ GRAY #318
⊡ YELLOW #743

center motifs from this point, following chart for placement of colors.

Following Engine Chart, work the border making 18 links vertically and 21 horizontally.

To Press: When embroidery is finished, press fabric, using a well-padded surface and steam iron, or regular iron and damp cloth. Embroidery should always be pressed lightly so that the stitching will not be flattened into the fabric. Place the embroidery face down on the padded surface and press from the center outward.

To Assemble Pillow: Trim edges of linen to $\frac{1}{2}''$ plus four threads beyond border all around.

Cut boxing strip to fit perimeter of pillow, plus $\frac{1}{2}''$ seam allowance on each end. Sew ends of boxing together with right sides facing, making $\frac{1}{2}''$ seam. With right sides facing, pin, then sew boxing to embroidered piece, making $\frac{1}{2}''$ seam. With right sides facing, pin, then sew back piece and boxing together making $\frac{1}{2}''$ seam, leaving 9" opening in center of one side. Turn to right side; push out corners neatly. Insert foam form. Turn edges of opening in $\frac{1}{2}''$ and slip-stitch closed. Make all cushions in same manner.

EMBROIDERED SIGNS
Shown on page 184

EQUIPMENT: Colored pencil. Pencil. Ruler. Scissors. Tape measure. Dressmaker's tracing (carbon) paper. Dry ballpoint pen. Straight pins. Sewing and embroidery needles. Embroidery hoop. Sewing machine. Steam iron. Padded surface. Knitting needle.

MATERIALS: Fabric: see individual directions. DMC six-strand embroidery floss, one skein of each color in color keys (unless otherwise indicated in parentheses). Twisted cord: see individual directions. Thread to match fabrics. Polyester fiberfill. All-purpose glue.

GENERAL DIRECTIONS: see "Four Methods of Cross-Stitching." (See Contents for all General Directions.) Press fabrics carefully; zigzag or whipstitch raw edges to prevent raveling. Mark pillow outline, following individual directions. Squares on charts represent threads on fabric; X's indicate length and position of stitches. Insert area to be embroidered in hoop to keep fabric taut; embroider as directed. Begin stitching by leaving end of

Red #666
Yellow #973
Dark Gray #414
Red cord, 33"

Green #702
Blue #334
Yellow #973 (sm. amt.)
Yellow cord, 38½"

floss on back and working over it to secure. To end strand or begin a new one, weave end of floss under stitches on back. Do not make knots. Cut out pieces; steam-press embroidery gently on padded surface. With right sides facing, pin and sew pillow pieces together, making $\frac{1}{4}''$ seams; leave 3" opening in center of one long side for turning. Turn to right side; gently poke out corners with knitting needle. Press pillow; stuff with fiberfill until plump, poking stuffing into corners with knitting needle. Turn raw edges at opening $\frac{1}{4}''$ to inside; slip-stitch opening closed.

Glue ends of twisted cord to prevent raveling. Starting at upper right corner of pillow with one end of cord, slip-stitch cord over seams all around pillow. When all seams are covered, slip-stitch other end of cord to upper left corner of pillow for hanger.

SIGN A: Size: 7" × 5". "Davos" counted-thread fabric, 18 threads-to-the-inch, $7\frac{1}{2}'' \times 5\frac{1}{2}''$. Muslin, $7\frac{1}{2}'' \times 5\frac{1}{2}''$ red twisted cord, 33".

Embroider the pillow design in cross-stitch, following chart and color key; start at upper left corner by counting 21 threads down from top and in from side edge to begin working border. Make cross-stitches over two threads as indicated on chart, using three strands of floss in needle. Embroider border and base of bulbs in dark gray, bulbs in yellow, and letters in red.

Complete pillow following General Directions, using muslin as backing.

SIGN B: Size: 8" × $5\frac{3}{4}''$. "Davos" counted-thread fabric, 18 threads-to-the-inch, $8\frac{1}{2}'' \times 6\frac{1}{4}''$. Muslin, $8\frac{1}{2}'' \times 6\frac{1}{4}''$ yellow twisted cord, $38\frac{1}{2}''$.

Embroider design as for Sign A starting at upper left corner by counting 22 threads down from top and in from side edge to begin working border. Make cross-stitches over one thread of fabric, using two strands of floss in needle. Embroider border and stems in green, letters and flowers in blue, flower centers in yellow.

Complete pillow following General Directions, using muslin as backing.

FRITZIE PICTURE
Shown on page 182

SIZE: Design area (within mat), 9" × 12"; framed, $12\frac{1}{2}'' \times 15\frac{1}{2}''$.

EQUIPMENT: Ruler. Scissors. Embroidery hoop and needle. Steam iron.

MATERIALS: Zweigart "Aida" (white, even-weave fabric, 14 threads-to-the-inch), $14\frac{1}{2}'' \times 17\frac{1}{2}''$. DMC six-strand embroidery floss: one skein of each color listed in color key and one skein each Flesh #754, Red #666, Deep Red #816, Black #310. Illustration board, $12\frac{1}{2}'' \times 15\frac{1}{2}''$. Masking tape.

DIRECTIONS: Tape all raw edges of fabric to prevent raveling. Cut floss into 18" lengths. Work all cross-stitches (for "Stitch Details.") with two strands in needle, all other embroidery with one strand. To begin a strand, leave end on back and work over it to secure; end and begin subsequent strands by running end of floss through stitches on back of work. When working cross-stitches, work all underneath stitches in one direction and all top stitches in the opposite direction. Make all crosses touch by inserting needle in same hole used for adjacent stitch. All backstitches are worked over one fabric thread, vertically, horizontally, or diagonally.

Each square on chart represents one horizontal and one vertical fabric thread. Each symbol on chart represents one cross-stitch worked over one horizontal and one vertical thread; different symbols represent different colors. Heavy lines on chart represent flesh areas as well as additional embroidery.

Position fabric with long edges at top and bottom. Measure $4\frac{1}{4}''$ down and $4\frac{1}{2}''$ in from upper right corner for first cross-stitch (see arrows on chart); mark with a pin. Place fabric in hoop and embroider design, following color key to work all cross-stitches first; fill in all outlined areas for face and hands with flesh-color cross-stitches. Work additional embroidery as follows: Accent pajamas with blue backstitches, pink blanket with deep red, Teddy's face with black, and boy's hands with brown. Outline pillow with light blue backstitches and mouths with red. Work boy's eyes in black fly stitch, Teddy's eyes in black French knots.

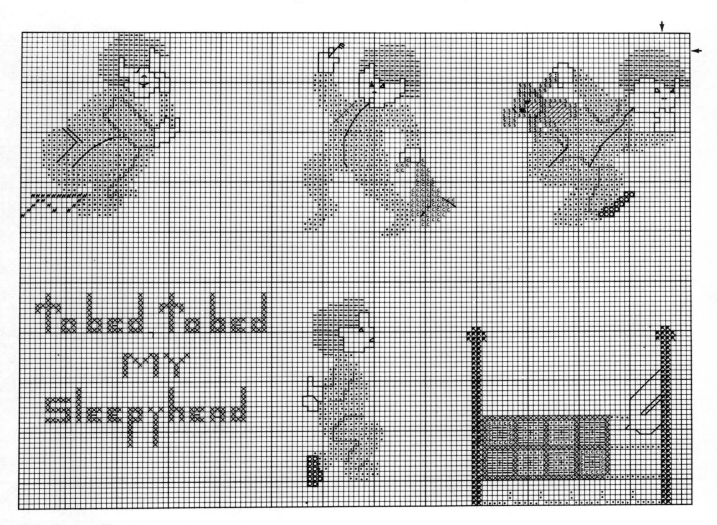

⊡ Light Blue	☒ Dark Blue	
⬛ Yellow	◢ Gold	
⑤ Brown	⊟ Lime Green	
⧄ Ecru	ℕ Olive Green	
⦙ Toast	⊞ Purple	
ⓒ Pink	⬜ White	

RUSSIAN PINAFORE
Shown on page 205

Work toothbrush handle with two close rows of deep red backstitches; add three black backstitch bristles.

Place finished embroidery face down on well-padded surface and steam-press lightly from center outward. Center illustration board on wrong side of stitched fabric; fold raw edges over board and tape in place. Mat, frame as desired.

EQUIPMENT: Scissors. Tape measure. Embroidery needle. Straight pins. Tracing wheel. Dressmaker's tracing (carbon) paper. Sewing machine with ruffler attachment. Steam iron.

MATERIALS: McCall's Pattern #5540, Misses' 6–16, or other, similar pattern. Red cotton fabric, 45″ wide, 1 yard. White Moygashel linen 45″ wide, 1 yard. Red and white narrow-striped cotton, 36″ wide, $\frac{3}{4}$ yard. Red and white wide-striped cotton, 36″ wide, $\frac{3}{4}$ yard. White Aida cloth 11 threads-to-the-inch, 42″ wide, $\frac{1}{4}$ yard. Wright's laces and trims:

white crocheted lace, 2″ wide, 4 yards; white eyelet ruffling, 6″ wide, 1¾ yards; woven tape (red, white, green floral on black background), ⅜″ wide, 3 yards; red flat-braid trim, ¾″ wide, 1½ yards; red-black geometric woven tape, 2″ wide, 1¾ yards; red-yellow floral woven tape, 1¼″ wide, 1 yard; red cotton bias tape, 2″ wide, 2 packages; black baby rickrack, 1 package; white medium rickrack, 1 package; lace edging, ½″ wide, 2 yards; red calico, single-fold bias tape, 2 packages. DMC six-strand embroidery floss, 2 skeins coral red #891; 3 skeins black #310. Red, white, and black sewing thread.

DIRECTIONS: (See Contents for all General Directions.) **Yoke:** The yoke is made without shoulder ties. Before cutting, mark line on yoke pattern for shoulder seam. When cutting out yoke, add ⅝″ to each shoulder for seam allowance. Cut two fronts and two backs from white linen. Put aside one back and one front for lining. Mark bottom seam line with carbon and tracing wheel on front yoke. Pin 1¼″-wide red-yellow woven tape just above bottom seam line; pin red floral bias tape just underneath at top and bottom edges of

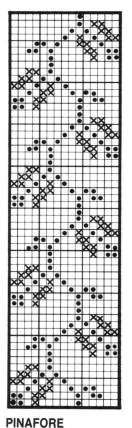

PINAFORE

⊠ RED
◉ BLACK

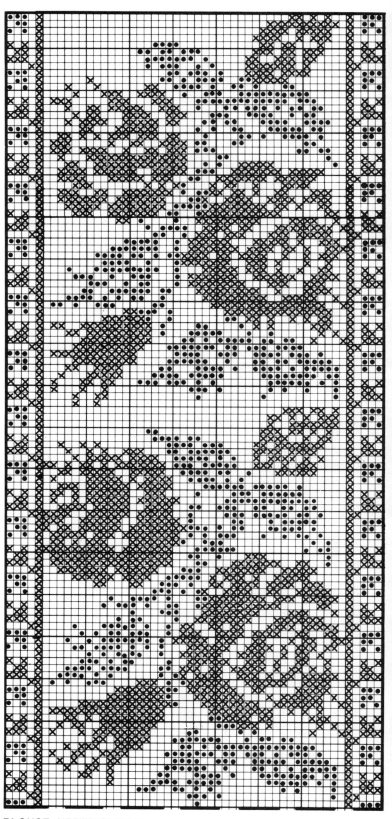

BLOUSE, UPPER SLEEVE

woven tape; pin black baby rickrack on top of each row of bias tape; add $\frac{5}{8}$" to each side of each tape for seam allowance. Stitch all tapes in place. Repeat for back yoke. Sew front and back yokes together at shoulders and sides; repeat without trim for yoke lining. With right sides together, sew yoke and lining all around neck edge. Turn yoke right side out. Baste lining to yoke at armholes on seam line; trim seam allowance to $\frac{1}{4}$". Bind armholes with red floral bias tape.

Skirt: Using skirt front and back patterns as guide, make fabric for skirt pieces by joining strips of fabric, with $\frac{1}{2}$" seams, in the following sequence and making front and back the same. Starting at top: 6" white linen; $4\frac{1}{2}$" narrow red and white stripe; 4" wide red and white stripe (stitch white rickrack and $\frac{1}{2}$"-wide white lace alternately over red stripes); $5\frac{1}{2}$" red cotton; 2" white crochet lace; $5\frac{1}{2}$" red cotton; $4\frac{1}{2}$" embroidered Aida cloth edged with $\frac{3}{8}$"-wide floral trim centered over red $\frac{3}{4}$"-wide woven braid (see specific instructions below for embroidering design on Aida cloth); 5"-wide striped red and white fabric; $5\frac{1}{2}$" red cotton; 2" white crochet lace; 7" red cotton; 2"-wide red-black geometric woven tape; 6" white eyelet ruffling.

Finishing: Following pattern instructions, join skirt pieces to yoke and stitch side seams.

To finish neck edge, unfold each package of 2"-wide red bias tape, opening out last fold and being careful not to twist tape, joining ends of each to form two circles. Place one circle inside another and pin long edges together; stitch along both sides $\frac{1}{4}$" in from edges. Gather tape with two rows of stitches $\frac{3}{4}$" in from one long side. Adjust gathers to make ruffle fit around neckline. Top-stitch ruffle to right side of yoke around neckline about $\frac{1}{2}$" down from neck edge.

Embroidery: Read "Four Methods of Cross-Stitching" and specifically the paragraph for even-weave fabric. Use three strands of floss in needle and work over one thread horizontally and one thread vertically, taking the stitches through the holes. Follow chart and color key to work design. Each square on chart represents one cross-stitch. The cross-stitch motif is $1\frac{1}{4}$" wide. With pins, mark this width centered across each strip of Aida cloth. Begin embroidery at one end of cloth within marked area. Repeat design until you reach the other end. Make two strips for front and back skirt. When embroidery is finished, steam-press.

RUSSIAN BLOUSE
Shown on page 205

EQUIPMENT: Scissors. Ruler. Ink marker. Embroidery needle. Embroidery hoop (optional). Straight pins. Sewing machine. Steam iron. McCall's Pattern #5663 (view B), Misses' 6–16, or other similar pattern.

MATERIALS: White Moygashel linen 45" wide, $\frac{3}{4}$ yard. Red cotton fabric 45" wide, $\frac{1}{2}$ yard. White Aida cloth 11 squares-to-the-inch, 45" wide, $\frac{1}{2}$ yard. Wright's trims: black double-fold bias tape $\frac{1}{4}$" wide, one package; black single-fold bias tape 1" wide,

BLOUSE, LOWER SLEEVE

1 package; black-red floral woven trim $1\frac{1}{4}''$ wide, 1 yard; red medium and red baby rickrack, one package each. Sewing thread to match fabric and trims. DMC six-strand embroidery floss, 6 skeins each red coral #891 and black #310.

DIRECTIONS: (See Contents for all General Directions.) **Sleeve Patterns:** Lay out the three patterns for lower sleeve (2B, 3B, 4B) and pin together to make one piece, overlapping inner seams. With ruler and ink marker, extend "length of goods" line on piece 2B to both ends of pattern. Using ink marker, mark off entire three-part pattern for lower sleeve into five horizontal bands, measuring widths on vertical line drawn and drawing lines at right angles to vertical line; starting at lower seam line (wrist) and working to upper seam line, mark bands as follows: $3''$, $3''$, $4\frac{1}{2}''$, $2\frac{1}{2}''$, $4\frac{3}{4}''$. **(Note:** If the sleeve length in your size makes it necessary to alter these widths, make adjustments in first, second, or fourth bands only, not the third or fifth bands.) When all horizontal lines are drawn, unpin pattern to make three separate patterns again.

Assembling Sleeves: Mark each section drawn on pattern 2B with an identifying number and cut apart pattern on horizontal lines, making five pattern pieces. Cut pieces from fabric as follows, going from lower to upper bands and adding $\frac{5}{8}''$ to inner horizontal edges: white linen, red cotton, embroidered Aida cloth (see below), red cotton, and embroidered Aida cloth. Cut apart patterns 3B and 4B and cut pieces from fabric in same manner, substituting white linen for the Aida sections. Cut pattern 1B from red cotton. Join sleeve pieces, first joining band sections of each piece. Bind wrist opening with $\frac{1}{4}''$-wide black bias tape. Cut cuffs from white linen; cut black-red floral trim the length of cuff plus $\frac{5}{8}''$ seam allowances for each sleeve. Fold cuff in half lengthwise, mark fold line with pins, unfold. Sew trim to cuff with one long edge along fold line. Sew cuff to sleeve, following pattern directions.

Assembling Blouse: Cut one front and one back from white linen. Cut and sew in facing at neck opening. Cut black-red woven trim $7''$ longer than twice the length of the opening. Pin trim along opening, mitering corners at bottom to turn; sew. Sew two rows of baby and one row of medium rickrack around woven trim. Sew sides of blouse together; sew sleeves in place. Follow pattern directions for finishing neckline, using $1''$-wide black bias tape to bind raw edges.

To Embroider: Read "Four Methods of Cross-Stitching." Put Aida fabric tightly in hoop, if desired. Be careful not to distort fabric. Use three strands of embroidery floss in needle and work over one mesh horizontally and one mesh vertically, through the holes.

Follow charts and color key to work design. Each square on chart represents one cross-stitch. Begin embroidery at one end and repeat design until you reach the other end. When embroidery is finished, cut out piece, leaving $\frac{5}{8}''$ seam allowance. Steam-press, if necessary.

GIRL'S LINEN APRON
Shown on page 205

SIZE: 6 years.
EQUIPMENT: Paper for pattern. Ruler. Scissors. Embroidery needle. Sewing machine. Straight pins. Tweezers. Penelope canvas, 12 mesh-to-the-inch, 1 yard.
MATERIALS: White Moygashel linen $72''$ wide, $\frac{3}{4}$ yard. DMC Six-strand embroidery floss, 6 skeins of desired color. Two snap fasteners. White sewing thread.
DIRECTIONS: (See Contents for all General Directions.) Enlarge patterns by copying on paper ruled in $1''$ squares. Place long dash line of apron half-pattern on fold of doubled linen; pin pattern in place. Cut out apron, adding $\frac{1}{2}''$ all around for hems. Cut four neck straps, reversing pattern for two. Cut four ties, each $2''$ wide and $26''$ long.

Fold under $\frac{1}{4}''$ along top edge of apron and stitch across near edge. Fold in $\frac{1}{4}''$ twice and baste for hems all around apron except across top. Fold top down to wrong side at short dash line of pattern. Stitch hems all around; continue stitching across top folded edge of apron.

Place two neck straps together, right sides facing; stitch with $\frac{1}{4}''$ seams along both long curved edges and top end. Turn right side out. Repeat with remaining two straps. Turn in open ends of neck straps; pin in place at either side of apron top, flush with side edges. Sew two snap fasteners at ends of straps as indicated by X's on pattern. For each tie, place two ties together, right sides facing; cut off one end of each at an angle. Stitch each tie with $\frac{1}{4}''$ seams, along long sides and angled end. Turn right side out. Turn in open ends. Stitch a tie to wrong side of apron sides at X's on pattern.

Cut a piece of penelope canvas about 7″ square. Pin canvas to right side of apron at top. Baste canvas in place and work cross-stitch over Penelope canvas as directed. Each cross on chart represents one cross-stitch. Work each stitch over two meshes horizontally and vertically. Use three strands of floss in needle and follow small chart, which is half of figure motif. Start at center of bib area of apron, $\frac{3}{4}''$ from top edge, and work from

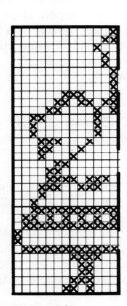

**CHART FOR
APRON BIB**

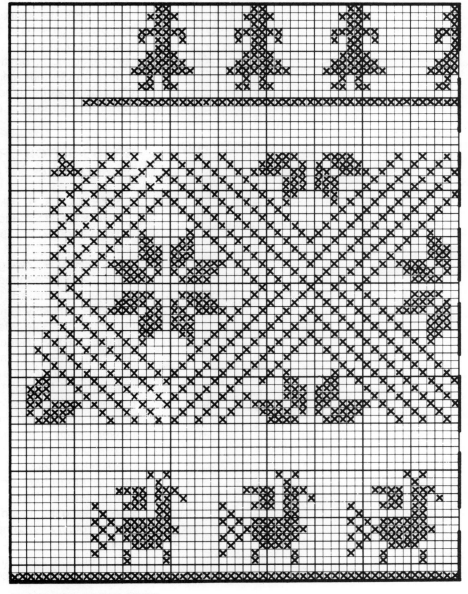

CHART FOR APRON SKIRT

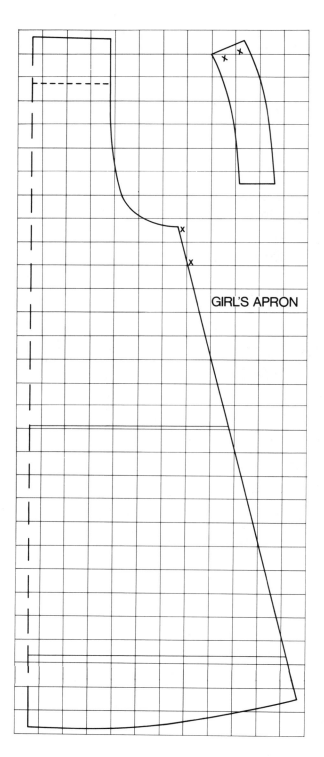

GIRL'S APRON

center of chart, marked by arrow, to the left. Be sure ends of crosses touch, by working stitches of adjacent crosses in same space of linen. Repeat chart to right in reverse, omitting vertical center line.

For bottom band, baste a piece of canvas about 14″ deep across lower portion of apron, about 2″ up from bottom edge.

Work cross-stitch, following wide-band design chart in same manner as top motif; fine lines on pattern indicate position of the two horizontal single rows of crosses in chart. Work complete chart from center of apron to left, then repeat chart in reverse to right, omitting center vertical line of crosses; note that animals are not reversed but continue in same direction (see illustration).

Remove strands of canvas.

CROSS-STITCH CRECHE BACKDROP
Shown on pages 206 and 207

SIZE: $11\frac{1}{2}″ \times 6″$ tall.

EQUIPMENT: Pencil. Ruler. Scissors. Embroidery hoop. Tapestry needle. X-acto knife. Straight pin.

MATERIALS: Zweigart Hardanger cloth (Art. 1008), 22 threads-to-the-inch, 14″ × 9″ piece blue. DMC pearl cotton #8, 1 ball white. Blue felt, piece 12″ square. Heavy cardboard or foamcore board for mounting. Glue. Masking tape.

DIRECTIONS: Read "Four Methods of Cross-Stitching." (See Contents for all General Directions.) With long edges of fabric at top and bottom, measure $1\frac{3}{4}″$ in and $3\frac{1}{4}″$ down from upper right corner for placement of first stitch, indicated on chart by arrow; mark mesh with pin. Follow chart to work each cross-stitch over two vertical and two horizontal fabric threads, using one strand pearl cotton in needle. Complete right half of creche, then reverse chart, omitting center vertical row, to work left half. Work eight or nine straight-stitch stars, placing them randomly (see illustration). After all embroidery is complete, remove fabric from hoop and steam-press lightly.

On cardboard or foamcore board, mark $11\frac{1}{2}″ \times 6″$ rectangle; place piece with long edges at top

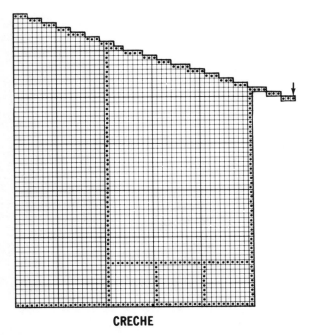

CRECHE

MATERIALS: Zweigart Hardanger cloth (Art. 1008), 22 threads-to-the-inch, 42" wide, ½ yard. DMC six-strand embroidery floss, one 8.7-yard skein of each color listed in color keys. White closely woven cotton fabric 36" wide, ¼ yard. White and dark-colored sewing threads. Fiberfill for stuffing. Cardboard.

DIRECTIONS: Read "Four Methods of Cross-Stitching." (See Contents for all General Directions.) Cut Hardanger cloth into eight 7" × 9" rectangles. Bind fabric edges as directed in how-to's. **For Each:** With short edges of Hardanger at top and bottom, measure 1½" down and 3½" in from upper right corner for placement of first stitch, indicated on chart by arrow; mark mesh with pin. Work design in cross-stitch, following chart, color key, and directions below. Separate floss and work with one strand in needle throughout. Each square on chart represents one cross-stitch worked over one horizontal and one vertical fabric thread; different symbols represent different colors. Outline faces and lamb with short black backstitches, following lines on chart. (For Angel, use peach floss.) Work facial features with black straight stitches. For Babe, fill halo with gold backstitches, using two strands. After all embroidery is completed, remove fabric from hoop and steam-press lightly.

Using dark-colored sewing thread, baste a line around figure, following solid line around chart. Cut out figure ¼" outside basting; use piece to cut matching back from white cotton.

With right sides facing and raw edges even, pin front and back together; machine-stitch in place, following basting thread; leave bottom edge open (for Babe, leave 1" open on one side). Trim seams; clip into curves. Turn right side out. Remove basting thread. Stuff with fiberfill until firm. Press all raw edges ¼" to inside. Slip-stitch Babe's opening closed. To make base for each of the others, stand figure on paper; trace around bottom for pattern. Cut out pattern and use to mark one base each on cotton fabric and cardboard; cut out, ¼" outside marked line on fabric and 1/16" inside marked line on cardboard. Press raw edges of fabric base ¼" to wrong side, then pin base to figure and slip-stitch in place halfway around. Slip cardboard in place; continue stitching to close.

and bottom. On each 6" side, mark a point 1¾" below top corner; draw line from each point to center of top edge; taper top of creche. Cut out creche carefully, using X-acto knife; use as pattern to cut matching piece from felt. Wrap embroidered fabric around board as shown in illustration; glue edges to back. Glue felt to back, covering fabric edges.

For stand, cut 2" × 4" rectangle from cardboard. Using X-acto knife, score (do not cut through) stand across width, 1" below top short edge. From felt, cut pieces 4" × 6" and 1½" × 3½". Cover stand with larger piece, gluing excess to wrong side. Glue smaller piece to center of wrong side. Spread glue on wrong side of stand between top and scoring. Position stand on creche back so that bottom edge of stand is flush with center bottom of creche; let dry.

CROSS-STITCH CRECHE FIGURES
Shown on pages 206 and 207

SIZE: 3¾"–6" tall.
EQUIPMENT: Pencil. Ruler. Scissors. Paper. Straight pins. Embroidery hoop. Tapestry needle. Sewing needle. Sewing machine.

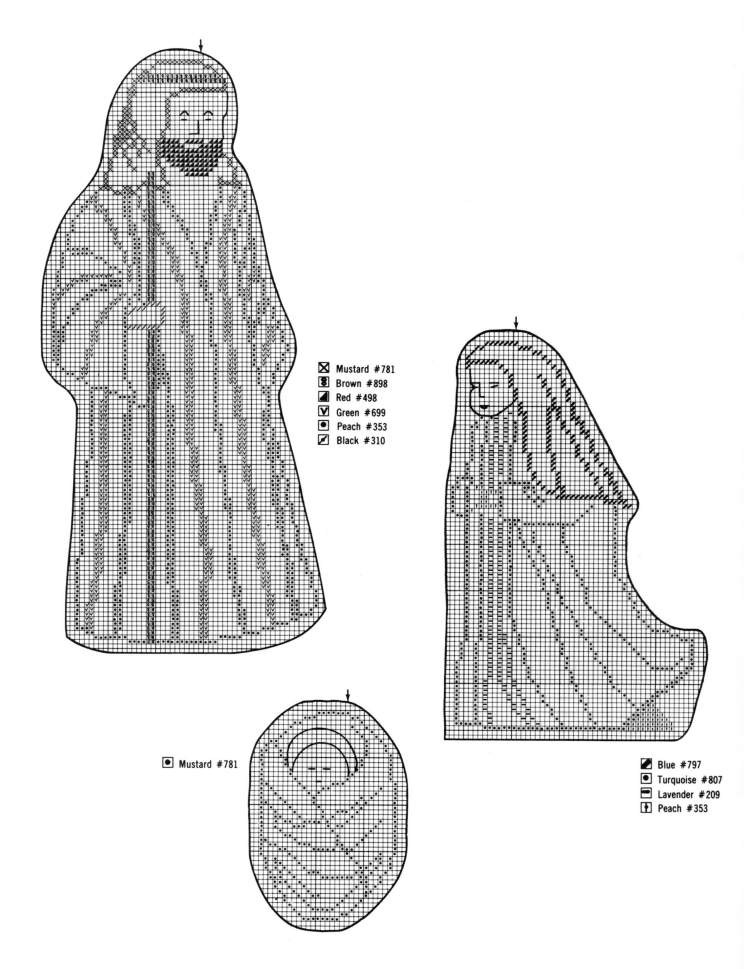

⊠ Mustard #781
⑧ Brown #898
◪ Red #498
Ⅴ Green #699
● Peach #353
◪ Black #310

⊡ Mustard #781

◪ Blue #797
● Turquoise #807
⊟ Lavender #209
✚ Peach #353

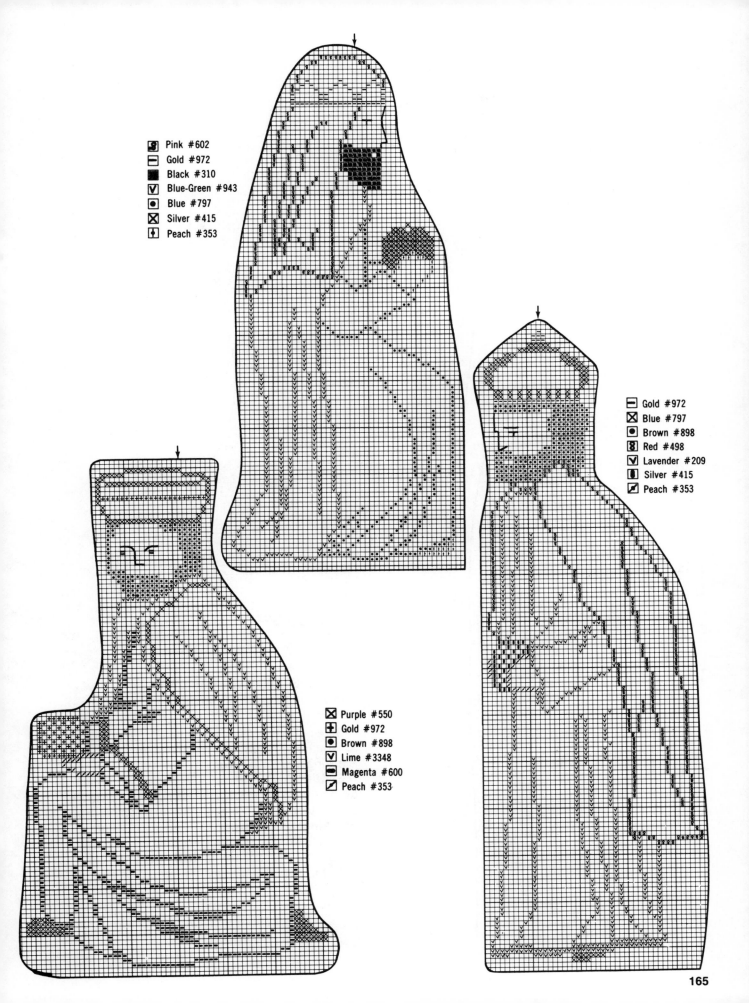

■ Pink #602
⊟ Gold #972
■ Black #310
V Blue-Green #943
⊙ Blue #797
⊠ Silver #415
✚ Peach #353

⊟ Gold #972
⊠ Blue #797
⊙ Brown #898
⊠ Red #498
V Lavender #209
◨ Silver #415
⊿ Peach #353

⊠ Purple #550
✚ Gold #972
⊙ Brown #898
V Lime #3348
⊟ Magenta #600
⊿ Peach #353

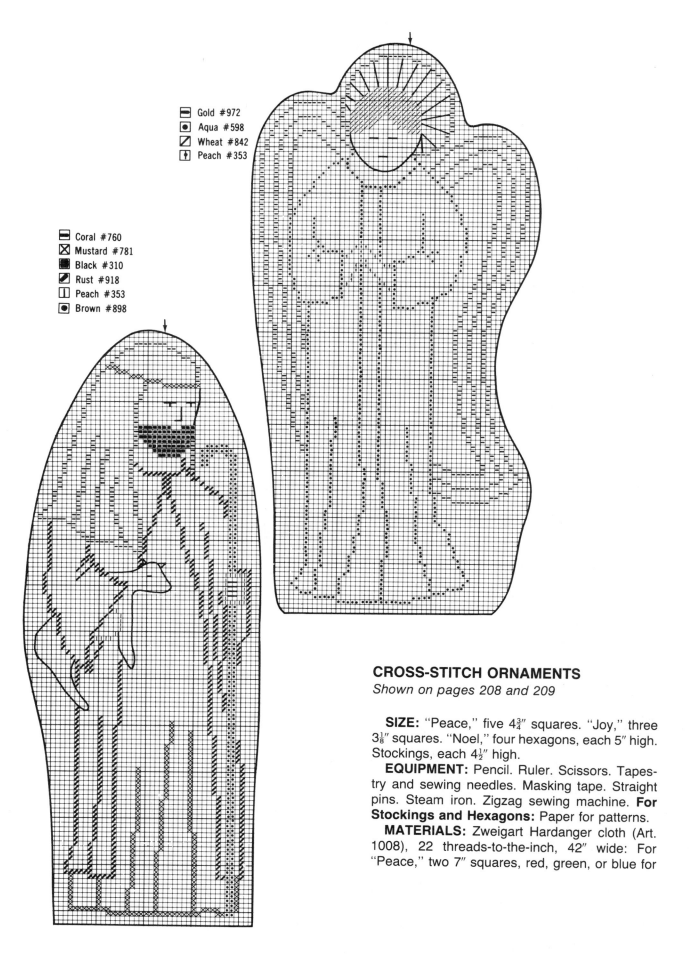

Gold #972
Aqua #598
Wheat #842
Peach #353

Coral #760
Mustard #781
Black #310
Rust #918
Peach #353
Brown #898

CROSS-STITCH ORNAMENTS

Shown on pages 208 and 209

SIZE: "Peace," five 4¾" squares. "Joy," three 3⅛" squares. "Noel," four hexagons, each 5" high. Stockings, each 4½" high.

EQUIPMENT: Pencil. Ruler. Scissors. Tapestry and sewing needles. Masking tape. Straight pins. Steam iron. Zigzag sewing machine. **For Stockings and Hexagons:** Paper for patterns.

MATERIALS: Zweigart Hardanger cloth (Art. 1008), 22 threads-to-the-inch, 42" wide: For "Peace," two 7" squares, red, green, or blue for each; for "Joy," one $5\frac{1}{2}'' \times 8''$ piece white for each; for "Noel," two $4\frac{1}{2}'' \times 7''$ pieces white for each. For Stockings, two $5\frac{1}{2}'' \times 7\frac{1}{2}''$ pieces white for each. DMC pearl cotton #8 in desired colors: one ball of each color used. Sewing thread to match fabrics. Satin ribbon in colors to match cross-stitching: $\frac{1}{8}''$ wide for "Joy," $\frac{1}{4}''$ wide for others, $\frac{3}{8}$ yard each. **For "Peace" and "Noel":** Polyester fiberfill. **For "Joy":** $3\frac{1}{8}''$ square lightweight cardboard for each.

DIRECTIONS: Read "Four Methods of Cross-Stitching." (See Contents for all General Directions.) Work each design with one strand pearl cotton in tapestry needle, making each cross-stitch over two threads or "squares" of Hardanger cloth each way.

"PEACE": Use white pearl cotton throughout. Begin by folding one square of cloth into quarters to find exact center and mark hole with a pin. Following chart for "P," count 32 squares to right of pin for center of first stitch, indicated on chart by arrow. Following chart, work entire border, then initial. In same manner, work remaining ornaments, counting 30 stitches from center to make first stitch on "A" chart, and 24 stitches for "E's" and "C." To finish, pin second square of cloth to back of worked piece with edges even. Count four squares out from border and backstitch three sides of design through both thicknesses, following solid outline on chart (see "Stitch Details"); stuff ornament with fiberfill and backstitch along fourth side. Using scissors, trim ornament to 1" beyond backstitching to measure about $4\frac{3}{4}''$ square for "C" and 5" square for others. To finish, fringe edges of both thicknesses by unraveling outside threads to within $\frac{1}{4}''$ of backstitching (see diagram). For hanger, cut piece of $\frac{1}{4}''$-wide ribbon in half; tack one end of each piece to back of upper corners of ornament; tie free ends into bow as shown.

"JOY": For red and green border, follow chart for final "E" in "Peace" series; use alphabet chart for "Joy" or your own initials. To begin, place piece vertically and measure $2\frac{1}{2}''$ down and $1\frac{1}{4}''$ in to make first green stitch, indicated on chart by star; work border, using red and green. Find center of bordered area by counting 23 squares down and 23 squares in from upper left inner corner of border; mark hole with a pin. **To Center Initials:** Find center of initial to be cross-stitched as follows: Count number of squares across width and number in depth of chart (omitting tail for Q). Starting at upper left corner, count half the depth down and half the width in to determine center stitch or space; mark on chart. Following chart and substituting initial from alphabet chart for "E," stitch initial; begin at center of both chart and cloth, and count outward from center to make stitches. In same manner, work remaining ornaments.

To finish, turn each piece face down and center cardboard square on wrong side of design. Fold side edges of cloth to back; secure with masking tape. Fold top edge of cloth to back and tape. Press bottom edge $\frac{3}{4}''$ to wrong side, then fold to back; pin. Using white thread in needle, slip-stitch side edges together through all thicknesses to make pocket on back of ornament. For hanger, cut 7" piece of $\frac{1}{8}''$-wide ribbon and tack one end to back of each upper corner. Halve remaining ribbon, tie two small bows, and tack one to each upper corner on front of ornament.

"NOEL": Using pencil and ruler, draw lines across patterns, connecting grid lines. Enlarge hexagon pattern by copying on paper ruled in 1" squares; complete half pattern indicated by dash line.

Begin by folding one square of cloth into quarters to find exact center and mark hole with pin. Following chart for "N," count 34 squares up from pin to center of first stitch, indicated on chart by arrow. Following chart, work top border; then turn piece upside down and work bottom border,

MAKING A SELF FRINGE

STOCKING
HEXAGON

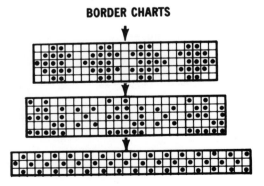
BORDER CHARTS

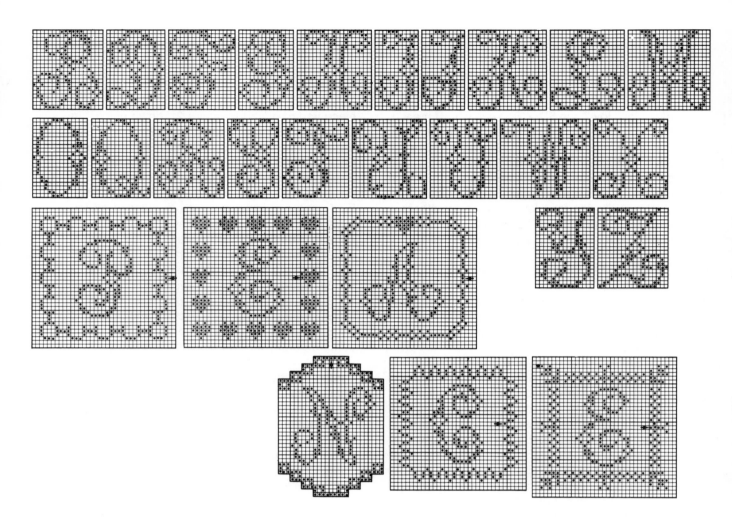

counting up from pin to find first stitch as for top border. Work initial. In same manner, work remaining ornaments, substituting initials on alphabet chart for "N" and following directions above for centering initial.

To finish, center pattern over design on wrong side of cloth and outline lightly with pencil; trim edges of piece to within $\frac{1}{2}''$ of line. Use as pattern to cut second piece of cloth for back. Place pieces together with wrong sides facing and edges even and stitch along pencil line, leaving 1" opening for turning; trim seam allowance, turn, stuff with fiberfill. Turn raw edges $\frac{1}{4}''$ to wrong side and slipstitch opening closed. For hanger, cut 8" piece of $\frac{1}{4}''$-wide ribbon, fold into a loop, and tack ends to back of ornament at center top. From remaining ribbon, make a small bow and tack to base of hanger on front as shown.

STOCKINGS: Using pencil and ruler, draw lines across patterns, connecting grid lines. Enlarge stocking pattern by copying on paper ruled in 1"

squares. Center stocking pattern on wrong side of one cloth piece so that top edge is even with crosswise grain of fabric and toe points right; outline stocking lightly with pencil. Using light thread in needle, baste outline with running stitch. On right side, count total number of squares across top edge of stocking. Beginning at upper left corner, count down six squares, then halfway across to determine first stitch or center, indicated on chart by arrow; work border in colors desired. On alphabet chart, count number of squares across chosen initial and mark center on top edge. To work initial on stocking, count 30 squares down and 22 squares in from upper left corner; mark hole with pin. Stitch initial, beginning at pin and top center of chart.

To finish, cut out stocking 1" from basting. Use as pattern to cut lining from second piece of cloth. Set machine for zigzag stitch and stitch along top of both pieces close to edge. Place pieces together, with right sides facing and raw edges even, and stitch along basting line except at top; trim seam allowance, clipping curves. Turn top edge of stocking 1″ to wrong side and slip-stitch. For hanger, cut 8″ piece of ¼″-wide ribbon, fold into loop, and tack ends to back of ornament at upper corner. Turn stocking to right side. From remaining ribbon, make a small bow and tack to base of hanger on front as shown.

HOLIDAY TABLE DRESSING
Shown on page 210

EQUIPMENT: Ruler. Scissors. Masking tape. Sewing and embroidery needles. Embroidery hoop. Straight pins. Sewing machine. Iron.
MATERIALS: Even-weave Aida Cloth with 11 squares-to-the-inch, 51″ wide (we used 2 yards

⊠ GREEN   ⊡ RED

for six squares; add 25½″ for every additional pair of squares you choose to make.) Six-strand embroidery floss: about four skeins emerald green and three skeins red for each square. 1½″-wide green grosgrain ribbon, 11¼ yards. White and emerald green sewing thread.

DIRECTIONS: (See Contents for all General Directions.) Cut cloth into 25½″ squares. Tape edges of squares to keep cloth from raveling. The cloth is stiff at first but will soften as it is handled.

To Embroider: Each chart supplied is one-quarter of a complete design. Each square represents one cross-stitch worked over a tiny square on fabric. Mark the center of each cloth square. Place cloth in embroidery hoop. Use two strands of the six-strand floss in needle, cutting into 20″ lengths.

Following the chart shown and the "Stitch Details," work cross-stitches on cloth in red and green floss. Turn chart one-quarter and repeat, omitting center (starred) rows. Repeat for remaining two quarters.

You can use one motif throughout or two alternating motifs as we have.

To Assemble: Remove tape from edges. With embroidered side down on ironing board, press carefully. Press $\frac{3}{4}''$ on all edges to right side. With white thread, stitch all around each square about $\frac{1}{8}''$ in from folded edge. Baste all the squares together, overlapping the edges slightly where they come together; stitch together.

On right side, pin and baste one strip of green ribbon down lengthwise center and two strips across over edges of squares as shown. You should have a $2\frac{3}{8}''$ margin of white between embroidered border and ribbon edge. With white thread in bobbin and green thread in needle, stitch along each edge of each ribbon strip.

Edge entire cloth with one long length of ribbon. Having approximately a $2\frac{3}{8}''$ margin of white between embroidered border and edge of ribbon, pin and baste ribbon in place, mitering corners. Stitch on ribbon along each edge. Sew mitered corners by hand with invisible stitches using green thread. Remove basting stitches. Press with iron.

SEASIDE PULLOVER
Shown on page 215

SIZES: Directions for misses' or men's size 34–36. Changes for sizes 38–40 and 42–44 are in parentheses.

Body Bust and Chest Size: 34"–36" (38"–40"; 42"–44").

Blocked Bust and Chest Size: 37" (41"–45").

MATERIALS: Reynolds Irish Fisherman Yarn, 12 (13–14) 2-oz. skeins. Fingering yarn, 1 1-oz. skein each of red and black, for embroidery. Knitting needles Nos. 5 and 7. Tapestry needle.

GAUGE: 5 sts = 1"; 6 rows = 1" (stockinette st, No. 7 needles).

Note: Designs are embroidered in cross-stitch when knitting is completed.

PULLOVER: BACK: Beg at lower edge, with No. 5 needles, cast on 92 (102–112) sts.

Ridged Border: K 8 rows, p 1 row, k 5 rows, p 1 row, k 1 row, p 1 row, k 4 rows. Change to No. 7 needles. Work in stockinette st (k 1 row, p 1 row) until piece measures 15" (16"–17") from start or desired length to underarm. Mark each side of last row for underarm. Check gauge; piece should measure $18\frac{1}{2}''$ ($20\frac{1}{2}''$–$22\frac{1}{2}''$) wide. Work even for 1" ($1\frac{1}{2}''$–2"), end p row.

Armhole Trim: Row 1: K 1, p 2, k 86 (96–106), p 2, k 1.

Row 2: Purl.

Row 3: K 3, p 2, k 82 (92–102), p 2, k 3.

Row 4: Purl. Repeat these 4 rows until piece measures $7\frac{1}{4}''$ ($7\frac{3}{4}''$–$8\frac{1}{4}''$) above underarm marker, end p row.

Top Ridged Border: K 5 rows, p 1 row, k 1 row, p 1 row, k 5 rows.

Shape Shoulders and Neckband: Bind off in k first 26 (29–32) sts; beg with a p 1, work in p 1, k 1 ribbing until there are 40 (44–48) sts from bound-off sts; drop yarn; join another strand of yarn, bind off in k last 26 (29–32) sts; end off. Change to No. 5 needles. Work in ribbing as established for $4\frac{1}{2}''$. Bind off loosely.

FRONT: Work same as for back until piece measures 1" ($1\frac{1}{2}''$–2") above underarm markers, end p row.

Armhole and Front Trim: Row 1: K 1, p 2, k 39 (44–49), p 2, k 4, p 2, k 39 (44–49), p 2, k 1.

Row 2: Purl.

Row 3: K 3, p 2, k 35 (40–45), p 2, k 8, p 2, k 35 (40–45), p 2, k 3.

Row 4: Purl. Repeat these 4 rows until piece measures same as back to start of top ridged border, end p row. Work ridges, shoulders and neckband same as back.

SLEEVES: Beg at lower edge, with No. 5 needles, cast on 44 (46–48) sts. Work bottom ridged border same as back. Change to No. 7 needles. Work in stockinette st, inc 1 st each side every $\frac{1}{2}''$ 18 (20–22) times—80 (86–92) sts. Work even until piece measures 21" (21"–22") from start or desired sleeve length, end p row. Check gauge; piece above last inc row should measure 16" ($17\frac{1}{4}''$–$18\frac{1}{2}''$) wide. Work the 13 rows of top ridged border. Bind off in p. Steam-press pieces lightly.

CHART 1

ROW 65

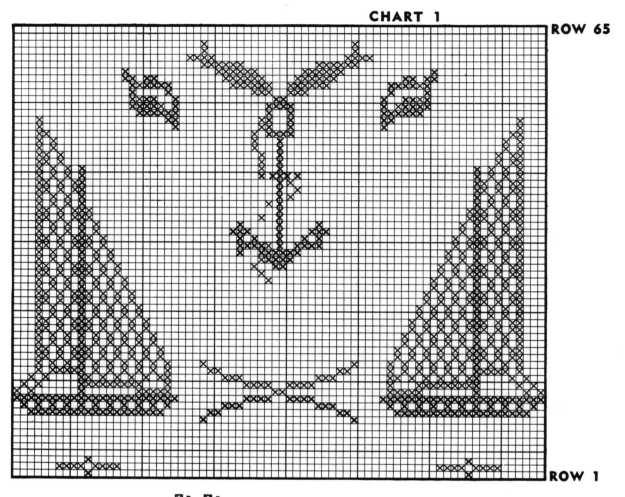

ROW 1

⊠ R ⊠ B

CHART 2

ROW 114

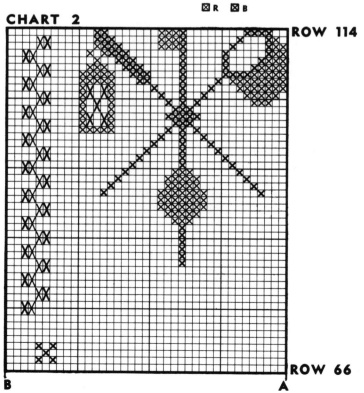

ROW 66

B   A

CHART 3

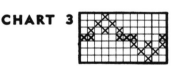

EMBROIDERY: Use tapestry needle with single strand of yarn to work design in cross-stitch. Run a basting thread down center front and center sleeve for a guide. Each square on charts equals one k st. Each row of squares equals 1 row. Each cross on charts represents 1 cross-stitch. Heavy crosses on charts are worked in black; light crosses are worked in red. On Chart 2, embroidery on front trim is worked over 2 rows as indicated. Repeat this embroidery for armhole trim.

Chart 1 is worked over 74 sts. The anchor post is worked between two sts as shown on chart. Count 114 stockinette st rows down from garter st ridge; mark this row for row 1 on Chart 1.

Chart 2 is worked over 78 sts. Work from A to B, then work back on same row from B to A.

For design on sleeve, mark 3″ down from garter st ridge, then count 35 rows down for start of anchor pat. Work and repeat Chart 3 around sleeve borders above ridges.

Work red and black cross-stitches over 2 rows between garter st ridges as illustrated. Work on front only; however, work around entire sleeve at top.

FINISHING: Sew shoulder and neckband seams. Sew in sleeves between underarm markers; sew side and sleeve seams. Steam-press seams open flat on wrong side. Turn half of neckband to wrong side; sew in place very loosely.

BUTTERFLY PILLOW OR DRESS
Shown on page 216

SIZE: Pillow, 14″ × 15″.
EQUIPMENT: Embroidery needle. Scissors. Sewing thread in pastel color. Penelope (cross-stitch) canvas, 7 mesh-to-the-inch, 14″ × 15″. Piece of cardboard, 2″ wide.
MATERIALS: For Pillow: White linen-like fabric, 15″ × 32″. White sewing thread. DMC six-strand embroidery floss: #703 green, 13 skeins; #947 orange, 3 skeins; #972 yellow, 1 skein. Inner pillow, 15″ × 16″.
Note: To embroider butterfly on a dress (or other article of clothing), follow directions as for

■ GREEN   ⊟ ORANGE   ⊡ YELLOW

pillow, but baste Penelope canvas to front of clothing where you wish to place design.

DIRECTIONS: Read "Four Methods of Cross-Stitching." (See Contents for General Directions.) Cut two pieces of white fabric, 15″ × 16″. On one piece, locate vertical center line (center of 16″ edges) and mark with running stitch in pastel thread, for placing the butterfly design. Center Penelope canvas over fabric and baste in place.

For embroidery, use full six strands of floss in needle. Follow chart and color key; each square of chart represents one cross-stitch. Start 5″ down from center top and work center top stitch of butterfly head (between antennae) with green floss. Continue center line of crosses down to bottom of body. Following chart, work to right, completing half of body, antenna, and right wing. Starting at left of center, work left side. When design is completed, remove basting and canvas threads.

Place back and front of pillow together, right sides facing; sew together ½″ from edge, leaving one side open. Turn to right side. Insert inner pillow in embroidered cover. Turn in remaining edges; slip-stitch across side.

With three skeins of green floss, make twisted cord as follows (method requires two people): Tie one end of yarn around pencil. Loop yarn over center of second pencil, back to and around first, and back to second, making as many strands between pencils as needed for the thickness of cord; knot end to pencil. Length of yarn between pencils should be three times length of cord desired. Each person holds yarn just below pencil with one hand and twists pencil with other hand, keeping yarn taut. When yarn begins to kink, catch center over doorknob or back of chair. Bring pencils together for one person to hold, while other grasps center of yarn, sliding hand down and releasing at short intervals, letting yarn twist to form cord. Sew around pillow over seam.

For tassels, use 2″ piece of cardboard and one skein of green floss for each tassel. Wrap floss around cardboard; tie strands together at one edge of cardboard. Cut strands at opposite edge. Wrap another piece of floss around all strands tightly, just below tie. Sew to corners of pillow.

LONG SLEEVE CROCHETED BLOUSE
Shown on page 217

EQUIPMENT: Steel crochet hook #9. Embroidery needle.

MATERIALS: McCall's Top Pattern 4876, Misses' 8–16, or other, similar pattern. Cotton gauze fabric (see pattern for yardage requirements). J. & P. Coats Knit-Cro-Sheen #A64, 2 (3, 3) balls (250 yds, each), Ecru #61. Six-strand embroidery floss, 1 skein in each of the following colors: green; gold; brown; red, rose. Penelope (cross-stitch) canvas 16 mesh-to-the-inch, one 12″ square.

DIRECTIONS: (See Contents for all General Directions.) Following pattern directions, cut out top minus back, which is crocheted.

To Embroider Front: Read "Four Methods of Cross-Stitching." (See Contents for all General Directions.) Center and baste canvas to fabric for front piece, with basting stitches running vertically, horizontally and diagonally. Floral cross-stitch design is worked with two strands of embroidery floss in needle. Take each stitch diagonally over the double mesh of canvas and through the fabric, being careful not to catch canvas. Work all underneath stitches of crosses in one direction and top stitches in opposite direction. Embroider design, centering on front of top. Chart is given for left side; reverse and work design for right side.

When design is embroidered, remove basting. Carefully draw out the horizontal threads of the

Continued on page 185

⊞ Mid Rose
◹ Signal Red
◺ Colonial Brown
⊟ Grass Green
⊡ Sun Gold

God Bless Our Home—a lasting and beautiful thought to make a special gift. Size is determined by the number of threads to the inch and the number worked over for each stitch. Directions and chart, page 130.

Counted cross-stitch spells out a unique sampler.
Use two shades of blue persian yarn to embroider alphabet and
flowers on ecru even-weave fabric. For directions,
turn to Alphabet Sampler, page 133.

*A stylized bouquet graces a meaningful
message in cross-stitch. Piece is
worked with embroidery floss
over 10-to-the-inch Penelope canvas.
Size: 16″ × 20⅛″.
Kindness Sampler, page 133.*

Wedding sampler's tender message is personalized with names of the bride and bridegroom; ring bearer's pillow matches. Directions on page 137.

be unto me
kind and true
as i be unto you

LOUIS
BARBARA
23 june 1979

*Traditional motifs—birds, flowers, and
an urn—are combined in a sampler that has a
sprightly freshness perfect for a kitchen
picture. Or, use the same easy cross-stitch-on-gingham
design to make
a pretty pillow
for an early
American setting.
Directions,
page 141.*

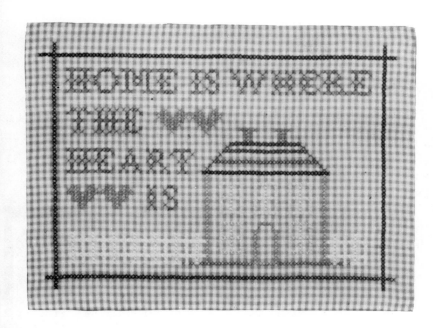

*Gingham samplers to brighten your home
are simple to stitch. When finished,
Home Sweet Home is 16" square,
Home is Where . . . measures 12" × 16".
Each is perfect for a kitchen or
family room. For directions, turn
to page 141.*

All aboard the Merriment Express! Start this delightful train moving with colorful embroidery floss for cross-stitching design, white linen for backing, and foam rubber padding for pillow forms.

Smoking locomotive pulls a hefty coal car,
a charming zoo wagon of lovable pets,
and a cozy caboose. Hang pillows for a
unique mobile of a chugging choo-choo!
Directions for Merriment Express, page 143.

Hang your message on a doorknob! Bright colors are cross-stitched onto 18 threads-to-the-inch even-weave fabric, then signs are stuffed and trimmed with twisted cord. Turn to page 154 for directions.

Stitch little Fritzie on his way to bed. Embroider crosses on 14 threads-to-the-inch even-weave fabric, then work the details in a few simple embroidery stitches. Picture measures $15\frac{1}{2}'' \times 12\frac{1}{2}''$ framed. See page 156 for directions.

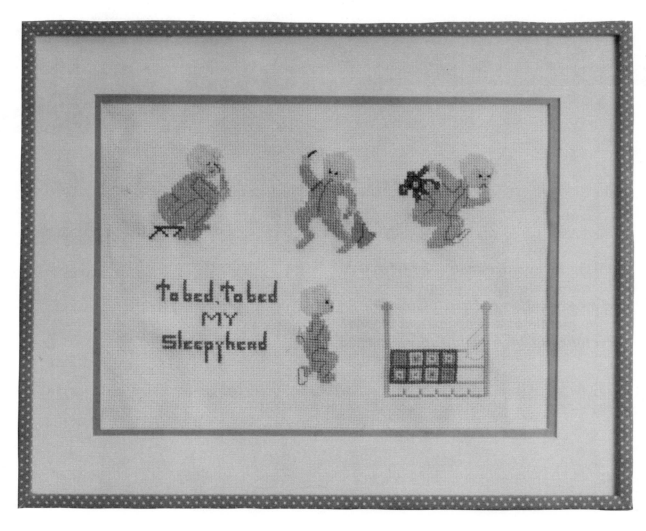

Continued from page 174

canvas, one strand at a time, then the vertical threads, leaving the finished cross-stitch design on the fabric.

CROCHET TRIMMING:

GAUGE: 4 sps or 4 rows = 1″

BLOCKING MEASUREMENTS: size 8 (10–12, 14).

Body Bust Size; $30\frac{1}{2}″$–$31\frac{1}{2}″$ ($32\frac{1}{2}″$–34, 36″).

Actual Crocheting Measurements: Width across back at underarm: 16 (17, 18). Length from shoulder to lower edge, excluding band at waist: 15 ($15\frac{1}{2}$, 16). Length of side seam, excluding band at waist: $9\frac{1}{2}″$ ($9\frac{1}{2}″$, $9\frac{1}{2}″$).

Crocheted Back: Starting at the lower edge, ch 197, (209, 221) to measure $17\frac{1}{2}″$ ($18\frac{1}{2}″$, $19\frac{1}{2}″$).

Row 1: Dc in 8th ch from hook—starting sp made; * ch 2, skip 2 ch, dc in next ch—sp made. Repeat from * across—64 (68, 72) sps in all. Ch 5, turn. **Row 2:** Skip first dc, dc in next dc—sp made at beg of row; * ch 2, dc in next dc—sp made. Repeat from * across to within last sp, ch 2, skip next 2 ch, dc in next ch—sp made at end of row. Ch 5, turn. **Rows 3–7:** Repeat Row 2. **Row 8:** Make 10 (12, 14) sps, 2 dc in next sp, dc in next dc—bl over sp made; work (10 sps, 1 bl) 4 times; work 9 (11, 13) sps. Ch 5, turn. **Row 9:** Make 8 (10, 12) sps, * bl in next sp, ch 2, skip 2 dc, dc in next dc—sp over bl made; bl in next sp, 8 sps. Repeat from * 3 more times; bl in next sp, sp over bl, bl in next sp, 9 (11, 13) sps. Ch 5, turn. **Row 10:** Repeat Row 8. **Rows 11–17:** Work sps across row. Ch 5, turn. Repeat rows 8–17 for pattern. Work even in pattern until back has 38 rows. Ch 1, turn at end of last row. **Armhole Shaping: Row 1:** Sl st in each dc and each ch st across first 3 sps; sl st in next dc, ch 5, dc in next dc, continue in pattern to within last 3 sps. Do not work over remaining sps. Ch 1, turn. **Rows 2 and 3:** Sl st in first dc in each of next 2 ch and following dc; ch 5, dc in next dc, continue in pattern to within last sp. Do not work over remaining sp. Ch 1, turn. At end of row 3, ch 5, turn—54 (58, 62) sps. Continue in pattern for 19 (21, 23) rows. Break off and fasten.

Front: Roll a $\frac{1}{4}″$ hem along lower edge, each side edge, neck and each shoulder edge of fabric front. Baste rolled edges. **Foundation Row:** Starting at corner of lower edge of fabric front, with right side facing, work across lower edge as follows: insert hook into fabric $\frac{1}{4}″$ from edge and draw up a loop, ch 5, * yarn over, inserting hook into fabric $\frac{1}{4}″$ from last st and $\frac{1}{4}″$ from edge and complete a dc, ch 2. Repeat from * across to opposite corner, making last dc in corner. Break off and fasten.

Left Shoulder Section: With right side of fabric front facing, attach yarn to left shoulder at armhole edge. **Row 1:** Making an uneven number of sps from armhole edge to left neck edge, work as for Foundation Row of Front. Ch 5, turn. **Row 2:** Work sps to within center sp, bl over sp, work sps to end of row. Ch 5, turn. **Row 3:** Work sps to within 1 sp before next bl, bl over sp, sp over bl, bl over sp, work sps to end of row. Ch 5, turn. **Row 4:** Repeat row 2. Ch 5, turn. **Row 5:** Work sps across. Ch 5, turn. **Rows 6–8:** Repeat rows 2–4. Break off and fasten.

Right Shoulder Section: With right side facing, attach yarn to right neck corner and complete as for opposite side.

Right Side Section: Foundation Row: With right side facing, attach yarn at right underarm of fabric front, ch 5 and work as for Foundation Row of Front across side edge, making last dc in 3rd ch of foundation row at lower edge—38 sps. Ch 5, turn. **Row 1:** Work 4 sps, * 1 bl and 5 sps. Repeat from * across, ending with 3 sps. Ch 5, turn. **Row 2:** Work 2 sps, * 1 bl, 1 sp, 1 bl and 3 sps. Repeat from * 5 times more. Ch 5, turn. **Row 3:** Repeat row 1. **Row 4:** Work sps across. Break off and fasten.

Left Side Section: Foundation Row: Attach thread to last dc of foundation row at lower edge, ch 2, work as for Foundation Row of Front, making last dc at underarm. Ch 5, turn. **Row 1:** Work 3 sps, * 1 bl and 5 sps. Repeat from * across, ending with 4 sps. Ch 5, turn. **Row 2:** Work 3 sps, * 1 bl, 1 sp, 1 bl, 3 sps. Repeat from * across, ending with 2 sps. Ch 5, turn. **Row 3:** Repeat Row 1. **Row 4:** Work sps across. Break off and fasten. Sew shoulder and side seams.

Pineapple Waistband: Starting at side edge, ch 42. **Foundation Row:** In 6th ch from hook, make 2 dc, ch 2 and 2 dc; ch 4, skip 9 ch, sc in next ch, ch 4, skip 8 ch, in next ch work 2 dc, ch 2 and 2 dc—shell made; ch 4, skip 5 ch, 8 dc in next ch, ch 4, skip 5 ch, shell in next ch, ch 3, skip 4 ch, dc in next ch. Ch 6, turn. **Row 1:** Make a shell in ch-2 sp of first shell—shell over shell made; skip next ch-4 loop, ch 3, dc in next dc, (ch 1, dc in next dc) 7 times; ch 3, shell over shell, skip next 2 loops, sc in ch-2 sp of last shell. Ch 3, turn. **Row 2:** Shell over shell, ch 4, skip next loop, sc in next ch-1 sp, (ch 3, sc in next ch-1 sp) 6 times; ch 4, shell over shell, ch 3, skip next 3 ch of turning chain, dc in next ch, Ch 6, turn. **Row 3:** Shell over shell, ch 4, skip next ch-4 loop, sc in next loop, (ch 3, sc in next loop) 5 times; ch 4, shell over shell. Ch 3, turn. **Row 4:** Shell over shell, ch 4, skip next ch-4 loop, sc in next loop, (ch 3, sc in next loop) 4 times; ch 4, in next shell sp make (2 dc, ch 2) twice and 2 dc—double shell made; ch 3, skip next 3 ch of turning chain, dc in next ch. Ch 6, turn. **Row 5:** Shell in first sp of double shell, ch 1, shell in second sp of same double shell, ch 4, skip next ch-4 loop, sc in next loop, (ch 3, sc in next loop) 3 times; ch 4, shell over shell. Ch 3, turn. **Row 6:** Shell over shell, ch 4, skip next ch-4 loop, sc in next loop, (ch 3, sc in next loop) twice; ch 4, shell over shell, ch 2, dc in next ch-1 sp, ch 2, shell over shell, ch 3, skip next 3 ch of turning chain, dc in next ch. Ch 6, turn. **Row 7:** Shell over shell, (ch 2, dc in next sp) twice; ch 2, shell over shell, ch 4, skip next ch-4 loop, sc in next loop, ch 3, sc in next loop, ch 4, shell over shell. Ch 3, turn. **Row 8:** Shell over shell, ch 4, skip 1 loop, sc in next loop, ch 4, shell over shell, ch 4, skip next ch-2 sp, 8 dc in next ch-2 sp, ch 4, shell over shell, ch 3, skip next 3 ch of turning chain, dc in next ch. Ch 6, turn. Repeat rows 1–8 for pattern. Work in pattern until band reaches around lower edge, ending with Row 7. **Sleeve Band:** make two: Starting at side edge, ch 34. **Foundation Row:** Dc in 10th ch from hook, ch 3, skip 5 ch, in next ch make *3 dc, ch 2 and 3 dc*—3-dc shell made; ch 3, skip 5 ch, sc in next ch, ch 3, skip 3 ch, dc in next 4 ch.

Do not work over remaining 5 ch. Ch 3, turn. **Row 1:** Dc in first dc and in next 3 dc, ch 7, in ch-2 sp of next 3-dc shell make 3 dc, ch 2 and 3 dc—3-dc shell over 3-dc shell made; ch 3, dc in next dc, ch 3, skip 3 ch, dc next dc. Ch 6, turn. **Row 2:** Skip first sp, dc in next dc, ch 3, 3-dc shell over shell, ch 3, sc in next loop, ch 3, dc in next dc. Ch 8, sc in top of turning chain. Ch 3, turn. **Row 3:** Dc in first loop (ch 1, dc in same loop) 11 times; ch 7, 3-dc shell over shell, ch 3, skip next sp, dc in next dc, ch 3, skip 3 ch, dc in next ch. Ch 6, turn. **Row 4:** Skip first sp, dc in next dc, ch 3, 3-dc shell over shell, ch 3, sc in next loop, ch 3, dc in next dc, (ch 2, dc in next dc) 11 times; ch 2, sc in last ch of foundation chain. Ch 3, turn. **Row 5:** * Skip 1 sp, dc in next sp, ch 3, 4 dc over dc just worked, ch 2. Repeat from * 3 more times; dc in next sp, ch 2, and mark this ch 2; (2 dc in next sp) twice; ch 3, skip next dc, dc in next dc, ch 7, 3-dc shell over shell, ch 3, skip next sp, dc in next dc, ch 3, skip 3 ch, dc in next ch. Ch 6, turn. **Row 6:** Skip first sp, dc in next dc, ch 3, 3-dc shell over shell, ch 3, sc in next loop, ch 3, 4 dc in next loop. Do not work over remaining sts. Ch 3, turn. Repeat rows 1–6 for pattern, working sc at end of row 4 in the marked ch 2 sp of row 5 of previous pattern until band fits lower edge of sleeve.

Sew sleeve seams. Roll a $\frac{1}{4}$" hem and work foundation row same as for Front around entire edge of each sleeve, starting and ending at seam. Join. Break off and fasten. Sew narrow ends of each Sleeve Band together. Sew to foundation row of each sleeve. Sew narrow ends of pineapple band together. Sew to lower edge of garment. **Neck Edging:** With right side facing, attach yarn to end sp of Foundation row at left neck. Work as for Foundation Row of Front along fabric front of neck to end sp at opposite side of right neck. Break off and fasten. Attach yarn at shoulder seam, ch 1, * dc in next sp, ch 1, 4 dc over dc just worked, skip 1 sp. Repeat from * around. Join with sl st to first ch 1. Break off and fasten.

BELL SLEEVE CROCHETED BLOUSE

Shown on page 217

EQUIPMENT: Steel crochet hook #9. Embroidery needle.

MATERIALS: McCall's Top Pattern 4876. Misses' 8–16, or other, similar pattern. Cotton gauze fabric (see pattern for yardage requirements). J. & P. Coats Knit-Cro-Sheen #A64, 3 balls (250 yds. each), Ecru #61. Six-strand embroidery floss #c.11, 1 skein in each of the following colors: Turquoise, canary yellow; dk. orange; dk. hunter green; fern green; watermelon; coral pink. Penelope (cross-stitch) canvas, 16 mesh-to-the-inch, one 14″ square piece.

DIRECTIONS: (See Contents for all General Directions.) Following pattern directions, cut out top.

To Embroider Front: Read "Four Methods of Cross-Stitching." Center and baste canvas to fabric for front piece, with basting stitches running vertically, horizontally and diagonally. Floral cross-stitch design is worked with two strands of floss

⊡ Canary Yellow	
⊞ Fern Green	⊞ Parakeet
⊠ Coral Pink	⊟ Dk. Orange
◪ Watermelon	⊟ Dk. Hunter Green

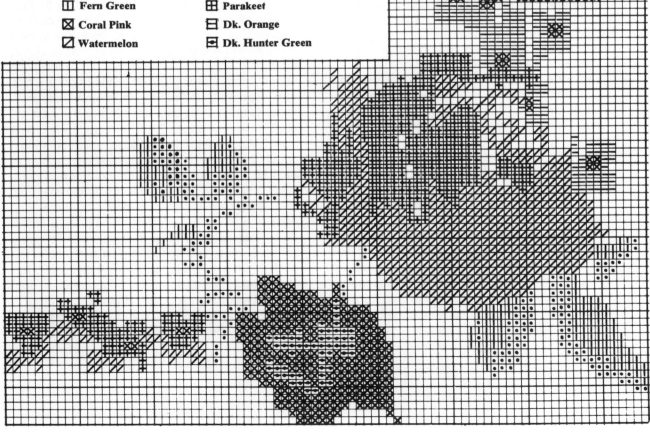

in needle. Take each stitch diagonally over the double mesh canvas and through the fabric, being careful not to catch canvas. Work all bottom stitches of cross in one direction and top stitches in opposite direction. Embroider design, centering on front of top. Chart is given for left side; reverse and work design for right side.

When design is embroidered, remove basting. Carefully draw out the horizontal threads of the canvas, one strand at a time, then the vertical threads, leaving the finished cross-stitch design on the fabric.

CROCHET TRIMMING: Edgings and inserts are adaptable to all sizes.

GAUGE: 4 sps = 1"; 4 rows = 1".

Right Side Panel: Row 1: Make a loop on hook; with right side of blouse front facing, working along hemmed edge, insert hook through material at upper edge of front $\frac{1}{8}$" in from outer edge, draw loop through material and through loop on hook. Ch 5, skip about $\frac{1}{4}$" along edge. Make 1 dc through material about $\frac{1}{8}$" from outer edge; * ch 2, skip $\frac{1}{4}$" along edge and make a dc as before. Repeat from * across. Ch 5, turn. **Row 2:** Skip first dc, dc in next dc, * ch 2, dc in next dc—sp over sp made. Repeat from * across to within last sp, ch 2, skip next 2 ch, dc in next ch. Ch 5, turn. **Rows 3–4, and 5:** Repeat row 2. At end of last row, break off and fasten. Sew last row of panel to right side edge of back.

Left Side Panel: With right side of blouse front facing, attach yarn over hemmed edge at lower edge of left side. Work same as for Right Side Panel. Sew last row of panel to left side edge of back.

Neck Edging: Rnd 1: With right side facing, attach yarn at center back seam, working along hemmed edge and being sure to have a number of ch-2 sps divisible by 4 (including sp formed by ch-5 at beg of rnd and last sp formed by ch-2 after joining) work same as for row 1 of Right Side Panel, to within about $\frac{1}{4}$" from ch-5 at beg of rnd, ch 2. Join with sl st to 3rd ch of ch-5. **Rnd 2:** In first sp make sc, hdc, 2 dc and tr—shell made; * skip next sp, shell in next sp. Repeat from * around to within last sp, skip last sp. Join to first sc. **Rnd 3:** Sl st to first dc of first shell, ch 1, sc in same

dc where last sl st was made, * ch 1, skip sc and hdc on next shell, dc in next dc, (ch 3, sc over bar of last dc made, ch 1, dc in same dc where last dc was made) twice; ch 3, sc over bar of last dc, ch 1, skip sc and hdc on next shell, sc in next dc. Repeat from * around, end last repeat with ch 1, skip last 2 dc on last shell, sl st to first sc on same rnd. Break off and fasten.

Waistband: Starting at narrow edge, ch 42. **Row 1:** Dc in 4th ch from hook and in each remaining ch—40 dc, counting turning chain as 1 dc. Ch 3, turn. **Row 2:** Skip first dc, dc in next 3 dc, (ch 2, skip 2 dc, dc in next dc) 11 times; dc in next 2 dc, dc in top of ch-3. Ch 3, turn. **Row 3:** Skip first dc, dc in next 3 dc, ch 5, skip first ch-2 sp, sc in next sp, ch 5, skip next sp, (dc in next dc, 2 dc in next sp) 5 times; dc in next dc, ch 5, skip next sp, sc in following sp, ch 5, skip next sp, dc in next 3 dc, dc in top of ch-3. Ch 3, turn. **Row 4:** Skip first dc, dc in next 3 dc, ch 2, skip next 2 ch, sc in next ch, ch 2, sc in next sc, ch 2, skip next 2 ch, sc in next ch, ch 2, (dc in next dc, ch 2, skip next 2 dc) 5 times; dc in next dc, ch 2, skip next 2 ch, sc in next ch, ch 2, sc in next sc, ch 2, skip next 2 ch, sc in next ch, ch 2, dc in next 3 dc, dc in top of ch-3. Ch 3, turn. **Row 5:** Skip first dc, dc in next 3 dc, ch 2, sc in next sc, ch 5, skip next sc, sc in following sc, ch 2, (dc in next dc, 2 dc in next sp) 5 times; dc in next dc, ch 2, sc in next sc, ch 5, skip next sc, sc in following sc, ch 2, dc in next 3 dc, dc in top of ch-3. Ch 3, turn. **Row 6:** Skip first dc, dc in next 3 dc, ch 2, sc in next sc, ch 2, skip next 2 ch, sc in next ch, ch 2, sc in next sc, ch 2, (dc in next dc, ch 2, skip next 2 dc) 5 times; dc in next dc, ch 2, sc in next sc, ch 2, skip next 2 ch, sc in next ch, ch 2, sc in next sc, ch 2, dc in next 3 dc, dc in top of ch-3. Ch 3, turn. **Row 7:** Skip first dc, dc in next 3 dc, ch 5, skip next sc, sc in following sc, ch 5, skip next sc, (dc in next dc, 2 dc in next sp) 5 times; dc in next dc, ch 5, skip next sc, sc in following sc, ch 5, skip next sc, dc in next 3 dc, dc in top of ch-3. Ch 3, turn. Repeat Rows 4 through 7 until Waistband measures about 1 inch shorter than desired length, ending with Row 5 of pattern. Ch 3, turn. **Next Row:** Skip first dc, dc in next 3 dc, (ch 2, dc in next sc) twice; ch 2, (dc in next dc, ch 2, skip 2 dc) 5 times; dc in next dc, (ch 2, dc in next sc) twice; ch 2, dc in next 3 dc, dc in top of ch-3. Ch 3, turn. **Last Row:** Skip first dc, dc in next 3 dc, (2 dc in next sp, dc in next dc) 11 times; dc in next 2 dc, dc in top of ch-3. Do not turn.

Waistband Edging (right side): Working along ends of rows, * ch 4, skip next row, dc in base of following row, ch 2, make 2 dc and 1 tr over bar of last dc made, skip next row, sc in base of following row. Repeat from * across, ending last repeat with skip next row, sc in base of corner st. Now, working along short edge, ch 4, skip first 4 sts, dc in top of next st and continue to work edging same as on long edge, skipping 4 dc instead of 2 rows, and ending with sc in top of corner st. Continue across next long and short edge in same manner as before, ending with sc in top of corner st. Break off and fasten.

With right side of blouse and Waistband facing, starting at back opening, sew one long edge of Waistband in place over lower edge of blouse, easing in fullness.

Sleeve Edging: Rnd 1: With right side facing, attach thread to lower edge of sleeve seam. Being sure to have a number of ch-2 sps divisible by 11, work same as for rnd 1 of Neck Edging. **Rnd 2:** Sl st in next sp, ch 3, in same sp make 2 dc, ch 2, 3 dc, * (ch 2, dc in next sp) 10 times; ch 2, in next sp make 3 dc, ch 2 and 3 dc—shell made; repeat from * around to within last 10 sps, (ch 2, dc in next sp) 10 times; ch 2. Join to top of ch-3. **Rnd 3:** Sl st in each of next 2 dc and ch-2 sp, ch 3, in same sp make 2 dc, ch 2, and 3 dc, * make ch 2 and dc in each ch-2 sp across to within next shell, ch 2, in ch-2 sp of next shell make 3 dc, ch 2 and 3 dc—shell over shell made. Repeat from * around, end with ch 2. Join to top of ch-3. **Rnds 4–6:** Repeat rnd 2 three more times—there are 15 sps between shells on rnd 6. **Rnd 7:** Sl st in each of next 2 dc and ch-2 sp, sc in same sp, * ch 15, sl st in 10th ch from hook, ch 1, turn. In ring make (sc, hdc, 3 dc hdc) 4 times; sc in ring, make 7 sc over remaining 5 ch sts, sl st in same ch-2 sp, (ch 3, skip next sp, dc in next sp, ch 5, sl st in 5th ch from hook—picot made; ch 2, in same sp make dc, picot, ch 2, dc, picot and ch 3, skip next sp, sc in next sp) 4 times. Repeat

from * around, ending with sl st to first sc. Break off and fasten. Steam lightly.

PEASANT PILLOWS
Shown on page 218

SIZE: Heart Pillow, 14″ square; Flower Pillow 13″ square.

EQUIPMENT: Scissors. Tapestry needles. Pencil. Ruler. Straight pins. Iron. Embroidery hoop (optional). Sewing maching. Steam iron.

MATERIALS: For each: Cream-colored Zweigart Florina fabric (100% viscose) 13½ threads-to-the-inch, 55″ wide ½ yard. Matching sewing thread. DMC Pearl Cotton #3 (16.4-yard skeins): orange-red #606, 3 skeins for Heart Pillow, 2 skeins for Flower Pillow; black #310, 2 skeins for each pillow. For inner pillow: Muslin 36″ wide, ½ yard. Polyester fiberfill.

GENERAL DIRECTIONS: (See Contents for all General Directions.) For each pillow, cut one square from fabric. Overcast edges of fabric to prevent raveling.

Embroidery is worked in cross-stitch. Read "Four Methods of Cross-Stitching." To work cross-stitch on pillows, use one strand of pearl cotton in needle and make stitches over three threads horizontally and three threads vertically.

Chart is given for one quarter of each design. Each square on chart equals one cross-stitch. Mark center of fabric with straight pin. Place fabric in embroidery hoop, if desired, pulling tautly. Embroider design, following charts, color key, and individual directions.

Steam-press the finished embroidery.

To finish outer pillow, cut square of fabric same size as embroidered one. Pin and sew back and front together, right sides facing, with ½″ seams; leave opening in center of one side. Turn to right side.

To make inner pillow, cut two squares from muslin 2″ larger than finished size of pillow. Stitch two pieces together with $\frac{1}{2}''$ seams, leaving an opening in center of one side. Turn to other side; stuff fully with fiberfill. Sew opening closed. Insert inner pillow in embroidered cover. Turn in raw edges; slip-stitch closed.

HEART PILLOW: Cut fabric 15″ square. Mark center of fabric and work one quarter of design from chart, starting at arrow on chart and center of fabric. For second quarter, repeat chart in reverse, omitting center row marked by arrow. Repeat in reverse for other half, omitting center rows marked by arrows. Assemble pillow as indicated above.

FLOWER PILLOW: Cut fabric 14″ square. Find center of pillow top; mark center thread with a pin. From center thread, count 38 meshes to the right; mark. At this point, begin base of the flower in upper right corner of pillow, placing lower left corner of first cross-stitch in marked mesh. Work two more cross-stitches to the right to complete base, then work entire flower, following chart and color key. Work flower in lower right corner of pillow top, reversing chart and colors; bases of two flowers are touching.

For flower in upper left corner of pillow top, count 38 meshes to the left of center thread, then 15 meshes down. At this point, begin base of flower in same manner as before, but working to the left; reverse colors. Work flower in lower left, reversing chart (see illustration).

PEASANT SHAWL
Shown on page 219

EQUIPMENT: Yardstick. Scissors. Tailor's chalk. Straight pins. Tapestry needle. Embroidery hoop (optional). Sewing machine. Iron.

MATERIALS: Cream-colored Zweigart Florina fabric (100% viscose) $13\frac{1}{2}$ threads-to-the-inch, 55″ wide, $1\frac{1}{2}$ yards. Matching sewing thread. DMC Pearl Cotton #3 (16.4-yard skeins): orange-red #606, 18; black #310, 7. Cotton fabric in red and black small print 45″ wide, $1\frac{1}{2}$ yards. Off-white cotton heavy lace ruffling, about 2″ wide, $3\frac{1}{2}$ yards.

DIRECTIONS: Lay fabric out flat. On two adjacent sides, mark a point 50″ from corner. Draw a diagonal line connecting the two points. Cut out triangle. Overcast edges of fabric to prevent raveling. Mark off 1″ for seam allowances all around.

Entire shawl design is worked in cross-stitch. Read directions for "Four Methods of Cross-Stitching." To do cross-stitch on shawl, use one strand of pearl cotton in needle and make stitches over three threads horizontally and three threads vertically. Place fabric in hoop if desired.

Each square on chart represents one cross-stitch. Fold shawl in half to find center; mark with line of basting or tailor's chalk. Work from center point of shawl (marked by arrows on chart) to the left, following chart and color key; repeat design until you have finished the entire left side, working

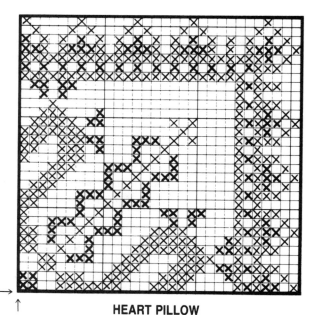

HEART PILLOW

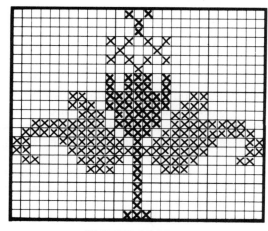

FLOWER PILLOW

outer border first, then main design, then inner border. For right side, repeat design in reverse, working again from center. Carefully steam-press embroidery. Trim seams to $\frac{1}{2}''$.

To line shawl, cut print fabric on the straight of goods, the same size as embroidered fabric; piece corner to complete triangle. Pin lace to lining around short sides, matching straight edges, with right sides facing, and easing fullness at center point; baste $\frac{1}{2}''$ in from edge. Pin shawl and lining together with right sides facing and lace edging between. Stitch all around with $\frac{1}{2}''$ seams, leaving opening in long side of shawl for turning. Clip corners and trim seams. Turn to right side and slip-stitch opening closed.

SHIRT AND BELT
Shown on page 218

EQUIPMENT: Scissors. Pencil. Ruler. Paper for patterns. Straight pins. Iron. Embroidery hoop (optional). Large-eyed embroidery and sewing needles. Steam iron. Sewing machine.

MATERIALS: For Shirt: McCall's pattern #5246 (view B) Misses' petite-large, or other, similar pattern. Muslin (see back of pattern envelope for yardage and other requirements). Ivory Aida cloth 14 threads-to-the-inch 43″ wide, $\frac{3}{8}$ yard. **For Belt:**

⊠ **BLACK**   ⊠ **RED**

Cream-colored Zweigart Florina fabric (100% viscose) $13\frac{1}{2}$ threads-to-the-inch, 55″ wide, $\frac{1}{8}$ yard. Buckram for interlining and muslin for lining, each 36″ wide, $\frac{1}{8}$ yard. Black satin twisted cord with tassel at each end (upholstery trim), $\frac{1}{4}$″ in diameter, 70″ long. Four large black-covered hooks. **For Both:** DMC Pearl Cotton #3 (16.4-yard skeins): orange-red #606, 8; black #310, 4.

DIRECTIONS: SHIRT: See charts and diagrams. Cut muslin fabric as specified in pattern. Measure cuff pattern without seam allowance; make pattern for front trim following Diagram 1; and make pattern for armband 3″ wide, length equal to the width of sleeve about 8″ up from bottom edge. Pin and mark two of each piece with pencil on Aida cloth, reversing pattern for second front trim (see Diagram 2). Leave at least $1\frac{1}{4}$″ between all pieces for seam allowances, but do not cut out yet. Overcast edges of Aida cloth to prevent raveling.

To Embroider: Read "Four Methods of Cross-Stitching.) (See Contents for all General Directions.) Work embroidered designs for shirt on Aida cloth. Put cloth in embroidery hoop, if desired. Use one strand of pearl cotton in needle and work over two threads horizontally and two threads vertically, taking the stitches through the holes.

Follow charts and color key to work design. Each square on chart represents one cross-stitch. Work front trims as given on chart, reversing de-

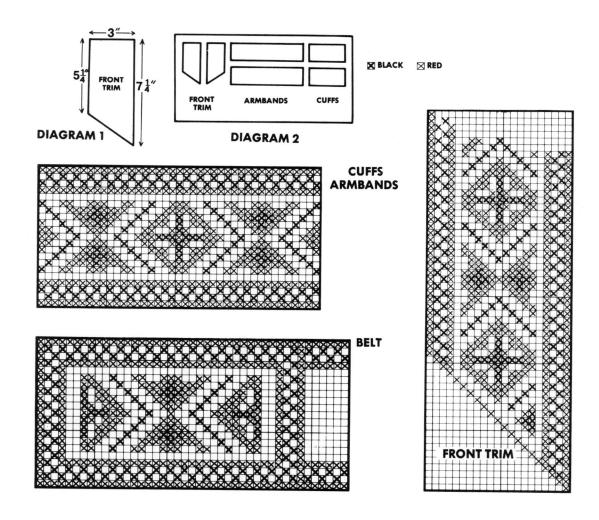

sign for second front trim. For armbands and cuffs, begin embroidery at one end and repeat design until you reach the other end.

When embroidery is finished, cut out all pieces with $\frac{5}{8}''$ seam allowances. Steam-press embroidery, if necessary.

To Assemble Shirt: For each armband, press long edges under and appliqué across a shirt sleeve 8″ above lower edge. Make cuffs by sewing one muslin and one embroidered cuff together for each, following pattern instructions. Assemble blouse; do not sew on neckline edge tie yet. Press seam allowance of front trim under and appliqué in place on shirt; cut away excess Aida cloth at top, flush with muslin neck edge. Complete neckline following pattern.

BELT: From Florina and muslin, cut one strip, each 4″ wide and the length of waist measurement. Overcast edges of Florina and muslin. Cut strip of buckram interlining, 3″ wide and 1″ shorter than the length.

Mark a line $\frac{1}{2}''$ in from all edges on Florina fabric, making design area 3″ wide. Starting at one end of fabric, work over two threads horizontally, two threads vertically. Repeat at other end. Continue border between each end.

Baste interlining to muslin strip, centered on wrong side. Stitch muslin lining and embroidered strip together, right sides facing; leave opening along one edge at center. Trim seams. Turn to right side; slip-stitch opening closed. Sew two hooks on each end, $\frac{1}{2}''$ from top and bottom. Lace satin cord through hooks, and tie.

BUNTING

Shown on page 221

SIZE: Directions are for size 1.
Fits Body Chest Size: 20″.
MATERIALS: Lion Brand Orlon Sayelle, 4 4-oz. skeins maroon, main color (MC); 1 skein turquoise, contrasting color (CC). Crochet hook size F. Large-eyed needle. 20″ zipper.
GAUGE: 4 sc = 1″; 4 rows = 1″.
To Dec 1 Sc: Pull up a lp in each of 2 sts, yo hook and through 3 lps on hook.

To Bind Off: At beg of row, sl st in each of specified number of sts; at end of row, leave specified number of sts unworked.
BUNTING: BACK: Beg at lower edge, with MC, ch 75.

Row 1: Sc in 2nd ch from hook and in each ch across—74 sc. Ch 1, turn each row.

Row 2: Sc in each sc across. Check gauge; piece should measure $18\frac{1}{2}''$ wide. Repeating row 2, dec 1 st each side of row 9, then every 10th row 7 times more—58 sc. Work even until 85 rows from start. End off; turn.

Shape Sleeves: With MC, ch 18, sc in each sc across back, ch 19. Turn.

Next Row: Sc in 2nd ch from hook and in each sc and ch across—94 sc. Ch 1, turn. Work 17 rows even.

Shape Top of Sleeve and Neck: Bind off (see To Bind Off) 12 sts, sc in each of next 25 sts; end off. Sk next 20 sts; with MC, sc in each of next 25 sts. End off.

RIGHT FRONT: Beg at lower edge, with MC, ch 39. Work in sc on 38 sts for 8 rows. Mark beg of last row for side edge. Dec 1 sc at side edge of next row, then dec 1 st at same edge every 10th row 7 times—30 sc. Work even until 84 rows from start, end center edge.

Shape Sleeve: Sc in each sc across, ch 19.

Next Row: Sc in 2nd ch from hook and in each ch across—48 sc. Work 17 rows even. Bind off 12 sts at side edge and 11 sts at center edge of next row. End off.

LEFT FRONT: Work as for right front for 8 rows. Mark end of last row for side edge. Work as for right front until 85 rows from start, end center edge. Drop yarn. Join another strand of yarn to side edge, ch 18. End off. Pick up dropped strand, sc in each sc and ch across—48 sc. Work 17 rows even. Bind off 11 sts at center edge and 12 sts at side edge of next row. End off.

HOOD: Beg at front edge, with MC, ch 33. Work in sc on 64 sc for 29 rows. End off.

Embroidery: Following Chart 1, embroider CC design in cross-stitch, working 1 cross-stitch over 1 sc. On back, start at outer edge, repeat patterns across to other edge. On left front, start at outer edge, repeat patterns to center. On bands with

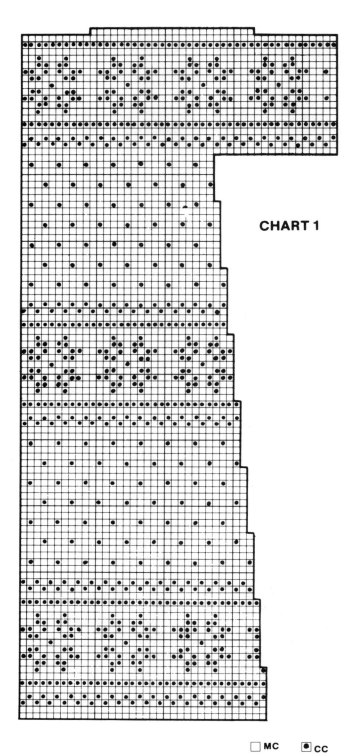

CHART 1

☐ MC ⦿ CC

star patterns, there should be 2 sts unworked at center. On right front, start at center edge, repeat all patterns except stars to outer edge. On bands with star patterns, leave 2 sts unworked at center edge, repeat stars across to outer edge. For hood, following Chart 2, work from A to B to top of chart, then repeat rows 4–9 to back of hood.

FINISHING: Sew sleeve and side seams; sew shoulder and top sleeve seams. Weave lower edge of back and fronts tog. Weave fronts from lower edge tog to top of row 18. Fold hood in half; weave back seam. Weave hood to neck edge.

Sleeve Cuff: From right side, with MC, work 24 sc around lower edge of sleeve. Join with a sl st in first sc. Ch 1, turn.

Rnd 2: Sc in each sc around. Join; ch 1, turn. Repeat rnd 2, 3 times. End off.

Front Edging: From right side, with CC, beg at lower edge of front opening, sc, * ch 1, sk 1 row, sc in edge of next row, repeat from * around front opening and hood. Join with a sl st in first sc. End off. Sew in zipper.

GIRLS' SNOWFLAKE SHIRT AND PUFF-SLEEVE BLOUSE

Shown on page 220

SIZES: Directions for size 4. Changes for sizes 6 and 8 are in parentheses.

Body Chest Size: 23″ (24″–26″).
Blocked Chest Size: 24″ (25½″–27″).
Fits Body Waist Size: 21″ (22″–23″).
MATERIALS: Lion Brand Orlon Sayelle, 4-oz

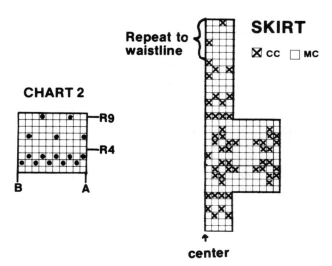

CHART 2

Repeat to waistline

SKIRT

☒ CC ☐ MC

R9
R4

B A

center

194

skeins: For Skirt, 2 (2–3) skeins maroon (MC); 1 skein turquoise (CC). For Blouse, 1 (1–2) skeins turquoise. Crochet hook size F. Large-eyed yarn needle. One button for skirt.

GAUGE: Skirt: 4 sc = 1″; 4 rows = 1″. Blouse: 3 V-sts = 2″; 2 rows = 1″.

To Dec 1 Sc: Pull up a lp in each of 2 sts, yo hook and through 3 lps on hook.

SKIRT: FRONT: Beg at lower edge, with MC, ch 78 (80–84).

Row 1: Sc in 2nd ch from hook and in each ch across—77 (79–83) sc. Working in sc, dec 1 sc (see To Dec 1 Sc) each side every 5th row 9 times—59 (61–65) sc. Work even until piece measures 12″ (13″–14″) from start or 1½″ less than desired skirt length.

Next Row (dec row): Dec 15 (15–17) sc evenly spaced across—44 (46–48) sc.

Waistband: Work 5 rows even. End off.

BACK: Work same as for front until piece measures 9″ (10″–11″) from start. Mark center st.

Divide Work: Work to within 1 st before center st, drop yarn; sk center st, with another strand of MC, sc in next sc and in each st across. Working on both sides at once, with separate strands of yarn, work same as for front until piece measures 12″ (13″–14″) from start—29 (30–32) sts each.

Next Row: (dec row): Dec 7 (7–8) sc across each half—22 (23–24) sts each side.

Waistband: Work 5 rows even. End off.

STRAPS (make 2); With MC, ch 6. Work in sc on 5 sts for 20″ (21″–22″) or desired length. End off.

CROSS-STRAP: Ch 15. Work in sc on 14 sts for 4 rows. End off. Weave edge of cross-strap to straps, 3″ above start of straps.

Embroidery: Run a basting line up center of back and front. With CC, following chart, begin at center and repeat chart to side edge of back and front. Work in cross stitch (see "Four Methods of Cross-Stitching."); each square on design chart represents 1 stitch. Embroider a cross stitch in every other st across 3rd row of waistband. Embroider a cross stitch in every other st across 2nd row of cross-strap and in every other st across 3rd row of cross-strap; do not place sts over sts.

FINISHING: Sew side seams. From right side, with MC, working from left to right, sc around lower edge and around entire outer edge of straps. Sew straps to front and back. From right side, work 1 row sc around back opening. Make chain loop on right side of waistband for button loop; sew button on left side.

TIE: With MC, ch 56″; sl st in each ch. End off. Draw through first row of waistband. Tie ends in front.

BLOUSE: BACK: Beg at lower edge with CC, ch 57 (60–66).

Row 1: (Dc, ch 1, dc) in 6th ch from hook (V-st made), * sk next 2 ch, V-st of (dc, ch 1, dc) in next ch, repeat from * to last 3 ch, end sk next 2 ch, dc in last ch—17 (18–20) V-sts. Turn each row.

Row 2: Ch 3 (counts as 1 dc), * V-st of (dc, ch 1, dc) in ch-1 sp of next V-st, repeat from * across, end dc in top of turning ch. Repeat row 2 for pat until piece measures 8″ (9″–10″) from start or desired length to underarm.

Shape Armhole: Sl st in each of first 2 dc, sl st in ch-1 sp, ch 3, V-st in ch-1 sp of next V-st, work in pat to within last V-st, end dc in ch-1 sp of last V-st—15 (16–18) V-sts. Work even until armholes measure 4½″ (5″–5½″) above first row of armhole shaping. End off.

FRONT: Work same as for back until 2 rows less than back.

Shape Neck: Next Row: Ch 3, work 4 (4–5) V-sts, dc in ch-1 sp of next V-st. Turn.

Next Row: Ch 3, dc in ch-1 sp of first V-st, work 3 (3–4) V-sts, dc in top of turning ch. End off. Sk 5 (6–6) V-sts on last long row, join yarn in ch-1 sp of next V-st, ch 3, V-st in ch-1 sp of next V-st, finish row—4 (4–5) V-sts. Complete to correspond to first shoulder.

SLEEVES: Beg at lower edge, ch 29 (31–33).

Row 1: (Dc, ch 1, dc) in 5th ch from hook, * sk next ch, V-st of (dc, ch 1, dc) in next ch, repeat from * to last 2 ch, end sk next ch, dc in last ch—12 (13–14) V-sts. Work in pat as established for 6 (6–7) rows or desired length to underarm.

Shape Cap: Repeat armhole shaping row 4 (4–5) times. End off.

FINISHING: Sew shoulder seams. Sew in sleeves; sew sleeve and side seams.

Edging: From right side, join yarn in underarm seam of sleeve. Ch 3, work 3 dc in each ch around lower edge of sleeve. Join with a sl st in top of ch 3. End off. From right side, work 2 dc in each st around neck edge. Join; end off.

BOYS' SNOWFLAKE SWEATER
Shown on page 220

SIZES: Directions for size 4. Changes for sizes 6 and 8 are in parentheses.
Body Chest Size: 23" (24"–26").
Blocked Chest Size (closed): 26" (28"–30").
MATERIALS: Lion Brand Orlon Sayelle, 2 (2–3) 4-oz. skeins maroon, main color (MC); 1 skein turquoise, contrasting color (CC). Crochet hook size F. Yarn embroidery needle. Separating zipper.
GAUGE: 4 sts = 1"; 4 rows = 1".
To Inc 1 Sc: Work 2 sts in same st.
JACKET: BACK: Beg at lower edge, above border, with MC, ch 53 (57–61).
Row 1: Sc in 2nd ch from hook and in each ch across—52 (56–60) sc. Ch 1, turn each row.
Row 2: Sc in each sc across. Check gauge; piece should measure 13" (14"–15") wide. Work in sc until piece measures 8" (9"–10") from start. Cut MC; join CC. With CC, work 11 rows. Cut CC; join MC. With MC, work 5 rows. End off.
RIGHT FRONT: Beg at lower edge above border, with MC, ch 27 (29–31). Work same as for back on 26 (28–30) sts. Piece should measure 6½" (7"–7½") wide.
LEFT FRONT: Work same as for right front.
SLEEVES: Beg at lower edge above border, with MC, ch 25 (27–29). Work same as for back for 2 rows—24 (26–28) sc. Working in sc, inc 1

sc (see To Inc 1 Sc) each side of next row, then every 3rd row 9 times more; **at the same time,** when piece measures 6" (6½"–7") from start, work 11 rows CC, 5 rows MC—44 (46–48) sc. End off.

Embroidery: Run a basting line up center of CC stripe on each sleeve and back. Following chart, beg at basting line, working in cross-stitch with MC, repeat the 11 sts of chart to each side edge of back and each sleeve (see "Four Methods of Cross-Stitching.") Beg at center front, repeat chart to side edge of each front. Each square on chart represents 1 stitch. With CC, embroider a cross st in each sc across 3rd MC row on lower edge of back, fronts and each sleeve. Work a cross-stitch in every other st across 5th and 6th MC rows on lower edge of back, fronts and each sleeve; across 3rd and 4th rows below CC stripe and across 3rd and 4th rows above each CC stripe.

FINISHING: Run in yarn ends on wrong side. Sew shoulder seams from outer edge for 3½" (4"–4½"), leaving 6" free at center back for neck. With center of sleeve at shoulder seam, sew in sleeves. Sew side and sleeve seams.
Lower Border: With CC, ch 7.
Row 1: Sc in 2nd ch from hook and in each ch across—6 sc. Ch 1, turn each row.
Row 2: Sc in back lp of each sc across. Repeat last row until piece, when slightly stretched, measures same as lower edge of body. End off.
Sleeve Border: Work same as for lower border until piece measures same as lower edge of sleeve.
Neck Border: Work same as for lower border until piece when slightly stretched measures 12". End off.

Sew borders to lower edge of body and sleeves. Fold neck border in half lengthwise; sew to neck edge. From right side, with CC, work 1 row sc on each front edge. Sew in zipper.

VICTORIAN AFGHAN
Shown on page 222

SIZE: 58" × 71", plus fringe.
EQUIPMENT: 14" aluminum afghan hook size 9 or J. Large-eyed tapestry and rug needles. Tape measure. Scissors. Cardboard, 3" piece.
MATERIALS: Knitting worsted: 16 4-oz. skeins

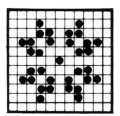

☐ **MC**
▣ **CC**

black for background, 1 skein each of the following colors for embroidery (or use tapestry wool, crewel wool, or leftover yarns):

Four reds: pale red, light red, medium red, cardinal.

Three purples: lavender, light purple, dark purple.

Three old-rose tones: light old rose, medium old rose, dark old rose.

Four greens: pale almond green, light almond green, medium almond green, dark almond green.

Four beige tones (white rose): oyster white, natural heather, celery, camel.

Five tans (horse and dogs): parchment, pale russet brown, light russet brown, medium russet brown, dark russet brown.

Four yellow-browns: tobacco gold, copper, wood brown, dark wood brown.

Two rusts: dark apricot, rustone.

Yellow.

GAUGE: 7 sts = 2″; 7 rows = 2″.

AFGHAN ST: Make a chain with same number of ch as desired number of sts.

Row 1: Pull up a lp in 2nd ch from hook and in each ch across, keeping all lps on hook.

To Work Lps Off: Yo hook, pull through first lp, * yo hook, pull through next 2 lps, repeat from * across until 1 lp remains. Lp that remains on hook always counts as first st of next row.

Row 2: Keeping all lps on hook, pull up a lp under 2nd vertical bar and under each vertical bar across. Work lps off as before. Repeat row 2 for desired number of rows.

CENTER SECTION: Ch 155. Work in afghan st on 155 sts for 112 rows. Piece should measure 44$\frac{1}{4}$″ wide, 32″ long.

Next Row: Sl st loosely under 2nd vertical bar and in each vertical bar across. End off.

Mark between 17th and 18th sts from right edge for right edge of cross-stitch design. Mark between 11th and 12th rows from bottom for bottom edge of design. Following chart, page 13, embroider horse in cross-stitch (see "Four Methods of Cross-Stitching.").

SIDE ROSE BORDERS (make 2): Ch 112. Work in afghan st on 112 sts for 46 rows. Piece should measure 32″ wide, 13″ deep.

Next Row: Sl st loosely under 2nd vertical bar and in each bar across. End off.

Mark between 3rd and 4th sts from right edge for right edge of design. Mark between 3rd and 4th rows for bottom of design. Following Chart 1, embroider rose border.

TOP AND BOTTOM ROSE BORDERS (make 2): Ch 155. Work in afghan st on 155 sts for 46 rows. Piece should measure 44$\frac{1}{4}$″ wide, 13″ deep.

Next row: Sl st loosely under 2nd vertical bar and in each bar across. End off.

Mark between 4th and 5th sts from right edge for right edge of design. Mark between 3rd and 4th rows for bottom of design. Following Chart 2, embroider rose border from A to B, then repeat end rose only from C to D.

CORNERS (make 4): Ch 46. Work in afghan st on 46 sts for 46 rows. Piece should be 13″ square.

Next Row: Sl st loosely under 2nd vertical bar and in each bar across. End off.

Dog Heads: Mark between 8th and 9th sts from right edge for right edge of design. Starting in 4th row, following chart, embroider head in cross-stitch. For second corner (top right), follow first corner, reversing design.

Monogram of Jesus: Mark between 6th and 7th sts from right edge for right edge of design. Starting in first row, following chart, embroider monogram in cross-stitch.

Date: Using illustration of afghan as guide and chart, plan date to fit space. Use graph paper, if necessary, to work out most pleasing arrangement of letters and numbers.

FINISHING: Weave in yarn ends on wrong side. Pin out pieces to correct measurements; steam-press. When pieces are dry, sew them together with black yarn. Cover joinings with cross-stitch in palest tone of horse. With same tone, work 1 row of sc around edge, making sc in each st or row, 3 sc in each corner. Join in first sc; end off.

FRINGE: Row 1: Use 4 strands of black yarn, cut 24″ long, in large-eyed rug needle. Hold afghan right side up with edge of afghan toward you. Bring needle up from wrong side through a st on edge. Pull yarn through leaving 2″ end in back. Hold this 2″ end in left hand. Put needle from right to left under end in left hand, bring it up forming loop at right. Insert needle from top to bottom through loop; pull tight, forming knot on

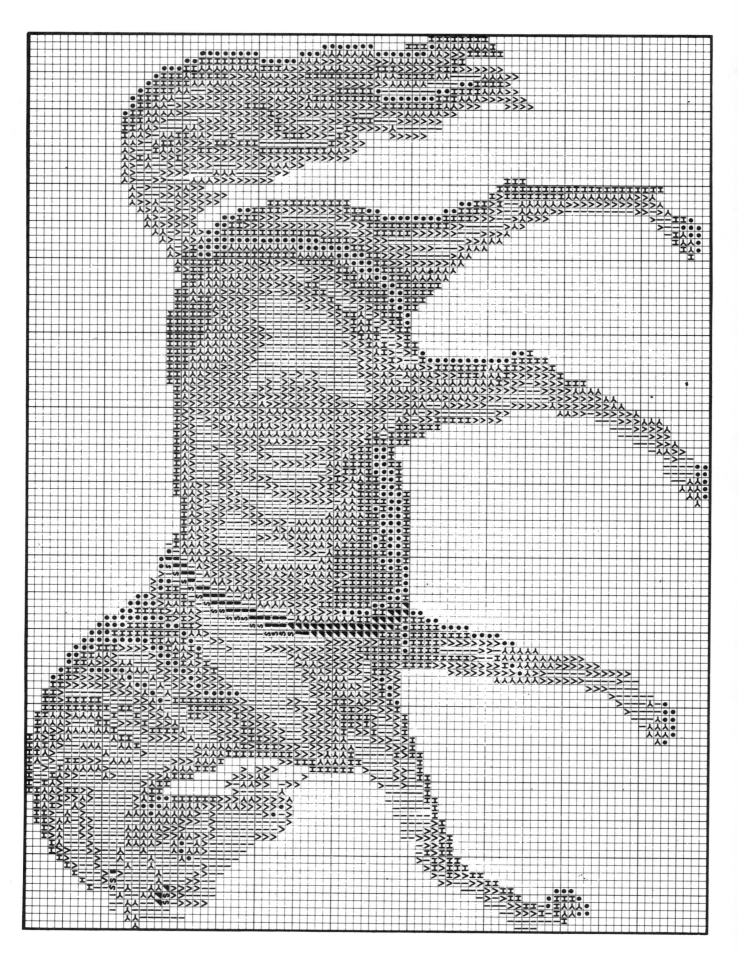

PALE RED
LT. RED
MED. RED
CARDINAL
LAVENDER
LT. PURPLE
DK. PURPLE
LT. OLD ROSE
MED. OLD ROSE
DK. OLD ROSE
PALE ALMOND GREEN
LT. ALMOND GREEN
MED. ALMOND GREEN
DK. ALMOND GREEN
OYSTER WHITE
NATURAL HEATHER
CELERY
CAMEL
TOBACCO GOLD
COPPER
WOOD BROWN
DK. WOOD BROWN
DK. APRICOT
RUSTONE
YELLOW
PARCHMENT
PALE RUSSET BROWN
LT. RUSSET BROWN
MED. RUSSET BROWN
DK. RUSSET BROWN

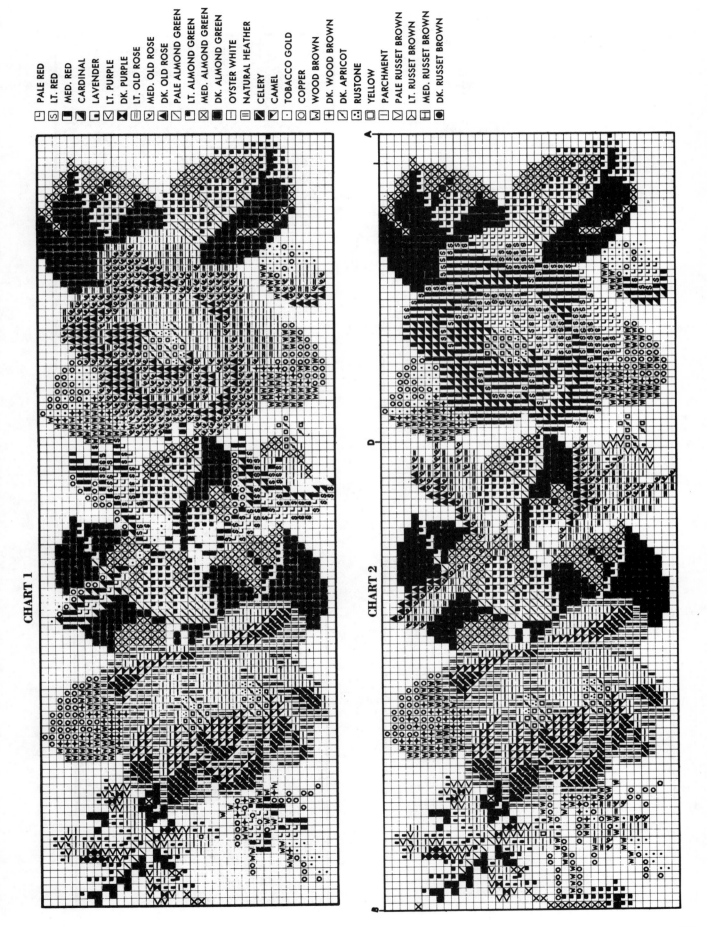

CHART 1

CHART 2

199

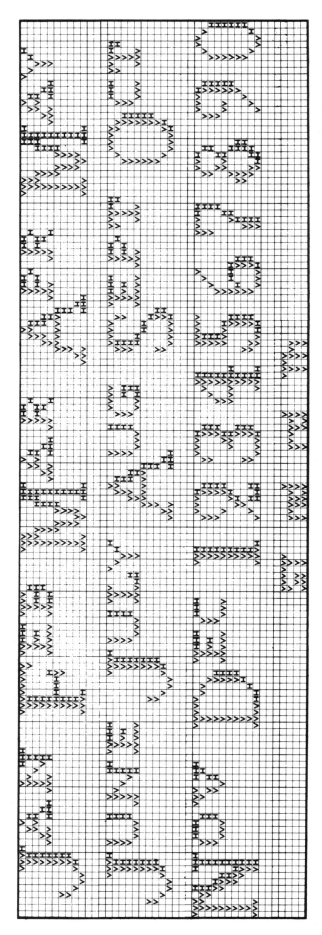

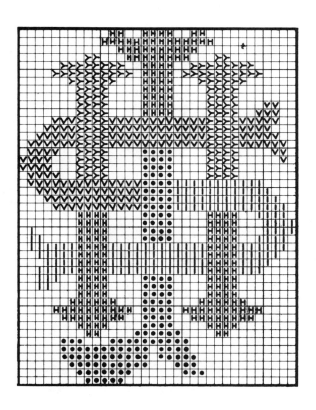

- ⊞ PARCHMENT
- ☑ PALE RUSSET BROWN
- ⊠ LT. RUSSET BROWN
- ⊞ MED. RUSSET BROWN
- ⬤ DK. RUSSET BROWN
- ■ DK. ALMOND GREEN
- ◨ DK. APRICOT
- ◻ YELLOW

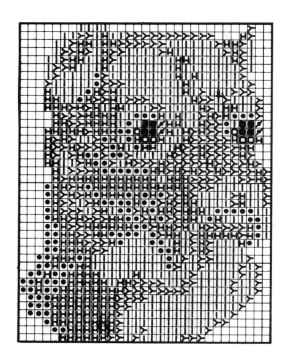

edge. Drop 2″ end. * Skip 3 sc to left on edge, bring needle up from wrong side through next st on edge. Pull yarn through forming scallop of yarn on edge. Insert needle from front to back through scallop. Pull yarn through forming loop. Insert needle from top to bottom through loop (see Fringe Detail); pull tight, forming knot on edge. Repeat from * around edge. Weave in ends on wrong side.

Row 2: Thread 4 strands of black yarn in large-eyed needle. Tie yarn in center of any scallop, leaving 3″ end. Working from right to left as before, * bring yarn up through next scallop and down through scallop just formed, forming a loop. Insert needle from top to bottom through loop; pull tight, forming knot. Repeat from * around, alternating one deep scallop with one scallop straight across. Finish off strands by tying knot and leaving 3″ of yarn hanging. Start new strands with a knot on next scallop, leaving 3″ of yarn hanging. Tie these ends together in a deep scallop and cut ends close.

Tassels: Finish each deep scallop with a tassel of yarn tied to center of scallop. To make tassel, wind several strands of yarn of different colors around a 3″ piece of cardboard 4 or 5 times. Slide a strand of yarn under one edge and knot it as tightly as possible to hold strands together. Cut through yarn on opposite edge. Wrap and tie a strand of yarn around tassel 1″ from top. Tie tassel to scallop by inserting threaded needle up through tassel, over scallop, then back through tassel. Knot yarn close to wound part of tassel; clip even with bottom of tassel.

TREE OF LIFE BEDSPREAD AND PILLOW SHAMS
Shown on pages 224–225

SIZE: Bedspread: 100″ × 104″; Sham 25″ × 35″.

EQUIPMENT: Masking tape. Pencil. Ruler. Scissors. Tapestry needles. Straight pins. Large embroidery hoop or frame. Sewing machine. Steam iron.

MATERIALS: Ecru Zweigart Florina fabric (100% viscose) $13\frac{1}{2}$ (or 14) threads-to-the-inch, 55″ wide, $6\frac{3}{4}$ yards (for bedspread and two pillow shams). Matching sewing thread. Paragon 3-ply Persian Yarn, 8.8-yard skeins, in colors listed in color key (number of skeins are given in parentheses). Lining fabric for pillow shams 48″ wide, $1\frac{1}{2}$ yards. Off-white wide hem facing for bedspread, $8\frac{3}{4}$ yards.

DIRECTIONS: From Florina fabric, cut one center panel for embroidery 55″ wide (the full width of fabric) and 102″ long. For each side piece, cut a panel 26″ wide and 102″ long. For two pillow shams, cut two pieces, each 26″ × 36″. Tape all raw edges of fabric to prevent raveling.

Bedspread: To Embroider: Work embroidery on the center panel only. The entire design is worked in cross-stitch; refer to "Four Methods of Cross-Stitching." Each cross-stitch is worked over two threads vertically and two threads horizontally. Each square on chart (pages 202–204) represents one cross stitch. Place area to be embroidered in hoop or frame.

To begin embroidery, leave end of yarn on back and work over it to secure; to end, run strand through stitches on back. Do not secure ends with knots. Use one strand of yarn in needle.

Mark the exact crosswise center of center panel, 23″ down from one 55″ edge (this will be the top). Begin cross-stitching at center point marked by arrow on chart. Follow chart and color key to work entire right half of design. Then, repeat design in reverse, omitting center row to complete design. Within the outlined areas, place initials (of husband and wife) and date, using chart below for alphabet and numbers. Then work the border across bottom where indicated and continue along sides up to top edge (there is no border across top).

When embroidery is complete, steam-press entire panel.

To Assemble: With right sides facing, pin and sew long edge of each side panel to each long edge of center panel, making $\frac{1}{2}$″ seams. Mark bottom edge of each side panel to round off; trim. Make a $1\frac{1}{2}$″ hem at top edge. With $\frac{1}{2}$″ seams and right sides facing, stitch hem facing along remaining edges. Press hem facing to wrong side; slip-stitch remaining edge of hem facing to wrong side of bedspread.

Pillow Sham: Work border as for bedspread all around each sham, $\frac{3}{4}''$ from raw edge. Steampress.

To Line and Assemble: For each, cut two pieces of lining fabric, each $26'' \times 24''$. Make $3''$ hem on one $26''$ edge of each lining piece. Overlap $5''$ of one piece along hemmed edge with the hemmed edge of the other piece; pin to hold in place. With right sides facing, pin and sew edges of sham front and lining together with $\frac{1}{2}''$ seams. Turn to right side. Topstitch all around sham $3\frac{1}{2}''$ in from seamed edges.

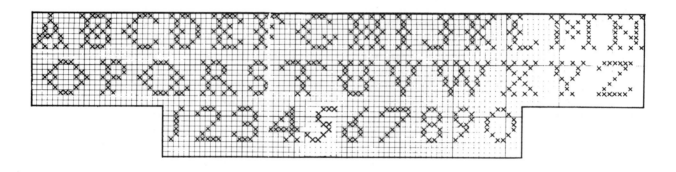

Note: Bedspread chart is divided into thirds: stitch from left to right of each chart (from top to bottom of design), leaving *no* extra space between sections of design.

203

Influenced by Russian folk dress, these peasanty clothes add just the right color and warmth to holidays or long, wintry nights. Woman's colorful blouse and floor-length pinafore dress are perfect for the holiday hostess.
Girl's linen apron is patterned with folk motifs; it's cute as can be when worn with a long, ruffled dress. Directions for blouse, pinafore, and girl's apron begin on page 157.

205

Tell the Christmas story in cross-stitch this year.
Each tiny creche figure (3¾" to 6" tall; Babe is 2" long)
is worked with just one strand of floss on a fabric that
counts 22 threads-to-the-inch. Backdrop, cross-stitched too,
gives the effect of looking out on a starry night.
Worked with DMC embroidery floss and pearl cotton on
Zweigart Hardanger cloth. For directions and charts, see page 162.

*Ornaments come in all shapes and sizes;
some carry little gifts, too. PEACE
is stitched on plump little sachets with
a variety of borders. Mix and match as you*

*please! All the letters in our alphabet
will fit within the simple borders of NOEL.
Tiny stockings and pockets of JOY are
gift holders. Directions on page 166.*

*Christmas colors are magnificent in cross-stitch
designs. Only one theme in two variations is used,
so the patterns work up quickly. Embroider with
six-strand embroidery floss on counted-thread cloth, then
sew squares to ribbon: nine squares make a great
tablecloth, three make a terrific table runner, or use
each separately for distinctive place mats!
Holiday Table Dressing, page 169.*

CRIB SET
Shown on page 226

SIZE: Coverlet, $22\frac{1}{2}'' \times 33''$ (without ruffle). Pillowcase, $10'' \times 12''$ (without ruffle).

EQUIPMENT: Scissors. Tape measure. Embroidery and sewing needles. Embroidery hoop (optional).

MATERIALS: Blue checked gingham, 7 squares-to-the-inch, $3\frac{1}{2}$ yards. DMC six-strand Embroidery Floss (8.7-yard skeins): 1 skein each orange #947, brown #780, royal blue #796; 2 skeins yellow #973; 4 skeins medium blue #322; 6 skeins medium green #469. White sewing thread. Unbleached muslin for pillow, $21'' \times 12\frac{1}{2}''$. Fiberfill for stuffing.

DIRECTIONS: Cut gingham fabric for coverlet top and lining, each $23'' \times 33\frac{1}{2}''$. Cut four strips, each $10\frac{1}{2}'' \times 58''$ for coverlet ruffle. Cut two gingham pieces for pillowcase, each $10\frac{1}{2}'' \times 12\frac{1}{2}''$; cut ruffle for pillowcase, $4'' \times 62''$.

Coverlet: Fold gingham for coverlet top in half twice to find center. Use four strands of floss in needle to work cross-stitch. Following directions for working cross-stitch on gingham under "Four Methods of Cross-Stitching", begin embroidering the tree design at center of gingham, starting at center of tree (arrows on chart). Following chart and color key on next page, complete cross-stitch tree and saying.

For cross-stitch border, measure 3" in from edge of fabric around entire coverlet top. Work solid row of green cross-stitches around entire coverlet. Skip one row of gingham checks; work a second row of solid cross-stitch in yellow within green border.

To assemble ruffle, stitch strips together, end to end, right sides facing, for length approximately $6\frac{1}{2}$ yards long; stitch ends of length together. Fold in half lengthwise and gather double raw edges with running stitches.

Keeping raw edges of ruffle out and flush with raw edges of embroidered piece, baste ruffle to right side of coverlet all around, adjusting gathers evenly. Stitch ruffle in place. Place gingham lining on top of embroidered piece, over ruffle; baste and stitch around with $\frac{1}{4}''$ seams, leaving a 6" opening for turning. Turn coverlet right side out and slip-stitch opening closed.

Pillowcase: Starting $\frac{3}{4}''$ up from one $12\frac{1}{2}''$ edge of gingham piece, work border as shown on chart, extending cross-stitch rows to within $\frac{1}{4}''$ from fabric edges (seam allowance). Work remainder of design as charted.

Fold strip for ruffle in half lengthwise. Using running stitch, gather strip for ruffled edge.

With right sides together and making $\frac{1}{4}''$ seams, stitch pillow front and back together around three sides, leaving open at bordered end. Having raw edges even and right sides together, stitch ruffle around pillowcase opening.

To make inner pillow, cut two pieces of muslin each $10\frac{1}{2}'' \times 12\frac{1}{2}''$. Stitch muslin pieces together, making $\frac{1}{4}''$ seams. Leave a 4" opening for turning. Turn case to right side; stuff firmly with fiberfill. Turn in raw edges and slip-stitch opening closed.

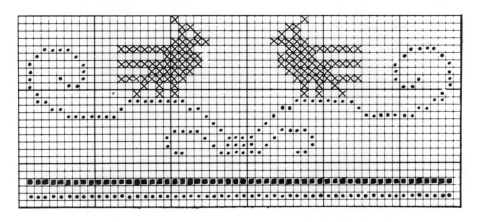

Under The Lovely Dreamland Tree

Are Many Happy Dreams For Thee

Sleep, Baby Sleep.

	Orange
V	Brown
◥	Royal Blue
■	Yellow
●	Medium Green
☒	Medium Blue

DELLA ROBBIA AFGHAN

Shown on page 223

SIZE: 50″ × 56″.

MATERIALS: Bernat Berella "4", 12 100-gram balls white, main color (MC), 3 balls dark leaf green #8864, contrasting color (CC). Bernat-Aero afghan hook size 6 mm (J). Bernat-Aero crochet hook size 5 mm (H). For embroidery: Bernat 1-2-3 Ply Persian-Type Yarn, 12½-yd. skeins, 2 skeins each of #096 light yellow, #092 dark yellow, #538 light orange, #534 dark orange, #833 medium leaf green, #335 light red; 3 skeins each #333 red, #332 dark red; 5 skeins each #836 light

• Dark Green	○ Light Orange
X Medium Leaf Green	╱ Dark Orange
◆ Light Green	● Light Red
G Dark Yellow	R Dark Red
Y Light Yellow	△ Red

green, #832 dark green. Bernat-Aero Quickpoint needle.

GAUGE: 4 sts = 1″; 7 rows = 2″ (afghan stitch).

AFGHAN ST: Row 1: Draw up a lp in 2nd ch from hook and in each ch, leaving all lps on hook. Work off lps as follows: Yo hook, draw through 1 lp, * yo, draw through 2 lps, repeat from * across. Lp that remains on hook counts as first st of next row.

Row 2: Sk first upright bar, draw up a lp in next upright bar and in each bar across, leaving all lps on hook. Work off lps as for row 1. Repeat row 2 for required length.

AFGHAN: CENTER SECTION: With afghan hook and MC, ch 110. Work even in afghan st on 110 sts for 110 rows. Sl st across last row. Do not end off.

Edging: Using crochet hook, ch 3, sc in corner sp, * sc in each row to next corner sp, sc, ch 2, sc in corner sp, sc in each of next 2 sts, (sk 1 st, sc in next 3 sts) 25 times sk 1 st, sc in each of last 6 sts, ch 2, sc in corner sp, repeat from * once, sl st in first ch of ch 3 at beg of rnd. End off.

EMBROIDERY: Following chart, embroider wreath in cross-stitch, using all 3 strands of embroidery yarn.

BORDER: Rnd 1: With crochet hook and CC, from right side, join yarn in upper right-hand corner, ch 3, 2 dc, ch 2, 3 dc in corner sp, * sk next 2 sts, 3 dc in next st (shell), repeat from * to next corner sp, 3 dc, ch 2, 3 dc in corner sp, repeat from first * around, end sl st in top of ch 3 at beg of rnd—29 shells across each end, 38 shells across sides.

Rnd 2: Ch 3, turn, 2 dc in first sp, * 3 dc in each sp to ch-2 corner sp, 3 dc, ch 2, 3 dc in corner sp, repeat from * around, sl st in top of ch 3.

Rnd 3: Ch 3, turn, 2 dc in next sp, 3 dc in each

Cross-Stitch on Afghan Stitch

sp, 3 dc, ch 2, 3 dc in each corner sp around. Join; end off.

Rnd 4: Turn. Join MC in same place as sl st, ch 3, 2 dc in next sp, 3 dc in each sp, 3 dc, ch 2, 3 dc in each corner sp around. Join.

Rnds 5–26: Continue to work shell pat in MC for 22 more rnds. Join, ch 3, turn each rnd. At end of rnd 26, end off. Turn.

Rnd 27 (right side): Join CC in any corner sp, ch 3, dc, ch 2, 2 dc in corner sp, dc in each dc around, 2 dc, ch 2, 2 dc in each corner sp. Join in top of ch 3.

Rnd 28: Ch 3, turn, dc in each dc around, 2 dc, ch 2, 2 dc in each corner sp. Join in top of ch 3.

Rnd 29: Ch 1, turn, sc in 3rd dc before corner, ** 10 dc in corner sp, * sk next 2 sts, sc in next sk, sk next 2 sts, 7 dc in next st, repeat from * to next corner, repeat from ** around. Join; end off.

BLUE LACE AFGHAN
Shown on page 227

SIZE: About 60″ square.

MATERIALS: 4-ply Knitting worsted weight acrylic yarn, 12 4-oz. balls white, 2 balls each of crystal blue and cadet blue, 1 ball each of baby blue and dark blue. 20″ aluminum afghan hook or flexible hook size G. Plastic crochet hook size G. Tapestry needles. Cardboard scrap, 5″ wide.

GAUGE: 4 sts = 1″; 7 rows = 2″.

AFGHAN: With white and afghan hook, ch 234.

Row 1: Pull up a lp in 2nd ch from hook and in each ch across, keeping all lps on hook.

To Work Lps Off: Yo hook, pull through first lp, * yo hook, pull through next 2 lps, repeat from * across until 1 lp remains. Lp that remains on hook always counts as first st of next row.

Row 2: Keeping all lps on hook, pull up a lp under 2nd vertical bar and under each vertical bar across. Work lps off as before. Repeat row 2 until there are 203 rows. Sl st loosely under 2nd vertical bar and in each vertical bar across. End off. Weave in ends on reverse side. Steam top and bottom edges lightly so that edges lie flat.

EMBROIDERY: Following chart and color key,

Continued on page 235

Nautical motifs brighten the front and sleeves of a natural wool pullover for men or women. Designs, worked in red and black cross-stitch, include sailboats, anchors, shells, fishnets and Portuguese lanterns. Directions for knitting and embroidery begin on page 171.

Butterfly pillow in fresh outdoor colors is worked over Penelope canvas on linen-like fabric. Twisted cord and tassels complete pillow measuring 14" × 15". Butterfly can also decorate a dress or T-shirt. Simply follow embroidery directions for pillow, using clothing fabric instead. Directions on page 173.

Embroidered gauze makes
perfect peasantries:
A beautiful bell-sleeved
blouse tops any softly wrapped
skirt. Brightly cross-
stitched flowers complement
crocheted waistband,
panels and edgings.
Bell-sleeve Crochet, page 187.
Lovely, long-sleeved top
with crocheted back is shown
with loose drawstring pant,
but it would pair well with
a long skirt, too. Crocheted
borders enhance delicate
floral cross-stitchery.
Long-Sleeve Crochet,
see page 174.

As a blouse or tunic, here's a great way to borrow dash from a Russian cossack! Tie-on belt cinches the waist, creates the soft, peasanty gathers. The shawl for all seasons is richly bordered in cross-stitch, edged with a flirtation of lace, and lined with a sprightly calico print. Don't just put the peasant look in your closet! Let it pattern pillows, too—like the ones shown here. Select shimmering pearl cotton for the embroidery and even-weave fabric for the background. Directions for Peasant Cross-Stitch begin on page 189.

Patterns of snowflakes on children's crochets
are just the thing to greet the winter.
Boy's sweater is worked in single crochet
with zippered front; snowflakes are
embroidered in cross-stitch on yoke and
sleeves. Girl's drawstring skirt
with suspenders is also single crochet
with snowflake embroidery. It pairs
with a pretty puff-sleeve blouse in
double crochet. Directions for all
begin on page 194.

Baby is snug for the
winter in his snow-
flake bunting, worked
in single crochet
with cross-stitch
snowflake patterns.
Bunting has front
zipper, attached hood.
Directions on page 193.

*This 19th-century carriage throw is embroidered in
Victorian style with flowers, animals, religious symbol,
and date. Each section is worked in afghan crochet,
embroidered with cross-stitch, and then joined for the afghan.
Directions on page 196.*

*Crochet a holiday
afghan in Bernat's
Berella "4" yarn and
embroider with a
sumptuous Della Robbia
wreath. 50" × 56".
Directions on
page 213.*

A handsome Tree of Life motif is worked in the rich colors of a Colonial palette. Recreate this traditional motif for a bedspread that will become a family heir-

loom. To stitch, just count the threads on the ecru even-weave background. Repeat the graceful scalloped frame on pillow shams as well. Directions on page 201.

A magical tree with heart-shaped leaves gives the sampler look to a ruffled coverlet for baby. Simple sentiment tells a bedtime story. Matching ruffled pillow repeats a bird motif from the coverlet. Embroidery is worked all in cross-stitch using DMC floss. Coverlet is 22½″ × 33″, plus ruffled edge. Directions on page 211.

Cuddle up through the long winter nights with an elegant afghan, made all in one piece of frosty white yarn, with cross-stitched "lace" patterns in four blues, and an all-around fringe. Blue Lace Afghan, page 214.

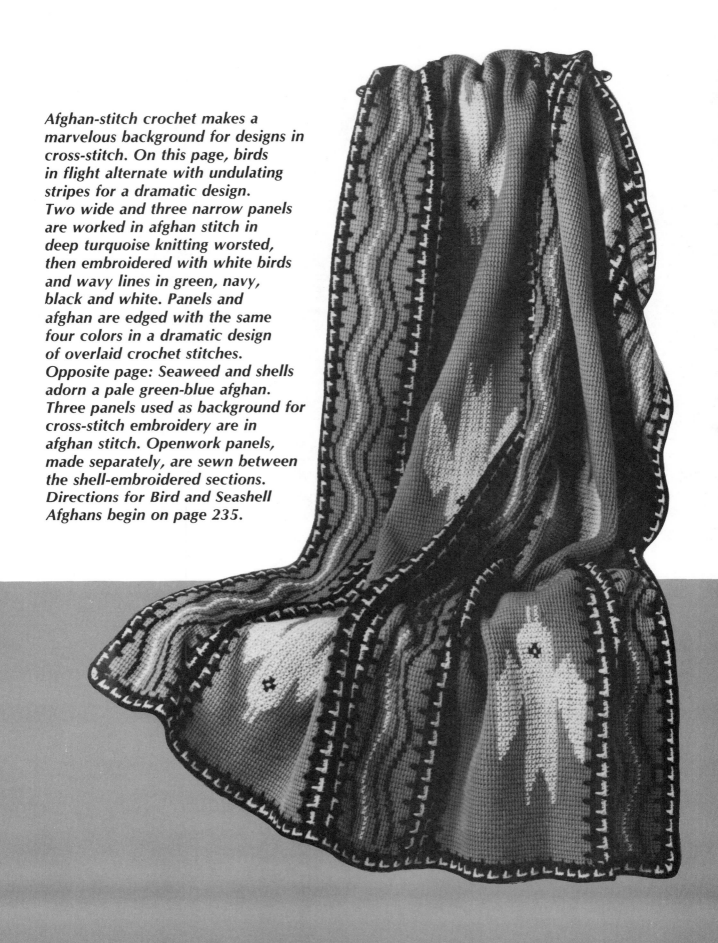

Afghan-stitch crochet makes a marvelous background for designs in cross-stitch. On this page, birds in flight alternate with undulating stripes for a dramatic design. Two wide and three narrow panels are worked in afghan stitch in deep turquoise knitting worsted, then embroidered with white birds and wavy lines in green, navy, black and white. Panels and afghan are edged with the same four colors in a dramatic design of overlaid crochet stitches. Opposite page: Seaweed and shells adorn a pale green-blue afghan. Three panels used as background for cross-stitch embroidery are in afghan stitch. Openwork panels, made separately, are sewn between the shell-embroidered sections. Directions for Bird and Seashell Afghans begin on page 235.

American folk art motifs—stylized flowers, animals, birds, a charming couple—give this coverlet its delightful air. Designs are cross-stitched in red and two blues on white squares of afghan-stitch crochet. Folk Art Afghan, page 240.

Our favorite morning glory, "Heavenly Blue," brightens parchment-colored squares crocheted in afghan stitch. Embroidered blocks alternate checkerboard fashion with solid olive-green squares. See Morning Glories, page 246.

Dramatic Eagle Afghan is crocheted, with
a cross-stitch center motif and border.
Entire afghan is 72" × 86", plus fringe. Made in three
separate panels. See Eagle Afghan directions, page 243.

*Reminiscent of Florentine needlepoint, afghan
repeats shaded motif in four colors. Design is worked in
cross-stitch on an afghan-crochet background, either in one piece
or in panels. Size is 54" × 72". Directions for Florentine Afghan, page 246.*

*Stylized tulips
are lavishly
sprinkled on a
soft afghan and
pillows. Pillow,
15" square, is crocheted front and back,
while afghan, 50" × 66", is worked in panels,
then both are embroidered in cross-stitch.
Turn to page 248 for directions.*

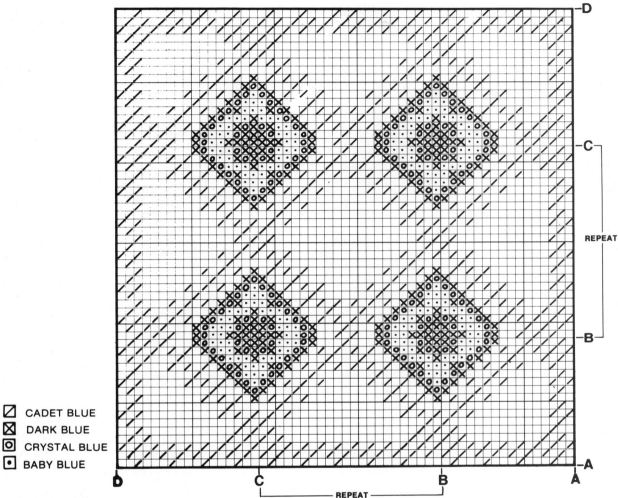

D **C** **B** **REPEAT** **A**

- ⊘ CADET BLUE
- ⊠ DARK BLUE
- ⊙ CRYSTAL BLUE
- ⊡ BABY BLUE

REPEAT

Continued from page 214

embroider design in cross-stitch, following directions in "Four Methods of Cross-Stitching." Working horizontally, work from A to B, repeat from B to C 9 times, work from C to D. Working vertically, work from A to B, repeat from B to C 7 times, work from C to D.

FINISHING: With white and crochet hook, work 1 row of sc around afghan, working 1 sc in each st or row and 3 sc in each corner. Join with sl st in first sc. End off.

FRINGE: Wrap crystal blue around 5″ cardboard; cut at one end. Using 2 strands tog, fold strands in half, insert hook from wrong side through sc on edge, draw fold through, draw ends through loop. Tighten knot. * Skip 1 sc, knot a fringe in next sc, repeat from * around. Trim fringe evenly.

BIRD AFGHAN
Shown on page 228

SIZE: 52″ × 72″.

MATERIALS: Knitting worsted, 10 4-oz. skeins turquoise, Main Color (MC); 2 skeins white (A); 1 skein each of kelly green (B), light navy (C) and black (D). Afghan hook size G or No. 6. Tapestry needle.

GAUGE: 9 sts = 2″; 3 rows = 1″.

AFGHAN: WIDE STRIP (make 2): With MC, ch 56. **Row 1:** Keeping all lps on hook, sk first ch from hook (lp on hook is first st), pull up a lp in each ch across—56 lps.

To Work Lps Off: Yo hook, pull through first

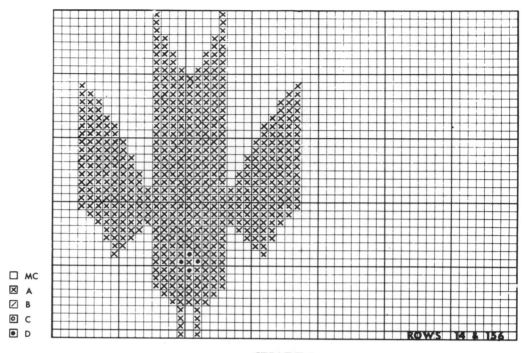

□ MC
☒ A
☑ B
◉ C
◉ D

ROWS 14 & 156

CHART 1

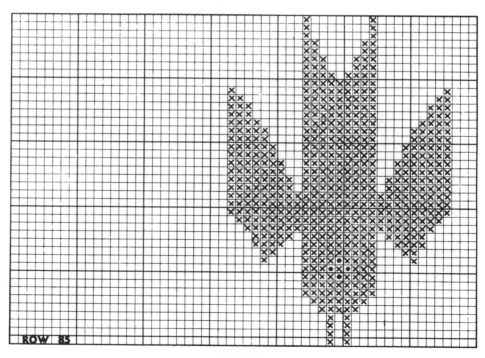

ROW 85

CHART 2

lp, * yo hook, pull through next 2 lps, repeat from * until 1 lp remains. Lp that remains on hook always counts as first st of next row.

Row 2: Keeping all lps on hook, sk first vertical bar, pull up a lp in next vertical bar and under each vertical bar across. Work lps off as before. Repeat row 2 until 209 rows from start. Sl st in each vertical bar across. End off. Check gauge; piece should measure 12½" wide, 70" long.

NARROW STRIP (make 3): With MC, ch 24. Work same as for wide strip. Check gauge; piece should measure 5½" wide.

EMBROIDERY: Note: Each square on charts is one stitch; each row on charts is one row of afghan st (lps pulled up on hook and worked off).

Wide Strips: Beg on row 14, embroider Chart 1 in cross st; beg on row 85, embroider Chart 2; beg on row 156, embroider Chart 1.

Narrow Strips: Beg on row 2, work and repeat the 22 rows of Chart 3, end on row 208.

EDGING: Row 1: With C, make lp on hook. From right side, working on side edge of wide strip, * sc in each of 3 rows, long dc under bar of st 2 rows below edge, repeat from * across. End off.

Row 2: With B, make lp on hook. From right side, sc in back lp of each of 2 sc, * long dc inserting hook at base of next sc, sc in back lp of next 3 sts, repeat from * across. End off.

Row 3: With A, make lp on hook. From right side, sc in back lp of first sc, work from first * to 2nd * of row 2. End off.

Half Cross-Stitch on Afghan Stitch

Cross-Stitch on Afghan Stitch

Row 4: With D, make lp on hook. From right side, sc in each of 4 sc, work from first * to 2nd * of row 2. End off.

Work same edging on each side edge of wide strips, each side edge of one narrow strip (center strip), one side edge of remaining 2 narrow strips.

Join Strips: With D, working through back lps, weave a wide strip to edges of center narrow strip having birds face opposite direction. Weave a narrow strip to each wide strip.

Work border same as edging around afghan, increasing at corners.

SEASHELL AFGHAN
Shown on page 229

SIZE: 46" × 62".

MATERIALS: Bucilla Winsom, 13 2-oz. skeins blue (A), 1 skein in each of winter white (B), brown (C), green (D), melon (E). Afghan hook size J/10 (6 mm). Crochet hook size H/8 (5 mm).

GAUGE: 4 sts = 1"; 3 rows = 1".

AFGHAN STITCH PANEL (make 3): With A and afghan hook, ch 40.

Row 1: Keeping all lps on hook, pull up a lp in 2nd ch from hook and in each ch across.

To Work Lps Off: Yo hook, pull through first lp, * yo hook, pull through next 2 lps, repeat from

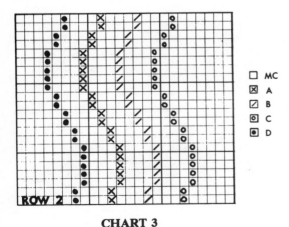

CHART 3

☐ MC
☒ A
☑ B
◉ C
◉ D

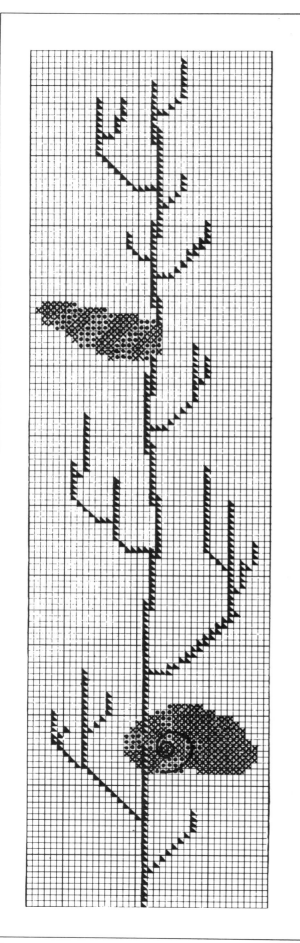

□ A
☒ B
◈ C
◪ D
⊡ E

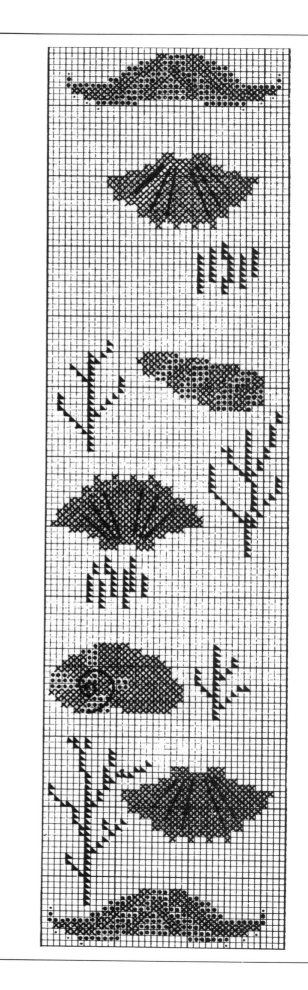

Fig. 1

* across until 1 lp remains on hook. Lp that remains on hook always counts as first st of next row.

Fig. 2

Row 2: Keeping all lps on hook, sk first vertical bar (lp on hook is first st), pull up a lp under next vertical bar and under each vertical bar across—40 sts. Work lps off as before.

Fig. 3

Repeat row 2 until there are 181 rows, about 60″ from beginning. Mark first row of panel for lower edge.

Last Row: Work sl st in each vertical bar across. End off. Block each panel to 10″ × 62″.

OPENWORK PANEL (make 2): With A and size H hook, ch 34 loosely.

Row 1 (right side): Sc in 2nd ch from hook, * ch 1, sk next ch, sc in next ch, repeat from * across—33 sts.

Row 2: Ch 4, turn, sk first ch-1 sp, dc in front lp of next sc, * ch 1, sk next ch-1 sp, dc in front lp of next sc, repeat from * across—33 sts; 16 sps.

Row 3: Ch 1, turn, sc in front lp of first dc, * ch 1, sk ch-1 sp, sc in front lp of next dc, repeat from * across, end ch 1, sk 1 ch of turning ch 4, sc in next ch. Repeat rows 2 and 3 until there are 121 rows, about 60″ from beg, end with row 3. End off. Mark first row for lower edge. Block each panel to 8″ × 62″.

EMBROIDERY: Beg on 16th row from lower edge, embroider one panel in cross-stitch following chart for center panel. Embroider coiled line on lower shell in outline stitch with C. Beg on 13th row from lower edge, embroider two panels in cross-stitch following chart for side panels. Embroider coiled line as for center panel. Embroider straight lines in E. Work French knots with E around outer curves of top and bottom shells. Note: See "Embroidery Basics."

FINISHING: Arrange panels as shown in illustration. With A, sew panels tog from right side, using overhand st and sewing 2 rows of openwork panel to 3 rows of afghan st panel, keeping seam as elastic as crochet fabric.

With A and size H hook, from right side, work 1 row sc around entire afghan, keeping work flat and working 3 sc in each corner; join with sl st in first sc. End off.

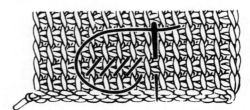

Half Cross-Stitch on Afghan Stitch

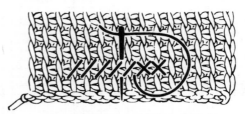

Cross-Stitch on Afghan Stitch

Outline Stitch

French Knot

FOLK ART AFGHAN

Shown on page 230

SIZE: 48″ × 66″.

MATERIALS: Bernat Berella 4, 13 4-oz. balls white. For embroidery, Bernat Berella Sportspun, 1 2-oz. ball each of red, light blue and medium blue. Bernat-Aero afghan hook size 4 mm (F). Tapestry needles.

GAUGE: 9 sts = 2″; 4 rows = 1″.

AFGHAN STITCH SQUARE (make 12): Ch 67.

Row 1: Keeping all lps on hook, sk first ch from hook, pull up a lp in 2nd ch from hook and in each ch across—67 lps.

To Work Lps Off: Yo hook, pull through first lp, * yo hook, pull through next 2 lps, repeat from * across until 1 lp remains. lp that remains on hook always counts as first st of next row.

Row 2: Keeping all lps on hook, sk first vertical bar (lp on hook is first st), pull a lp under next vertical bar and under each vertical bar across. Work lps off as before. Repeat row 2 until there are 60 rows. Sl st in each vertical bar across. End off. Block square.

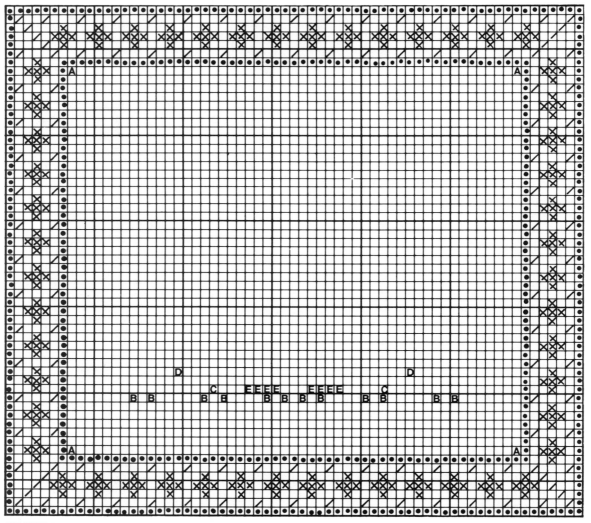

CHART 1

⊠ **Red**
⊡ **Med. Blue**
⟋ **Lt. Blue**

EMBROIDERY: Embroider squares in cross-stitch before assembling them. Following Chart 1 for border, work border around each square. Beg at lower right-hand corner of chart and square, work first medium blue st on 2nd row of square and 2nd st. Following Chart 2, make 4 squares for corners of afghan, beginning at each A on Chart 1 for each corner square.

Following Chart 3, make 2 squares for center top and center bottom of afghan, beginning first row of sts at B on chart 1.

Following Chart 4, make 2 squares for center of afghan, 2nd and 3rd rows, beginning first row of sts from C to C on chart 1.

Following Chart 5, make 2 squares for right edge, 2nd row, and left edge, 3rd row, beginning first

CHART 2

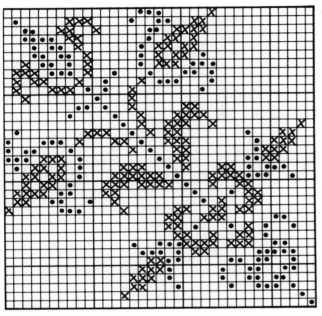

⊠ **Red**
⊙ **Med. Blue**
⧄ **Lt. Blue**

CHART 3

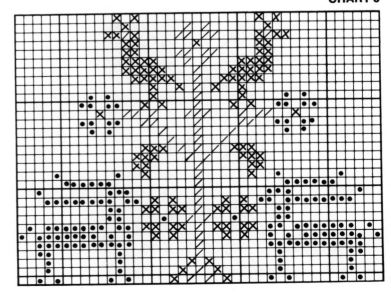

row of **skirt** sts from D to D on chart 1. Mouths on Charts 5 and 6 are small straight red sts. Following Chart 6, make 2 squares for right edge, 3rd row, and left edge, 2nd row, working first row of feet at E on Chart 1.

JOINING SQUARES: See diagram for joining squares.

First Row: Join yarn in upper left corner of square 1, * ch 6, sk 3 rows on left side of square, sc in next row, repeat from * to lower left corner of square, ch 4, sc in lower right corner of square 2; ** ch 3, sc in next ch-6 lp, ch 3, sk 3 rows on right side edge of square 2, repeat from ** to top, ch 4, sl st in joining st at top of square 1; end off.

CHART 4

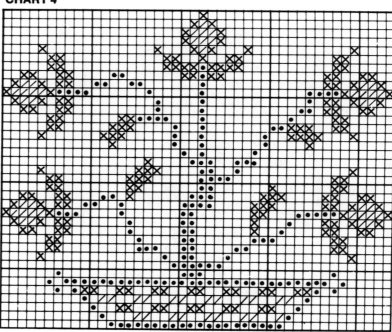

CHART 5

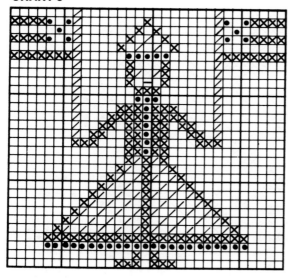

☒ **Red**
⊙ **Med. Blue**
⧄ **Lt. Blue**

12	11	10
9	8	7
6	5	4
3	2	1

Join yarn in upper left corner of square 2, work lps and join square 3 to square 2, as first 2 squares were joined. In same way, join next 3 rows of squares.

JOINING ROWS: Join yarn in upper right corner of square 1. * Ch 6, sk 3 sts on top edge of square, sc in next st, repeat from * across top of square, end 2 sts from corner, ch 6, sc in ch-4 lp between squares, repeat from first * across, end sc in left corner of square 3, ch 4, sc in lower left corner of square 6. ** Ch 3, sc in next ch-6 lp, ch 3, sk 3 sts on lower edge of square, sc in next st, repeat from ** across to lower right corner of square 4, ch 4, sl st in upper right corner of square 1. End off.

CHART 6

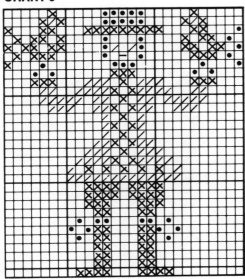

Join 3rd and 2nd rows of squares tog in same way. Join 4th and 3rd rows of squares tog in same way.

FINISHING: From right side, work 1 row of sc around outer edge of afghan, working 1 sc in each st or row, 4 sc in each ch-4 lp, and 3 sc in each corner. Working from left to right, work reverse sc in each sc around.

EAGLE AFGHAN

Shown on page 232

SIZE: 72″ × 86″, plus fringe.
MATERIALS: Bear Brand De Luxe Knitting Worsted, 30 4-oz. skeins white. 14″ afghan hook size 3 or F. DMC tapestry wool, 15-yd. skeins (see color key on page 245 for amounts). Tapestry needle.
GAUGE: 6 sts = 1″; 5 rows = 1″.
AFGHAN ST: To work panels see directions under "Afghan Stitch Basics."
AFGHAN: Center Panel: Ch 160. Work in afghan st on 160 sts for 404 rows. End off.
Side Panel (make 2): Ch 130. Work in afghan st on 130 sts for 404 rows. End off.
FINISHING: Mark row 131 of panel for first row of embroidery (bottom row of chart, next page). Mark 3rd st in from left edge of panel as left edge of chart. Embroider center panel in cross-stitch (see "Four Methods of Cross-Stitching") before joining panels.

From wrong side, sl st panels tog, working in back lp of edge sts. Work 1 row sc around entire afghan.

Embroider border in gold (one 4-oz. skein of knitting worsted can be used for border). Start corner design (Chart 1) in 5th row up and 5th st in from any corner. Work corner design, then repeat scroll design (Chart 2) across to 12th st from next corner, work corner design (point of corner design points to corner of afghan).

Fringe Edging: From right side, join yarn in lower corner of afghan. Ch 3; * pull up a ½″ lp in each of next 4 sc, yo hook and through 5 lps on hook, ch 3, repeat from * across lower edge, end

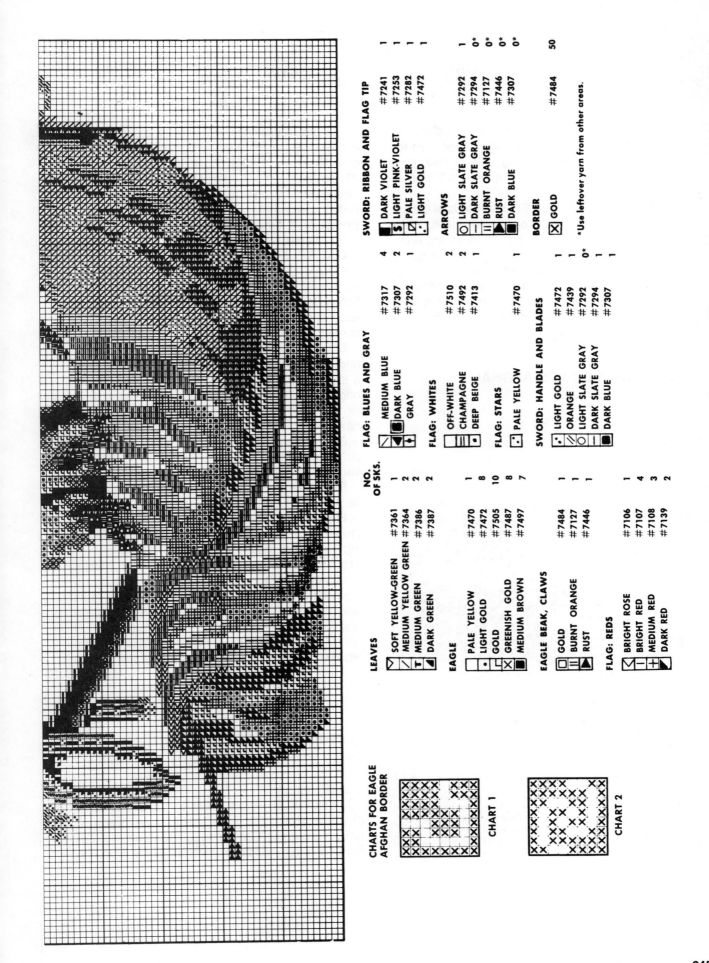

NO. OF SKS.

LEAVES

▽	SOFT YELLOW-GREEN	#7361	1
╱	MEDIUM YELLOW GREEN	#7364	2
T	MEDIUM GREEN	#7386	2
◤	DARK GREEN	#7387	2

EAGLE

	PALE YELLOW	#7470	1
•	LIGHT GOLD	#7472	8
L	GOLD	#7505	10
X	GREENISH GOLD	#7487	8
■	MEDIUM BROWN	#7497	7

EAGLE BEAK, CLAWS

□	GOLD	#7484	1
=	BURNT ORANGE	#7127	1
▲	RUST	#7446	1

FLAG: REDS

∨	BRIGHT ROSE	#7106	1
—	BRIGHT RED	#7107	4
+	MEDIUM RED	#7108	3
◤	DARK RED	#7139	2

FLAG: BLUES AND GRAY

╱	MEDIUM BLUE	#7317	4
▼	DARK BLUE	#7307	2
◆	GRAY	#7292	1

FLAG: WHITES

‖	OFF-WHITE	#7510	2
	CHAMPAGNE	#7492	2
•	DEEP BEIGE	#7413	1

FLAG: STARS

∴	PALE YELLOW	#7470	1

SWORD: HANDLE AND BLADES

∴	LIGHT GOLD	#7472	1
╱	ORANGE	#7439	1
O	LIGHT SLATE GRAY	#7292	1
—	DARK SLATE GRAY	#7294	0*
■	DARK BLUE	#7307	1

SWORD: RIBBON AND FLAG TIP

■	DARK VIOLET	#7241	1
S	LIGHT PINK-VIOLET	#7253	1
◢	PALE SILVER	#7282	1
∴	LIGHT GOLD	#7472	1

ARROWS

O	LIGHT SLATE GRAY	#7292	2
I	DARK SLATE GRAY	#7294	2
▲	BURNT ORANGE	#7127	1
■	RUST	#7446	
	DARK BLUE	#7307	1

BORDER

X	GOLD	#7484	50

*Use leftover yarn from other areas.

CHARTS FOR EAGLE AFGHAN BORDER

CHART 1

CHART 2

ch 3, sl st in corner. End off. Repeat edging on top edge of afghan. Cut 10″ strands of yarn for fringe. Holding 4 strands tog, fold in half, knot around ch-3 loop. Repeat in every ch-3 loop at both ends.

Embroidery: Refer to "Four Methods of Cross-Stitching" to cross-stitch on afghan stitch. Work eagle following color key and chart where numbers and amounts of yarn are given. Scraps of yarn may be used for the embroidery providing you have a sufficient amount of yarn to embroider all of the area indicated on the chart by the symbol for that color. (One yard works about 25 cross-stitches.)

MORNING GLORIES AFGHAN
Shown on page 231

SIZE: About 45″ × 72″.
MATERIALS: Bernat Sesame (2-oz. pull pouches), 15 Parchment (A), 9 Lt. Olive (B), 6 Olive (C). For embroidery, Bernat Tapestria (12½-yd. skeins), 4 skeins R1653 (Royal), 3 each R1656 (Horizon Blue), R1984 (Avocado), R1986 (Medium Olive) and R1362 (Dark Rust), 2 each R1657 (Robin Blue), R1658 (Blue Mist) and R1988 (Pale Olive), and 1 each R1096 (Goldenrod) and R1428 (White). Bernat-Aero afghan hook size 5 mm (H). Bernat-Aero crochet hook size 5 mm (H). Tapestry needle.

GAUGE: 5 sts = 1″; 4 rows = 1″.
SQUARE (make 18 A and 17 B): With afghan hook, ch 33. Work even in afghan st (see "Afghan Stitch Basics") on 33 sts for 32 rows. Work sc in each st and row around square and 3 sc in each corner. Sl st in first sc.

Edging: Rnd 1: From right side, with crochet hook, join C in any corner sc, (yo hook, draw up a lp in same st) twice, yo and through 5 lps on hook (puff st), ch 1, * puff st in next sc, ch 1, ** sk 1 sc, puff st in next sc, ch 1, repeat from ** to next corner, repeat from * around. Join. End off.

Rnd 2: Join A in any puff st, ch 1, sc in each puff st and in each sp between puff sts, 3 sc in each corner st. Join.

Rnd 3: Ch 1, sc in each st, 3 sc in each corner st. Join. End off.

FINISHING: Following chart, work design in cross-stitch (see "Four Methods of Cross-Stitching") on 18 A squares. Sew squares tog, checkerboard fashion, working in back lp only, having A squares in each corner and making afghan 5 squares wide and 7 squares long. Working in sc and working 1 sc in each st and in each joining and 3 sc in each corner, work 1 rnd each of A, B and C. End off. With C, work a cross-stitch at point where 4 squares are joined. Steam lightly.

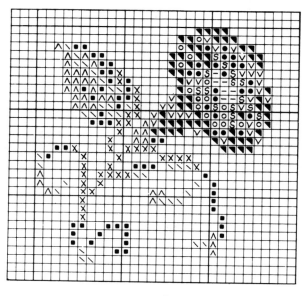

KEY TO CHART

◥ = R1653 Royal
V = R1656 Horizon Blue
O = R1657 Robin Blue
● = R1658 Blue Mist
\ = R1986 Medium olive
■ = R1984 Avocado
∧ = R1988 Pale olive
X = R1362 Dark Rust
– = R1096 Goldenrod
S = R1428 White

FLORENTINE AFGHAN
Shown on page 233

SIZE: About 54″ × 72″.
MATERIALS: Bernat Berella "4", 13 4-oz. balls of brown (MC); For embroidery, 1 ball each of Baby Yellow (A), Old Gold (B), Roman Gold (C), Pale Olive (D), Medium Olive (E), Baby Blue (F),

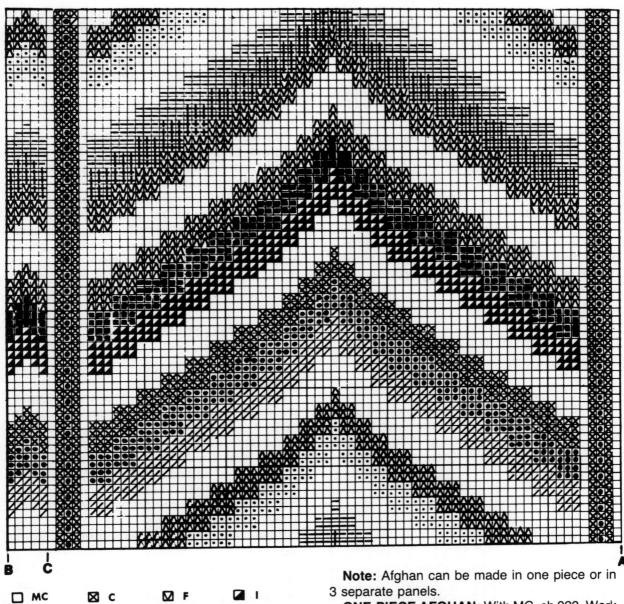

B   C

□ MC	⊠ C	☑ F	◩ I
◪ A	⊡ D	⊞ G	◪ J
◉ B	◩ E	⊟ H	◪ K

Wedgwood Blue (G), Marine Blue (H), Rose (I), China Rose (J), Burgundy (K). Bernat-Aero afghan hook size I (5½ mm). Crochet hook size H (5 mm). Tapestry needles.

GAUGE: 4 sts = 1″; 3 rows = 1″.

Note: Afghan can be made in one piece or in 3 separate panels.

ONE-PIECE AFGHAN: With MC, ch 223. Work in afghan stitch on 223 sts, following directions, under "Afghan Stitch Basics," until 221 rows have been completed. Work sl st in each vertical bar across. End off.

AFGHAN IN PANELS: With MC, ch 71. Work in afghan stitch on 71 sts, following directions, under "Afghan Stitch Basics," until 221 rows have been completed. Work sl st in each vertical bar across. End off. Make one more panel the same.

For center panel, with MC, ch 81. Work in afghan stitch on 81 sts until 221 rows have been completed. Work sl st in each vertical bar across. End off.

FINISHING: If afghan is made in panels, sew panels tog with MC having wider panel in center. With MC, work 1 row sc along each long edge of afghan. Following chart, embroider afghan in cross-stitch (See "Four Methods of Cross-Stitching"): work from A to B twice, then from A to C once. When top of chart is reached, repeat from bottom of chart twice, then repeat from bottom of chart until top of afghan is reached.

Steam. For fringe, cut strands of all colors 10". Using 2 strands of MC and 1 strand each of 3 colors, knot fringe in every other st across top and bottom of afghan, alternating the 4-color groups. Trim ends.

CROCHETED TULIP PILLOW
Shown on page 234

SIZE: 15" square.
MATERIALS: Pingouin Pingoland, 50-gram skeins: 6 skeins Ecru #853, 1 skein each Petrole #810, Jade #806, Vieux Rose #839, Eveque #823, and Bouteille #845. Crochet hook size K/10½ (6½ mm). Pillow form.
GAUGE: 5 sc = 2"; 6 rows = 2".

- ⊡ Eveque or Petrole
- ☑ Vieux Rose or Jade
- ☒ Bouteille

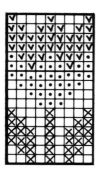

PILLOW

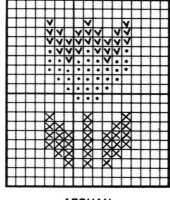

AFGHAN

PILLOW (make 2 pieces): With Ecru, ch 36.
Row 1: Sc in 2nd ch from hook, sc in each ch across—35 sc. Ch 1, turn.
Row 2: Sc in each sc across, ch 1, turn each row. Repeat row 2 until 47 rows have been completed. End off.
Embroidery: Using double strand of yarn, embroider tulips on one piece following chart (see "Four Methods of Cross-Stitching.") Center one tulip with bottom of stem on row 18. Place a tulip of contrasting color separated by 1 st on both sides of center tulip.
FINISHING: From right side, with Ecru, sc pieces tog on 3 sides, working sc in each st or row, 3 sc in each corner. Insert pillow form, close last side. With Bouteille, work 2 rows sc around pillow, working 3 sc in each corner. Join; end off.

CROCHETED TULIP AFGHAN
Shown on page 234

SIZE: 50" × 66".
MATERIALS: Pingouin Pingoland, 50-gram skeins: 32 skeins Ecru #853, 6 skeins Bouteille #845, 1 skein each of Petrole #810, Jade #806, Vieux Rose #839, and Eveque #823. Wooden crochet hook size M/13 (9 mm). Yarn needle.
GAUGE: 17 sc and 20 rows = 8" square.
AFGHAN: PANEL (make 5): With Ecru, ch 18.
Row 1: Sc in 2nd ch from hook, sc in each ch across—17 sc. Ch 1, turn.
Rows 2–20: Sc in each sc across. Ch 1, turn each row.
Row 21: Ch 3 (counts as 1 dc plus 1 ch), * sk next st, dc in next st, ch 1, repeat from * across, end dc in last st. Ch 1, turn.
Row 22: Sc in first dc, * sc in ch-1 sp, sc in next dc, repeat from * across, end sc in last sp, sc in 2nd ch of ch 3. Ch 1, turn. Repeat rows 2–22, 5 more times, then repeat rows 2–20 (7 sc squares of 20 rows separated by openwork row). Working down side of panel, work sc in each sc row, 2 sc in each dc row to bottom, 3 sc in corner, sc in each ch across lower edge, 3 sc in corner; work sc on 2nd side as for first side to top of panel; end off.

Embroidery: Using double strand of yarn, work cross-stitches on sc squares, following chart. Each square on chart represents one stitch. On two panels for sides of afghan, work design in first square at bottom, using Vieux Rose and Eveque for tulip. Skip 1 square, embroider 3rd square using Jade and Petrole for tulip. Embroider 5th square as for first square; embroider 7th square as for 3rd square. On one panel for center, beg in first square at bottom, work tulip colors in reverse (start with Jade and Petrole).

On 2nd panel, beg in 2nd square from bottom, work tulip with Jade and Petrole. Skip one square, embroider 4th square with Vieux Rose and Eveque. Embroider 6th square as for 2nd square. On 4th panel, work tulip colors in reverse (work 2nd square from bottom with Vieux Rose and Eveque).

TO JOIN PANELS: Hold 2 panels to be joined with right sides tog. From wrong side, join Ecru in first sc on side of panel facing you. Ch 2, sl st in first sc on 2nd panel. Insert hook down in first sc of 2nd panel and up in 2nd sc, work sl st. Insert hook down in 2nd sc and up in 3rd sc, work sl st. * Sk 1 sc on first panel, dc in next sc, work 2 sl sts on 2nd panel (inserting hook in same sc as last sl st and up in next sc twice), repeat from * across, end dc in last sc on first panel. End off. Join all panels in same way.

BORDER: Rnd 1: With Ecru, from right side, work dc, ch 1 pattern all around afghan, working dc, ch 3, dc in each corner st. Join; end off.

Rnds 2–5: With Bouteille, work 4 rnds sc, working sc in each st, 3 sc in each corner. Join; end off.

Rnds 6–9: With Ecru, work 4 more rnds sc. Join; end off.

EMBROIDERY BASICS

Equipment and Material

SELECTING YOUR MATERIAL: The appearance of your work is greatly influenced by the materials that you choose. You can make a delicate piece of work with fragile fabric and a fine thread, or translate the identical design onto coarser fabric, using a heavier thread. The needle to use with each yarn or floss should have an eye large enough to accommodate the yarn, but not larger than needed. Embroidery needles are rather short and have a long, slender eye. They are readily available in sizes 1 to 10; the higher numbers are finest. Some types of embroidery traditionally use a certain yarn or floss, while others technically require a specific kind. Crewel wool, for example, is a fine, twisted 2-ply wool yarn used in traditional crewel.

NEEDLES: Keep a good selection of needles on hand and protect them by storing them in a needle case.

SCISSORS: You will need proper scissors. Embroidery scissors should be small, with narrow, pointed blades and must be sharp. Protect the blade points by keeping them in a sheath.

FRAMES/HOOPS: Embroidery is usually worked in a frame. With the material held tautly and evenly, your stitches are more likely to be neat and accurate than if the fabric were held in the hand while working. Many embroidery hoops and frames are equipped with stands or clamps to hold the embroidery piece and leave both your hands free.

THREADS: Before you begin work on a piece of embroidery, arrange a system for keeping your threads handy and colors neatly separated. Cut skeins into convenient sewing lengths—18″ or 20″ is usually best, as longer threads may become frayed. Place each strand between the pages of a book. Allow one end to extend beyond the edge of the page. Fold the other end back and forth on the page, or loosely braid all colors to be used together, pulling the end from the braid as each color is used.

Six-strand embroidery floss can be separated into one, two, or more strands for working in fine stitches. To separate strands after cutting thread length, count the desired number of strands and carefully pull them out, holding the remainder apart to prevent tangling and knotting. Piles of wool yarn can also be separated in the same manner for a finer thread.

Basic Embroidery Tips

THREADING THE NEEDLE: To thread yarn or floss through the needle eye, double it over the end of the needle and slip it off, holding it tightly as close as possible to the fold. Push the eye of the needle down over the folded end and pull the yarn through.

TO BEGIN A STITCH: Start your embroidery with two or three tiny running stitches on back of fabric toward the starting point, then take a tiny backstitch and begin. Do not make knots when beginning or ending stitches.

TO END A COLOR: Fasten off the thread when ending each motif, rather than carrying it to another motif. Pass the end of the thread through the last few stitches on the wrong side, or take a few tiny backstitches.

TO REMOVE EMBROIDERY: When a mistake has been made, run a needle, eye first, under the stitches. Pull the embroidery away from the fabric; cut carefully with scissors pressed hard against the needle. Pick out the cut portion of the embroidery. Catch loose ends of the remaining stitches on back by pulling the ends under the stitches with a crochet hook.

TO FINISH: When your embroidered piece is completed, finish off the back neatly by running ends into the back of the work and clipping off any excess strands. If wool embroidery or needlepoint is not really soiled but needs just a little freshening, simply brushing over the surface with a clean cloth dipped in carbon tetrachloride or another good cleaning fluid may be satisfactory. This will brighten and return colors to their original look. If fabric is soiled, wash gently. Embroideries made of colorfast threads and washable fabrics can be laundered without fear of harming them. Wash with mild soap or detergent and warm water, swishing it through the water gently—do not rub. Rinse in clear water without wringing or squeezing. When completely rinsed, lift from the water and lay on a clean towel; lay another towel on top and roll up loosely. When the embroidery is sufficiently dry, press as described below.

Finishing Techniques

FABRIC EMBROIDERY: Better results will be obtained by blocking rather than pressing an embroidered piece for a picture or hanging. However, articles that are hemmed, such as tablecloths or runners, should be pressed; blocking would damage the edge of the fabric. To press your embroidered piece, use a well-padded surface and steam iron, or regular iron and damp cloth. Embroideries that have been worked in a frame will need very little pressing. If the embroidery was done in the hand it will no doubt be quite wrinkled and may need dampening. Sprinkle it to dampen and roll loosely in a clean towel. Embroidery should always be pressed lightly so that the stitching will not be flattened into the fabric. Place the embroidered piece face down on the padded surface and press from the center outward. For embroidery that is raised from the surface of the background, use extra thick, soft padding, such as a thick blanket.

After blocking or pressing, an embroidered picture should be mounted right away to prevent creasing.

TO BLOCK: Using needle and colorfast thread, follow the thread of the fabric and take $\frac{1}{4}''$ stitches to mark guidelines around the entire picture, designating the exact area where the picture will fit into the rabbet of the frame. The border of plain linen extending beyond the embroidery in a framed picture is approximately $1\frac{1}{4}''$ at sides and top and $1\frac{1}{2}''$ at bottom. In order to have sufficient fabric around the embroidered design for blocking and mounting, $3''$ or $4''$ of fabric should be left around the embroidered section. Now, matching corners, obtain the exact centers of the four sides and mark these centers with a few stitches.

If the picture is soiled, it should be washed, but it should be blocked immediately after washing. In preparation, cover a drawing board or soft wood bread board with a piece of brown paper held in place with thumbtacks, and draw the exact original size of the fabric on the brown paper. Be sure linen is not pulled beyond its original size when the measurements are taken. (Embroidery sometimes pulls fabric slightly out of shape.) Check drawn rectangle to make sure corners are square.

Wash embroidery; let drip a minute. Place embroidery right side up on the brown paper inside the guidelines and tack down the four corners. Tack centers of four sides. Continue to stretch the fabric to its original size by tacking all around the sides, dividing and subdividing the spaces between the tacks already placed. This procedure is followed until there is a solid border of thumbtacks around the entire edge. In cross-stitch pictures, if stitches were not stamped exactly even on the thread of the fabric, it may be necessary to remove some of the tacks and pull part of embroidery into a straight line. Use a ruler as a guide for straightening the lines of stitches. Hammer in the tacks or they will pop out as the fabric dries. Allow embroidery to dry thoroughly.

TO MOUNT: Cut a piece of heavy white cardboard about $\frac{1}{8}''$ smaller all around than the rabbet size of the frame to be used. Stretch the embroidery over the cardboard, using the same general procedure as for blocking the piece. Following the thread guidelines, use pins to attach the four corners of the embroidery to the mounting board. Pins are placed at the centers of sides, and embroidery is then gradually stretched into position until there is a border of pins completely around picture, about $\frac{1}{4}''$ apart. When satisfied that the design is even, drive pins into the cardboard edge with a hammer. If a pin does not go in straight, it should be removed and reinserted. The edges of the fabric may be pasted or taped down on the wrong side of the cardboard or the edges may be caught with long zigzag stitches. Embroidered pictures can be framed with glass over them if desired.

FOUR METHODS OF CROSS-STITCHING

How To Cross-Stitch

Several different ways to do cross-stitch are described above and illustrated in photos. All yield equally good results if care is taken to make sure that the strands of thread or yarn lie smooth and flat. Begin by leaving an end of floss on back and working over it to secure; run end of strand in on back to finish off. Try not to make any knots.

It is important when working cross-stitch to have the crosses of the entire piece worked in the same direction. Work all underneath threads in one direction and all the top threads in the opposite direction. Keep the stitches as even as possible. Be sure to make all crosses touch; do this by putting your needle in the same hole as used for the adjacent stitch.

Monk's or Aida Cloth: The design can follow

ON MONK'S CLOTH

ON GINGHAM

OVER PENELOPE CANVAS

ON EVEN-WEAVE FABRIC

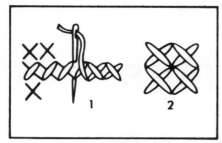

HOW TO MAKE CROSSES

the mesh of a coarse, flat-weave fabric, such as monk's cloth. Here the design may be worked from a chart simply by counting each square of fabric for one stitch.

Gingham: A checked material, such as gingham, can be used as a guide for cross-stitch. Crosses are made over checks, following a chart.

Even-Weave Fabric: The threads of an even-weave fabric, such as sampler linen, may be counted and each cross-stitch made the same size. For example, in the detail, a three-thread square is counted for each stitch.

Penelope Canvas: Penelope (or cross-stitch) canvas is basted to the fabric on which the design is to be embroidered. First, center canvas over linen, making sure that horizontal and vertical threads of canvas and linen match, then make lines of basting diagonally in both directions and around sides of canvas. The design is then worked by making crosses as shown, taking each stitch diagonally over the double mesh of canvas and through the fabric, being careful not to catch the canvas.

When design is completed, the basting is removed and the horizontal threads of the canvas are carefully drawn out, one strand at a time, then the vertical threads, leaving the finished cross-stitch design on the fabric.

Penelope canvas is available in several size meshes. Choose finer sizes for smaller designs; larger sizes are suitable for coarse work in wool.

AFGHAN STITCH BASICS

Plain Afghan Stitch: Work with afghan hook. Make a ch desired length.

Row 1: Keeping all lps on hook, sk first ch from hook (lp on hook is first st), pull up a lp in each ch across; Figure 1.

To Work Lps Off: Yo hook, pull through first lp, * yo hook, pull through next 2 lps, repeat from * across until 1 lp remains; Figure 2. Lp that remains on hook always counts as first st of next row.

Row 2: Keeping all lps on hook, sk first vertical bar (lp on hook is first st), pull up a lp under next vertical bar and under each vertical bar across; Figure 3. Work lps off as before. Repeat row 2 for plain afghan stitch.

Edge Stitch: Made at end of rows only to make a firm edge. Work as follows: Insert hook under last vertical bar and in lp at back of bar, pull up 1 lp; Figure 4.

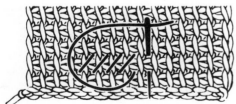
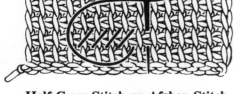

Half Cross-Stitch on Afghan Stitch

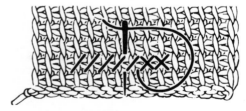

Cross-Stitch on Afghan Stitch

FIGURE 1   FIGURE 2

FIGURE 3   FIGURE 4

STITCH DETAILS

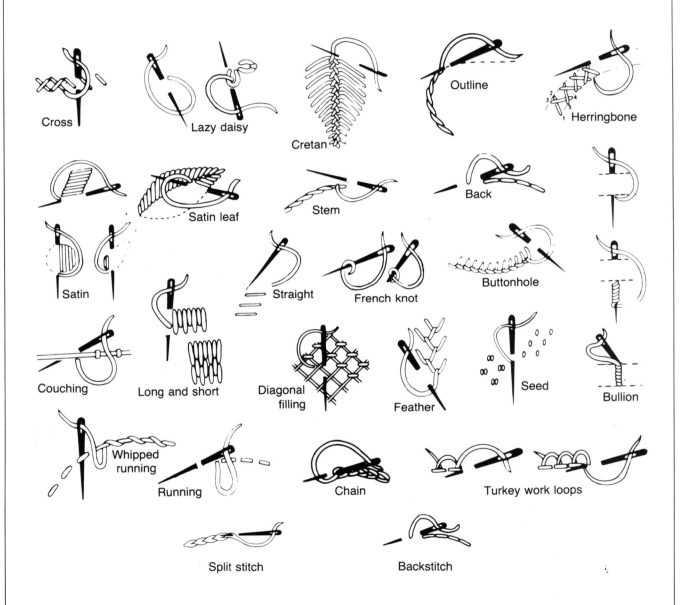

Cross

Lazy daisy

Cretan

Outline

Herringbone

Satin leaf

Stem

Back

Satin

Straight

French knot

Buttonhole

Couching

Long and short

Diagonal filling

Feather

Seed

Bullion

Whipped running

Running

Chain

Turkey work loops

Split stitch

Backstitch

INDEX

Page numbers in **bold** type refer to information in illustrations